Eating Disorders for the Primary Care Team

Margaret Perry

Quay Books

Mark Allen Publishing Ltd

Quay Books Division, Mark Allen Publishing Limited,
Jesses Farm, Snow Hill, Dinton, Wiltshire, SP3 5HN

British Library Cataloguing-in-Publication Data
A catalogue record is available for this book

© Mark Allen Publishing Ltd 2002
ISBN 1 85642 192 9

Printed in the UK by Bath Press, Bath

Contents

Introduction

For many individuals, 'weight watching' is an integral part of daily life and can become a constant battle that for some will continue for many years. In spite of this, obesity is a recognised problem for western nations where food is abundant, and receives its fair share of media attention because it is seen to be responsible for a number of related health problems.

Acceptable body shape and weight are influenced by culture, yet in affluent western societies people are taught from an early age to take an interest in, and to be concerned with, their appearance.

During the last thirty years the figure which women once sought to attain has changed quite dramatically, from a curvaceous image towards a slimmer, more slender physique, which is reflected in media personalities and other high profile persons.

Several studies have focused on the effect which images of rich, slim and often beautiful teenage idols have on adolescents.

Diet and fitness related articles regularly appear in the ever-increasing number of women's magazines and recent years have seen the introduction of several men's health magazines, some of which have similar inclusions.

The dieting industry appears to be one of growth with a wealth of books and videos related to this subject. Slimming clubs are evident in almost all towns and cities, alongside the emergence of health food shops.

The desire to be slim frequently commences in the teenage years: a quest that for many will continue into adult life. A small minority progress from merely wanting to lose a little weight to an existence where food rules their life. But, where does the need to shed a few pounds and the onset of an eating disorder begin, and can health professionals improve the outcome through earlier recognition and treatment?

A growing interest

The term eating disorders is used to describe a number of clinical conditions, all of which have an effect on the health and well being of the sufferer.

Anorexia nervosa and bulimia nervosa are two of the most widely publicised. Binge-eating disorder is a more recently acknowledged illness and is the least understood. In recent years, eating disorders in general have received a growing amount of media interest, accompanied by a comparable level of scrutiny from the medical profession. This, in turn, has lead to the spread of a number of self-help groups and charitable organisations that can offer advice to the general public and provide educational material to support health professionals.

The onset and predisposing factors which might potentially influence the onset of an eating disorder have been the subject of extensive research and discussion for many years. It is now evident that there are a wide spectrum of risk factors which precipitate the commencement of symptoms, although these vary between individuals and no two cases are identical. The issues involved are so complex that it is often difficult to determine a specific cause (or causes) for the person's illness. The link with psychiatry has been present for many years and originates from the fact that a number of these risk factors are shared with those attributed to some psychiatric conditions.

There appears to be a degree of overlap in the influences which have preceded the development of each of these illnesses, and it is now known that some of the aetiological factors that have been cited as relevant to their onset can be found in the past history of anorexia, bulimia and binge eater sufferers.

The quantity of research that continues to evolve serves to enlighten the medical profession; offering health professionals and the general public an insight into these complex conditions. Unfortunately, such conditions remain poorly understood and there is little training available for staff in the primary care setting, leaving them at risk of mismanagement and misdiagnosis.

Eating disorders require considerable expertise both in their recognition and treatment, and present a challenge for all those involved.

Given their potentially devastating effects if left untreated, there is a need for a greater awareness of both the aetiological factors and the early features which may precede the onset of these conditions. It is hoped that greater understanding will reduce the increasing numbers of those affected, and that earlier intervention will limit the health effects associated with an often long-term battle with an eating disorder.

Background information

Anorexia nervosa was first described by an English physicist William Gull in 1874 and its literal meaning is, 'loss of appetite for nervous reasons' (Blades, 1997). This definition is known to be inaccurate because there is no loss of appetite, just a refusal by the individual to permit themselves to gratify it. Bulimia nervosa was not truly recognised until the mid-nineteen seventies. Its appearance in the medical literature is credited to Russell in 1979, although other authors have reported references to behaviour patterns resembling the condition found in texts written much earlier than this. Historical writings have suggested that the Romans would adopt bulimic type behaviour as a means of enabling them to attend feasts, where they would consume vast quantities of food over a period of several hours without too much difficulty. The term bulimia is said to be derived from the Greek language, meaning 'ox hunger', although there has been little evidence to support the implication that the abnormal eating patterns adopted by those with this illness have any connection with hunger.

Many of the early descriptions of bulimia nervosa referred to the clinical features as greatly similar to those exhibited by anorexia sufferers and, in 1986, Fairburn and Garner indicated that anorexia and bulimia should be considered as different expressions of a single psychiatric disorder.

Binge-eating disorder is classified by the American Psychiatric Association as belonging to a category labelled as, 'eating disorder not otherwise specified' (American Psychiatric Association, 1994) and is relatively new in recognition. Early descriptions date back to the 1950s when Hamburger (1951) described a condition in which patients showed a craving for food, often uncontrollable and compulsive in nature. Preferred food choices are now known too include those high in calorie content, especially candy, ice cream, and other sweet foods. Little is currently known about the aetiology or epidemiology and there is some debate as to whether the condition is linked with the later onset of anorexia nervosa or bulimia nervosa.

The American Psychiatric Association cite a need for further research to clarify its clinical significance.

Anorexia nervosa: Characterised by intense periods of self-starvation with an accompanying drastic and excessive weight loss.

There are now two recognised subtypes:

Restricting type: Where the person does not adopt any regular additional binge/purge methods (laxative or diuretic abuse, and/or vomiting

Binge eating or purging type: The patient regularly uses binge/purge behaviour interspersed with periods of intense self-starvation.

Bulimia nervosa: Characterised by a cycle of binge eating followed by purging which may involve vomiting, the use of laxatives and/or diuretics to rid the body of food.

Binge-eating disorder: Characterised by periods of compulsive eating. Episodes of impulsive gorging are not accompanied by the purging behaviour which can occur with both anorexia nervosa and bulimia nervosa.

These conditions all have distinctive attributes which are unique to each of them, and despite some level of interaction between them (both in their aetiological factors and the clinical features which sufferers display), they remain highly complex illnesses which are little understood.

The difficulty for health professionals lies in the fact that the signs and symptoms vary widely from person to person, leading to the growing body of evidence to support the existence of a number of subclinical cases of eating disorders which do not fulfil the diagnostic criteria, but where patients present with a chaotic eating pattern (Button and Whitehouse, 1981). The classification of eating disorder not otherwise specified (EDNOS) as specified by the American Psychiatric Association, also incorporates those who present with a broad range of clinical features which are not easily categorised and do not fit the diagnostic criteria for either anorexia or bulimia nervosa.

It is estimated that approximately 45% of those with anorexia also exhibit symptoms of bulimia at some time during the course of their illness, and between a third and a half of patients with bulimia nervosa have met the strict diagnostic criteria for anorexia nervosa in the past, while many others have almost but not quite, met these criteria (Russell, 1988). It also appears that various interactions between the clinical manifestations of these diseases can occur making it extremely difficult to determine precisely which condition it is they are suffering from.

As already mentioned, binge-eating disorder remains a subject for future investigation. Research to date has concentrated on those elements which are shared with bulimia nervosa, with which it is believed to share the closest link; and specifically, whether individuals may progress from one condition to the other.

Both anorexia nervosa and bulimia nervosa commonly commence in the teenage years. The typical age of onset of anorexia nervosa is approximately sixteen to eighteen years of age (Morgan and Russell, 1975), while bulimia often presents at a slighter older age (Mitchell *et al*, 1987), approximately twenty-four, although this has been attributed to the fact that sufferers have managed to conceal their condition for a number of years prior to its discovery. This implies that the true age at which symptoms originally developed may have been several years earlier. The secrecy adopted by bulimics makes the true date of onset difficult to assess.

The pattern of binge-eating behaviour synonymous with that seen in binge-eating disorder typically commences in late adolescence or in the early twenties (American Psychiatric Association, 1995), although those presenting for treatment are often older, possibly indicating a similar level of reluctance to seek medical help as seen with bulimia nervosa.

Changes in adolescence

The beginning of an eating disorder heralds the start of a distressing period ahead for the patient, their relatives and friends. Since adolescence has been shown to be the most likely time for the early stages to evolve, it seems likely that the changes that occur at this time should be considered as potentially instrumental in their development.

The adolescent years are traumatic for many teenagers, and involve a multitude of physiological and emotional changes. Many young people are gaining increasing independence, are expected to take on new levels of responsibility at home and may be under pressure to achieve at school.

These physical and emotional changes occur alongside the desire for personal autonomy, achievement, and the desire to be physically attractive which, together with the combined pressures of cultural attitudes towards dieting, may contribute to the development of an eating disorder (McSherry, 1984). Some researchers believe that eating disorders develop as a means of stemming the tide of physical and emotional changes, enabling the individual to regain some control of their lives and avoid further changes which accompany the transition from child to adult. They are regarded by some as a manipulative scheme to avoid maturity and the pressures which adult life brings.

Rapid growth

In late childhood both boys and girls undergo a 'growth spurt' brought about by a sudden surge in hormones. The age at which this occurs varies from child to child as does the duration of this rapid period of physical and emotional change. Because of the wide variation among individuals in the timing of the growth spurt there is a wide range of physiologic variations in normal growth (Rogol *et al*, 2000). Girls commence the pattern of monthly menstrual periods and this can be as early as nine years of age or as late as sixteen or seventeen. Both sexes encounter alterations in physical appearance, and in many cases the growth spurt starts at an earlier age in girls than boys and often finishes earlier in girls. Somatic growth and maturation are influenced by several factors that act independently or in concert to modify an individual's genetic growth potential (Rogol *et al*, 2000).

Table Introduction.1: Secondary sexual characteristics	
Male	**Female**
Muscle development	Deposition of fat on hips, waists
Breaking of the voice	and thighs
Growth of body hair	Growth of body hair

The two principal hormones involved are testosterone in the male and oestrogen in the female. Both of these hormones are involved in the physical changes which occur and stimulate production of growth hormone. Under the influence of these hormones enlargement of long bones and vertebrae continue at a rapid rate which is reflected in a swift increase in height. When this process is complete, epiphyseal closure is facilitated with the cessation of any further expansion.

In boys the growth of facial hair begins as well as the development of the male sexual organs. Testosterone is active in several organs and tissues around the body, and has an influence on protein synthesis, which later plays a part in producing the increased muscle mass which is evident in adult males, but is not seen in adult females. In adolescent females breasts develop together with the growth of the uterus and vagina in preparation for childbirth, and the ovaries become functional at this time. The adult shape of females differs from that of males, and is influenced by the distribution of fat which is particularly evident on the hips and thighs.

Body image disturbance

Early studies suggested an interaction between rising concern with appearance and weight, which may play a leading role in encouraging those more vulnerable teenagers in society to commence dieting. In some cases this will lead to the onset of an eating disorder (Crisp, 1977).

The sudden change in body shape has been found to be a source of emotional distress for teenage girls in particular. Davies and Furnham (1986b) noted that the level of dissatisfaction towards body measurements increased as the age of girls increased. Despondency with such physical changes was reflected in the number of girls who cited hips and waist as particular features of dislike.

An over-perception of body size among adolescents in this age group is not a new finding and has been found in many countries in previous studies. One American study involving one thousand teenagers attending high schools across America reported that females in particular exhibited abnormal levels of preoccupation with body shape and weight (Abraham and Jones, 1984).

A sample of British female adolescent girls aged between twelve and eighteen years of age found that less than 4% of those included in the study were actually overweight, but ten times that number considered themselves to be so (Davies and Furnham, 1986a). Similar statistics to support the tendency to describe oneself as 'fat' are frequently documented, with some studies suggesting that as many as 70% of normal weight adolescents and young adults believe themselves to be overweight (Greenfield *et al*, 1987).

Greater dissatisfaction with personal appearance has been found among girls who experience an early menarche. The rapid change in physical appearance results in a body shape to which the child is unaccustomed. Girls who experience this at a young age may be very conscious of the fact that they are different from their friends. For some, it may be many months, even years before the same changes become visible in their peers, and the fact that this is not shared has been noted as a possible reason for starting to restrict food intake in an effort to rid the body of its new shape. Teenagers are anxious to be popular and do not like to be singled out as different from their associates.

O'Dea and Abraham (1999) found that young post-menarchal females described increased feelings of inadequacy, loss of personal self-control, and decreased self-esteem, which was associated with a desire to lose weight and a determination to eliminate eating between meals.

A recent American study of teenage perceptions of body image, and weight control practices used by these teenagers, identified some interesting findings. In common with other studies, older females exhibited more dissatisfaction with their appearance than younger girls, however this displeasure was far more prominent among white subjects. Black children, when asked to select a body size drawing which they felt they could identify with, chose larger body sizes as their ideal shape, and perceived less personal and family pressure about their weight when compared to their white counterparts (Adams *et al*, 2000).

Dieting in adolescence

Dieting behaviour and erratic meal patterns are said to be common occurrences among pre-adolescent and adolescent boys and girls (Casper, 1990; Field *et al*, 1993). In an Australian study, 38% of girls and 12% of boys were categorised as intermediate dieters, while a worrying 7% of girls and a further 1% of boys fell into a group categorised as extreme dieters. Other studies have identified similar findings. Field *et al* (1999) reported that approximately 29% of girls within their study admitted to having been on a diet in the previous year, while a further 14% reported that they were concerned with their weight a great deal of the time or always. Poor nutritional status among teenagers is of particular concern to health professionals and raises the question of its potential impact on long-term health. High fat intake is clearly linked with heart disease, while inadequate intake of vitamins, minerals and other nutrients can have both long- and short-term effects which, if drastic enough, are potentially fatal. Many teenagers have a liking for fast foods, and during the teenage years they may be introduced to smoking and alcohol intake, which have additional implications if these habits are sustained into adult life. The interaction between unhealthy dieting and disordered eating behaviours has the potential to adversely affect nutrient intake, mental health status and long-term health outcomes (Neumark-Sztainer and Hannan, 2000).

The extent and severity of this erratic nutritional intake has been implicated as an early indicator of a latent eating disorder.

Patton *et al* (1999) cited dieting in adolescence as the most important predictor of new eating disorders. He suggested that:

1. Adolescent females who diet at a severe level are potentially eighteen times more likely to develop an eating disorder than those who do not adopt dieting behaviour.
2. Those who diet at a moderate level are five times more likely to develop an eating disorder.
3. Around two thirds of new cases of eating disorders arise in females who have dieted moderately prior to developing their condition.

The age at which a young person begins to watch the content of their diet is a cause for concern and there are indications that in some cases this activity starts before the child reaches adolescence. Maloney *et al* (1989) studied a group of eight to thirteen-year-old girls and found that nearly half of those interviewed felt that they wanted to lose weight, nearly a third had tried to do so, adopting additional exercise, calorie restriction and occasionally vomiting as a means of achieving this. Particularly worrying is the fact that 6.9% of those included in Maloney *et al*'s study were found to meet the diagnostic criteria for anorexia nervosa, indicating that disturbed eating attitudes are present in a few subjects at a much earlier age than most of the research suggests. This requires separate investigation to determine whether earlier intervention might be effective in preventing more serious problems as these children progress towards the teenage years.

Early detection of suspicious dieting behaviour poses a considerable problem for health professionals, and there is a need to raise awareness of the potential dangers of abnormal eating patterns, particularly among those who may be in a position to educate and support teenagers through this difficult time in their lives. In spite of the help which primary care staff could offer young people, there is little information available within the primary care setting and very little training for the primary care team.

Recognition of problems early in their evolution is imperative if the growing number of teenagers who go on to develop eating disorders is to be abated.

A global issue

It would appear that eating disorders are gaining momentum in countries around the world where they were previously regarded as non-existent. Once labelled Western diseases, statistics are now suggesting a growing number of reported cases in less wealthy countries. Lee (2000) reported their emergence in low income Asian countries, such as Malaysia, India, China, the Philippines and Indonesia. A study of female high school students in three Chinese communities, found that there was general disillusionment with persona, with many of those interviewed expressing a desire for a slimmer, lighter physique. These findings were evident across all three areas, but Hong Kong students scored highest across all topics included for evaluation (Lee and Lee, 2000).

Much of the early research established eating disorders as being a phenomenon most prevalent among white communities. As a result, both the general public and health professionals may have inaccurate misconceptions relating to this issue. However, recent material has provided evidence to propose that minority populations appear to have substantial numbers of subjects similarly affected (Field *et al*, 1997). A study conducted in Bradford, found the prevalence of bulimia nervosa to be more common in first generation Asian females, with a rate of 3.4%. This was considerably higher than in white populations of a similar age group, where the rate was only 0.6% (Mumford and Whitehouse, 1988). This suggests that Asian girls who are being educated in Great Britain have adopted Western ideals and desire the same slim physique as their white peers. Similar findings have been discovered in other multi-racial communities around the world. Fitzgibbon *et al* (1998) studied binge eating among Hispanic and non-Hispanic white populations and found that patterns of bingeing and purging were more severe among the Hispanic group than their non-Hispanic equals.

A study conducted in Boston, Massachusetts, aimed to ascertain racial differences between black and white women and to determine the differences in the methods adopted by these women in an attempt to control their weight.

Obesity among black women was found to be a common problem with many women in the study concerned and distressed about their weight. These women were found to be as likely as white women to reveal that they had engaged in behaviours of binge eating and self-induced vomiting during the preceding three months, with a possible abuse of laxatives or diuretics as a further adjunct to weight control (Striegel-Moore *et al*, 2000)

They also expressed feelings of guilt at their inability to control their eating habits and employed other compensatory methods as an intermittent means of appeasing their distress. Fasting was also found to be regularly used as a means of implementing a rapid weight loss between binge episodes.

If these statistics are found to be replicated in other communities around the world, the number of people whose lives are affected by these illnesses may be many more than current statistics suggest. The implications of this are that eating disorders represent a public health challenge requiring substantial resources if the rising morbidity and mortality rates are to be avoided.

Suggested further reading

Eating attitudes in adolescence

O'Dea JA, Abraham S (1999) Onset of disordered eating attitudes and behaviours in early adolescence: interplay of pubertal status, gender, weight and age. *Adolescence* **34**(136): 671–9

Ricciardelli LA, Williams RJ, Kiernan MJ (1999) Bulimic symptoms in adolescent girls and boys. *Int J Eat Disord* **26**(2): 217–21

Neumark-Sztainer D, Story M, Dixon LB, Murray D (1998) Adolescents engaging in unhealthy weight control behaviors: are they at risk of other health compromising behaviors? *Am J Public Health* **88** (6): 952–55

Dieting and weight concerns in adolescence

Neumark-Sztainer D, Hannon PJ (2000) Weight related behaviours among adolescent girls and boys: Results from a national survey. *Arch Paediatr Adolescent Med* **154**(6): 569–77

Patton GC, Johnson-Sabine E Wood K., Mann AH, Wakeling A (1990) Abnormal eating attitudes in London schoolgirls: a prospective epidemiological study: outcome at twelve months follow-up. *Psychol Med* **20**(2): 383–94

Patton GC, Selzer R, Coffey C, Carlin JB, Wolfe R (1999) Onset of adolescent eating disorders: population based cohort study over three years. *Br Med J* **318**: 765–768

Global issue

Striegel-Moore RH, Wilfley DE, Pike KM, Dohm F. Fairburn CG, (2000) Recurrent binge-eating in black American women. *Arch Fam Med* **9**(1): 83–87

Yanovski SZ (2000) Eating disorders, race, and mythology. *Arch Fam Med* **9**(1): 88

Section I: Anorexia nervosa

Section 1 Anorexia nervosa

1

Anorexia nervosa

Epidemiology of anorexia nervosa

Anorexia nervosa of the restricting subtype is rarely seen, however a number of girls will present with a subthreshold version of the illness, requesting help for a subthreshold disorder (Freeman and Newton, 1995). The condition is far more common in females with estimates of the male:female prevalence ratio ranging from 1:6 to 1:10 (*American Journal of Psychiatry*, 2000), and this female bias has been replicated in many epidemiological studies of anorexia nervosa

In Third World countries where food supplies are often scarce, anorexia is extremely rare, in fact, in some countries obesity is regarded as a luxury and is seen as a sign of beauty. The incidence of anorexia in previous published papers has been closely linked to higher social classes (Morgan and Russell, 1975), and in 1976 Crisp *et al* identified a prevalence rate of ten per thousand girls at private schools in England. The distribution of anorexia and its apparently greater affinity for adolescents from wealthier families, has been evident from the earliest research papers on this subject, right through to the most current research material. A recent study into the aetiology of anorexia found that 73% of sufferers recruited to take part were from social classes 1 and 2 (Fairburn *et al*, 1999), which would suggest that this has remained a constant feature of the disorder.

The suspected rise in incidence of the condition has evoked considerable interest both from the media and the medical profession. Between 1970 and 1976 the number of reported cases of anorexia almost doubled rising from 0.35 to 0.64 per 100,000 (Thompson, 1993). By 1991, a Dutch research project reported a rate of 6.3 anorexia sufferers per year per 100,000 (the second highest figure to be reported at that time) (Hoek, 1991).

More recent statistics suggest a lifetime prevalence of anorexia nervosa among women of between 0.5% and 3.7% (Walters and Kendler, 1995).

The portrayal of the disease as one occurring specifically in the Western world has been well documented in earlier papers. Gordon

(1990) identified two factors that he felt were influential and were specifically related to the rising incidence of the illness among women:

1. Women taking on roles in society that were once seen as a man's domain. Women are encouraged to achieve both in their personal lives and alongside their male colleagues in the work environment.

2. A greater interest in personal appearance, and a preoccupation with weight, which is culturally influenced. Over the last thirty years, the role of women in Western societies has changed. Many of the world's most successful women are slim and beautiful.

In the anorexic the initial interest in personal appearance becomes obsessional, to a point where the person exhibits a gross distortion of body image, the individual believing themselves to be overweight, even though to those around them they may be severely underweight.

A decade ago anorexia nervosa was rare outside the developed West (Lee, 2000), but there are now reported cases in countries once untouched by these diseases.

In Japan, the increasing incidence of anorexia has been attributed to a loss of spiritual wealth which has accompanied the rise in national wealth enjoyed by this nation in recent years (Anderson, 1998). She describes children of this era as being unable to express their loneliness or feelings of solitude to their families and loved ones. This inability to communicate manifests itself as the resulting physical and emotional problems which accompany these feelings of distress.

The extent to which Japanese communities are becoming affected by these illnesses is reflected in the figures which suggest that rates are comparable to, or above, those in the United States (Nadaoka *et al*, 1996).

Recorded estimates of known cases of eating disorders vary from area to area and are dependent on a number of external factors, including the assessment and sampling methods used to detect the disorder.

The issue of whether the number of people affected by eating disorders has continued to follow a growing trend is surrounded by criticism. Although epidemiological studies have indicated that the incidence of anorexia nervosa has been steadily rising, some controversy has existed since the majority of these studies have been conducted in clinic or hospital environments, with little emphasis on community or population studies. Data related to this issue is collected from a variety of sources, including community surveys, outpatient clinics, inpatient hospital records and psychiatric units. One of the problems in comparing prevalence studies across countries and over time is that various definitions have been used in published studies, with differences made in the adherence to strict diagnostic criteria and the inclusion of partial syndromes (Fombonne, 1995). There is also the question of the detection and documentation of partial syndromes, with an indication that those who do not fully meet the diagnostic criteria may outnumber those who have full blown anorexia nervosa (Meadows *et al*, 1986). This is supported by Lucas (1993) who suggested that the increased prevalence rates may be partly accounted for by the growing number of patients with milder forms of the illness who are now identified because of increased awareness and a greater interest in eating disorders.

Aetiology of anorexia nervosa

Factors linked to the onset of anorexia:
- ⌘ Family background.
- ⌘ Genetic factors.
- ⌘ Personality traits.
- ⌘ Exposure to adverse events.
- ⌘ Sexual abuse.

Family background

Individual parenting styles and family background have provided a subject for debate. In 1991, Kenny, looked at the characteristics which could be applied to the families of adolescents who develop anorexia nervosa and described them as adopting the following parenting styles:

1. A home environment where social interaction outside the family is frowned upon. Making outside contact with others and forming friendships is not encouraged.
2. The parents adopt a repressive approach.This may be more evident in one parent who is overtly dominant in the family group.

3. The child is subjected to pressure from their family who express high expectations for their child (which the child may feel unable to live up to).

Once popular theories, these early notions may be inaccurate. [Webster and Palmer (2000) indicated that adversity in childhood did not play a part in the development of anorexia nervosa, and that most sufferers in their study reported little family disturbance prior to the onset of the condition, suggesting that the distress which the illness brings to loved ones may well be responsible for the spread of family disruption. [Rearing practices, such as rejection and overprotection (which were once thought to play a fundamental role in the aetiology of the disorder) may not always be relevant, indeed, the majority of anorexia nervosa patients who are still in their teens and who have a short evolution of the history of the disease have a perception of rearing style that is similar to that of the normal population (Castro *et al*, 2000). It would seem logical to expect anguish within the family to intensify at a later date, once the illness starts to progress, and the patient's condition deteriorates.

An alternative theory is that events which have occurred in the early years may somehow influence the child's vulnerability to develop an eating disorder at a later date.

Shoebridge and Gowers (2000) studied parental over-concern in the early years of children who later went on to develop anorexia nervosa in adolescence. Mothers of anorexic teenagers were found to have endured events such as loss of a previous child either pre-natally or postnatally, the presence of obstetric complications particularly a prolonged spell in the neonatal unit following the delivery, and difficulties in conceiving the child. When compared to the control group high incidences of such experiences were found to have occurred among those mothers whose daughters later developed anorexia nervosa.

Hypothalamic dysfunction

Babies born prematurely or those who experience a traumatic delivery are obviously a cause of parental apprehension, but there is some indication that the clinical significance of such a start in life may be greater than once thought. Cnattingius *et al* (1999) used data collected from birth records rather than relying on information supplied by the mother which would rely on exceptional memory recall. Perinatal factors (the most important being the possibility of brain damage which occurred either during delivery or in a baby born prematurely) were found to have an independent association with anorexia nervosa, suggesting that even though this particular risk factor may account for only a few cases of the disease, it may uncover the mechanisms underlying the development of the disorder (Cnattingius *et al*, 1999). It is thought possible that such events may lead to hypothalamic dysfunction, which subsequently interferes with the normal hypothalamic mechanism. The consequences of a dysregulation in this function, although not well understood, may affect appetite and feeding behaviours (Brewerton, 1995). Children who are difficult to feed are a source of parental distress and may be subjected to numerous visits to the GP and in some cases are referred for further investigation. Rastam (1992) suggested that such early problems with food intake may predispose the child to an increased risk of developing an eating disorder in adolescence. The patho-physiology surrounding hypothalamic dysfunction and its possible influence has been the subject of debate in earlier studies, with an alternative argument which suggests that such disturbances in normal body processes are usually secondary to malnutrition and weight loss, and occur as a result of the lack of adequate nourishment (Palmer, 1990). Which of these two arguments has the most impact on the course of events remains unresolved.

Genetic influences

Genetic and other biological, gender related, psychological and familial risk factors are among those subjects identified as important areas for future research by the American Psychiatric Association (American Psychiatric Association, 2000).

Further investigation is required to determine whether single risk factors are capable of precipitating onset of an eating disorder or whether a multifactorial existence (including a genetic predisposition) is required.

The risk for the onset of dieting is believed to increase among those who have lived in an environment where dieting among other family members is a frequent occurrence. High rates of parental eating disorders, indicates that the child may have had considerable exposure to an unhealthy interest in food, probably from a young age (Fairburn *et al*, 1999). Such a family history has aroused suspicion that there may be a degree of heritability among offspring who develop these illnesses.

Because restrictive type anorexia nervosa is relatively rare, a number of studies have included the detection of partial syndromes and subclinical conditions in their findings. In an earlier study Strober *et al* (1990) reported higher rates of anorexia nervosa among female relatives of patients with the disease.

A later study conducted a controlled family study of both anorexia and bulimia nervosa to determine whether there was evidence of transmission of these conditions among the relatives of ill subjects (Strober *et al*, 2000). Because all the cases who formed the proband were female, only female relatives were studied.

Statistical analysis revealed that true anorexia nervosa was rare among the families of the comparison subjects, this was not the case among the families of the anorexia and bulimia sufferers, with the relative risk of anorexia increasing to 11.3 and 12.3 in female relatives of anorexic and bulimic probands respectively (Strober *et al*, 2000). Both full and partial syndromes of anorexia nervosa were evident among the families of both anorexic and bulimic patients.

Identical twins of parents who have problems with anorexia have been found to develop similar problems once they themselves reach adolescence. Walters and Kendler (1995) were able to establish an association between the development of a severe case of anorexia in one twin and a corresponding, but much less severe syndrome, in the other twin. They found the co-twins of those twins diagnosed with the illness had significantly lower body mass indices than the co-twins of those who were well. The severity of this weight loss was far greater in the co-twins of the most severely affected anorexics.

Strober suggested that there are higher rates of anorexia and bulimia in relatives of ill subjects, supporting a familial tendency and a cross transmission in families which might indicate a common or shared familial diathesis (Strober *et al*, 2000).

Personality traits

Fairburn *et al* (1999) studied the concept that the risk factors for anorexia can be broadly categorised into one of two classes, those that increase the risk for psychiatric disorder in general and those that increase the risk for dieting. Within this study the personality traits of anorexics were found to be:

- perfectionism
- negative statements when asked to give a self-evaluation
- low self-esteem.

The drive for perfectionism is accompanied by low self-esteem and a belief that they are inadequate and incompetent in most areas of life. They often exhibit rigid behaviour patterns preferring to adhere to orderly and predictable routines in their daily life. They are often reluctant to encompass new experiences and prefer to resist change wherever possible.

Negative self-evaluation and associated personality traits are evident prior to onset of the illness, but are accentuated once the disease progresses and have been shown to persist even in the event of a recovery (Casper, 1990).

Exposure to adverse events

Garner and Garfinkel (1980) suggested that a 'trigger' factor may be all that is needed in the presence of such traits to act as a catalyst for the onset of the illness. Horesh *et al* (1995) focused on separations, deaths, negative or bad experiences with parents (which included physical and emotional abuse) and family disruptions (which included parental fighting and verbal hostility but not necessarily directed at the child). Such stressors might include:

❖ A single traumatic event: Events severe enough to trigger onset would include parental separation, death of a close relative, rape, or abortion.

❖ An extended period of emotional pain. Problems with sexuality appear to be specifically related.

It is clear that there are individuals who experience a multitude of problems in their early years, and yet are able to mature both physically and emotionally, reaching adulthood relatively unscathed by these early experiences. The complex multifactorial nature of the condition does not allow health professionals to determine which individuals will make an emotional recovery with relatively few health effects, or those who will progress to a chronic condition with a poor prognosis.

A comparison of forty healthy adolescents with seventy-nine non-anorexic psychiatric patients and twenty-one severely anorectic hospitalised patients confirmed an association between stressful life events in the family and psychopathology in adolescence (Horesh *et al*, 1995).

Troop and Treasure (1997) studied a group of women, with the aim of identifying distressing personal situations or episode events in the year preceding onset of the condition and whether these events differed significantly to those experienced by women who continued to remain in good health.

Little variation was found in the nature of life events encountered by the two groups, but differences were shown to exist in the way that individuals dealt with such events, indicating that those who went on to develop anorexia coped poorly with life crises.

Schmidt *et al* (1997) found that 67% of anorexia sufferers had experienced a severe event of marked difficulty in the previous twelve months, which in 37% of cases related to family relationships. Distressing situations included recurrent arguments, which in some cases lead to separation or divorce of parents, in which the patient appeared to be indirectly involved.

Garner and Garfinkel (1980) suggested that there are many people in society who possess the individual, familial or cultural antecedents and that these become pathogenic within the context of stressors which initiate the cycle of dieting, weight loss and pursuit of thinness.

Sexual abuse

Much has been written about the possibility that sexual abuse may play a part involved in the aetiology of eating disorders. Unwanted sexual experiences at any age are a distressing event in the majority of cases, and there are a number of authors who feel that such a history might provide a plausible link to the later development of psychiatric illness in some individuals.

Palmer *et al* (1990) described incidents involving sexual abuse among young anorexics, which in two cases had involved full sexual intercourse in children below the age of thirteen. In the older age group (aged 13–15), there were considerably more subjects who reported having been subjected to full sexual intercourse (against their will in 97% of cases), which was accompanied by force (41%), some degree of threat (38%) and severe or moderate distress at the time of the event in 75% of cases (Palmer *et al*, 1990). In many cases the offender was a known family member.

Schmidt *et al* (1997) found similar high rates of sexual shame and disgust, which when compared to the control group, were more prevalent among the anorexia group than either the bulimics or the controls. The content of these experiences were described by participants as premature sexual incidents, or inappropriate acts or situations which posed a moral dilemma for the person involved. Although the personal information offered by those who are willing to impart such details varies from study to study, as many as 60% of subjects in one study gave a past history of sexual interference, although the nature of these experiences were not detailed (Calam and Slade, 1989).

Diagnosis of anorexia nervosa

The diagnostic and statistical manual of mental disorders (DSM-IV American Psychiatric Association, 1994) is the tool which acts as a guide in assisting health professionals skilled in this field to confirm a diagnosis. Understanding and application of the tool and its categories requires a considerable level of expertise and eating disorders are just one example of several conditions which the DSM-IV is used to assess.

Diagnostic criteria for anorexia nervosa: DSM-IV (American Psychiatric Association, 1994)

1. Active and relentless and persistent pursuit of a low body weight which is achieved by an inappropriate level of rigorous exercise and self-starvation (in some cases intermittent use of laxatives and/or diuretics may accompany this regime to enhance the weight loss).
2. Absolute dread of weight gain.
3. Abnormal perception of own body image and a denial of weight loss and associated practices.
4. If the individual has commenced onset of menstrual periods, the criteria include cessation of menstruation as a diagnostic inclusion. Guidelines suggest that in these instances the female should have missed at least three monthly periods prior to the diagnosis.

Eating disorder not otherwise specified

1. History should include all the elements within the diagnostic criteria for anorexia nervosa, but does not require the cessation of menstruation as a component.

2. Encompasses all the diagnostic criteria for anorexia nervosa as above, but the patient does not appear to have abnormal perceptions regarding their body size.

In addition, there are an array of questionnaires and structured interview techniques designed to extract information on the nature and severity of the patient's illness. The instruments described briefly below are by no means exhaustive. Among those used for anorexia are:

❖ The Eating Attitudes Test (Garner *et al*, 1982): Designed to assess symptoms and concerns of patients with an eating disorder. Originally devised for use in anorexia, however its use has also extended to bulimia nervosa.

❖ The Eating Disorders Examination (Fairburn and Cooper, 1993): Assesses both the existence and severity of clinical features and can also provide information relating to additional DSM-IV diagnoses.

❖ The Eating Disorders Inventory (Garner *et al*, 1993; Garner, 1991). Provides information relating to both symptamology, behaviour patterns and psychological traits.

Difficulties in diagnosis

There is some controversy surrounding the weight criteria which is presently used to make a diagnosis, based around the fact that the current assessment measures do not take into account changes between the male and female shape, or the vast amount of growing which occurs in adolescence and the transition to adulthood. Hebebrand *et al* (2000) suggested that although the weight criterion for a diagnosis of anorexia nervosa is a weight less than 85% of what is considered normal for that particular person, the body mass index of a patient can only be interpreted appropriately when the age and sex specific distribution of the body mass index is known.

Teenagers and pre-adolescent children can be 'finicky' in their choice of preferred foods, and because of the wide variations in height and weight which exist among young teenagers it is highly likely that there are a number of teenagers who are 'awkward' with regard to food preferences, who meet the weight criteria for anorexia but do not have the disease. There are some individuals who, rather than actually losing weight, simply fail to gain weight as their height increases, giving them the appearance of a child who is significantly underweight (Lask and Bryant Waugh, 1997).

Onset and clinical features

The impact of anorexia on the individual can be divided into three broad categories: behavioural, psychological and physical. *Table 1.1* is not exhaustive but gives a brief insight into the manifestations of this disease.

Table 1.1: Behavioural, psychological and physical aspects of anorexia nervosa

Behavioural	Psychological	Physical
Refusal of food	Obsessive symptoms	Rapid weight loss
Secrecy	Preoccupation with food	Low blood pressure
Lying about food	Ritualistic behaviour pattern	Low metabolic rate
Denial of weight loss	Abnormal dread of weight gain	Tiredness
Excessive exercise	Addictive behaviour	Constipation
	Emotional and psychological disturbance	Susceptible to cold
	Body image disturbance	

Behavioural effects of anorexia

Any obese individual who attempts to diet in an effort to lose weight needs to exercise a considerable amount of personal willpower if they are to achieve the desired target. Avoidance of fattening foods requires a measure of self-control which is often too difficult for the individual to sustain, particularly when such foodstuffs have been a regular inclusion in the daily diet. Many experience even greater difficulties in maintaining this once they cease to exercise such vigilance over their nutritional intake. Herman and Polivy (1991) believe dieting to be a struggle for control because the process of staying on a diet requires the individual to exercise personal self-control. In anorexia nervosa, the subject's behaviour begins as an initial desire to lose weight, but later becomes centred around an absolute avoidance of weight gain.

Genuine dieters are usually delighted when their intense efforts are rewarded with a barrage of positive comments complimenting them on their new, slimmer appearance. Anorexics, on the other hand, will go to extreme lengths to conceal their weight loss, often expressing intense denial of a problem, and adopting a baggy style of dress in an attempt to achieve this (Freeman and Newton, 1995). The brain requires an adequate supply of glucose to function correctly and the effects of depriving this vital organ of its daily needs has been independently researched. While commencing a diet may have been a conscious choice, when illness supervenes patients become trapped in weight reducing behaviour (Tiller *et al*, 1993).

By denying the body of adequate nourishment, the anorexic is capable of maintaining a steadfast refusal to satisfy their hunger. They may adhere to a stringent calorie intake often comprising their diet of foods which are particularly low in calories and/or may be of poor nutritional value. Foods are often divided into categories, usually good or bad, which allows patients to select only those foods which they perceive to offer little threat to their stringent dietary regime. The patient allows themselves to exist on bulky, low calorie foods such as celery, crispbreads or cottage cheese (Thompson, 1993) and may resort to lying about daily food intake in an attempt to persuade other family members that they are not hungry, hence offering an explanation for not finishing meals.

The pursuit of thinness is further enhanced by the accompanying rigorous exercise regime which the individual adopts. This is usually excessive and ritualistic in nature, and may be performed in secret to avoid detection. The patient vehemently denies any interference with their well being and is somehow able to pursue an exercise regime despite their severely emaciated state. Adoption of such an exercise regime has been viewed as an addictive behaviour, and may reflect pathological cognition about exercising (Davis *et al*, 1999).

The ability to refuse sustenance constantly becomes increasingly difficult to sustain and may result in a lapse in self-control. The binge which follows is then replaced by purging, a practice which allows the anorexic to appease their guilt, having allowed their resolve to falter. Often consumption of a relatively small amount of a particular food which is not normally permitted is sufficient to provoke an episode of bingeing and purging (Herman and Polivy, 1991). As previously mentioned, many anorexics will adopt a pattern of behaviour which will alternate between restrictive anorexia nervosa and the presence of bulimic symptoms at different times throughout their illness (Kassett *et al*, 1988; Beumont *et al*, 1976).

Psychological symptoms

Reluctance to recognise that they have a problem is a feature of anorexia nervosa, with a lack of identification of any abnormal behaviour patterns on the part of the individual concerned. Denial of the severity of their illness and emaciated state has serious implications, and is instrumental in the patient's refusal to accept that there is any need for medical intervention. Alongside these dysfunctional thought processes is low personal self-esteem. A number of theories have emerged in an attempt to understand the reasons why these patients develop such negative opinions of themselves.

Cooke and Striegel-Moore (1997) described two distinct pathways which might culminate in body image disturbance and negative schemas which encourage the development of anorexia nervosa. The first is one in which the child's life experiences with those adults who are most important to them (eg. sexual abuse) leaves them with a negative perception of their physical self. The second involves a traumatic process where the child is left feeling that achieving body changes is a method of self-regulation (Cooke and Striegel-Moore, 1997). Once such thoughts are embedded they become a powerful tool for perpetuating the anorexic illness and intensive therapy is required to effect a change.

An increasing level of obsessive behaviour occurs alongside a protracted interest in food. Kaye (1993) suggests that anorexics do not themselves regard their obsessive-like symptoms as strange or abnormal and make no attempt to seek treatment or advice or, indeed, to repress such thoughts.

Food preoccupation takes over the person's life, accompanied by an increasing level of irritability and depressive symptoms which lead to social isolation and a withdrawal from normal activities. They may become self-absorbed preferring to spend time alone, becoming more and more introverted as their illness progresses.

Many anorexics are known to satisfy their heightened interest in food by appearing to have a curiosity for food and its nutritional value. They may devote time to cooking elaborate meals for those around them, and yet have no intention of partaking of the meal themselves.

Diminishing energy levels manifest themselves in poor levels of concentration which may result in schoolwork of a lesser quality than would normally be expected of the child, a warning sign for school staff in a previously conscientious, hardworking individual. The mental strength which the individual is able to exhibit in their continued refusal of food is parallelled by an increasing amount of physical weakness and emaciation which is clearly visible to those around them, although denied by the anorexic.

When the illness continues to become one of prolonged duration, it appears that the associated behavioural and psychological symptoms increase in intensity. Takei *et al* (1989) found that where the duration of illness had continued for a period of ten years or more the frequency of abnormal eating behaviour, and the extent of physical and psychotic symptoms were greater, with potentially irreversible damage to the health of the individual.

Physical effects of starvation

The patient may present at their GP surgery for a consultation concerning one of the physical features which accompany their eating disorder. Anorexics often do not feel that they have a problem and relatives may be the force which makes them seek medical attention.

The most obvious physical sign is that of severe weight loss brought about by a gradual process of self-starvation. The severity of symptoms are highly variable from patient to patient, and the degree of dieting is reflected in the amount of weight lost. Nylander (1971) suggested that the disorder may be expressed in mild or incipient forms, where those individuals who meet the usual diagnostic criteria may represent extreme points on a continuum.

The ability of the patient to conceal their weight loss may enable them to escape the concern of friends and family, particularly in the early stages of their illness. The body will attempt to compensate for poor nutritional intake by using conservation mechanisms in an attempt to minimise the amount of energy consumption needed for daily living. A reduction in the metabolic rate occurs in an attempt to utilise what little food intake occurs more sparingly. A study of sixteen anorexic women found that basal metabolic rate was considerably diminished, but had reverted to normal in the comparison group of recovered subjects (Polito *et al*, 2000).

The effects of rigorous dieting in the adolescent years has serious health risks, some of which will give acute symptoms which occur as a direct result of malnutrition. The long-term medical implications hold the risk of serious and in some cases irreversible complications which cannot be rectified.

Loss of body fat leaves the individual susceptible to the cold (which may be a symptom the patient complains of regularly) and as a compensatory mechanism a growth of fine hair develops (termed lanugo) in an effort to counteract this.

Palla and Litt (1988) reported postural changes in blood pressure and pulse as frequent findings. In their study, among those patients who adopted strict dieting practices, 62% of restricting anorexics and 83% of those who used vomiting and purging were found to have postural hypotension on examination. These changes were found to manifest themselves as light-headedness, dizzy spells and more rarely syncope (Palla and Litt, 1988). These physiological changes are accompanied by a diminished ability to enjoy life, leaving the sufferer feeling lethargic and interfering with their ability to participate in activities which they would once have enjoyed.

Suggested further reading

Epidemiology

Hoek HW, Bartelds AI, Bosveld JJ, van der Graaf Y, Limpens VE, Maiwals M, Spaaij CJ (1995) Impact of urbanization on detection rates of eating disorders. *Am J Psychiatry* **152**(9): 1272–8

De Azevedo MHP, Ferreira CP (1992) Anorexia nervosa and bulimia nervosa: a prevalence study. *Acta Psychiatr Scand* **86**: 432–6

Aetiology

Horesh N, Apter A, Lepkifker E, Ratzoni G, Weizmann R, Tyano S (1995) Life events and severe anorexia nervosa in adolescence. *Acta Psychiatr Scand* **91**(1): 5–9

Fairburn CG, Cooper Z, Doll HA, Welch SL (1999) Risk factors for anorexia nervosa: Three integrated case comparisons. *Arch Gen Psychiatry* **56**(5): 468–76

Strober M, Lampert C, Morrell W, Burroughs J, Jacobs C (1990) A controlled family study of anorexia nervosa: evidence of familial aggregation and lack of shared transmission with affective disorders. *Int J Eat Disord* **9**: 239–53

Diagnosis

Garner DM, Olmsted MP, Bohr Y, Garfinkel PE (1982) The eating attitudes test: psychometric features and clinical correlates. *Psychol Med* **12**(4): 871–8

Garner DM, Garfinkel PE (1979) The eating attitudes test: an index of the symptoms of anorexia nervosa. *Psychol Med* **9**(2): 273–9

Cooper Z, Fairburn CG (1987) The Eating Disorder Examination: a semi structured interview for the assessment of the specific psychopathology of eating disorders. *Int J Eat Disord* **6**: 1–8

Onset and clinical features

Matsunaga H, Kiriike N, Iwasaki Y, Miyata A, Yamagami S, Kaye WH (1999) Clinical characteristics in patients with anorexia nervosa and obsessive compulsive disorder. *Psychol Med* **29**(2): 407–14

Takei M, Nozoe S, Tanaki H, Soejima Y, Manabe Y, Takayami I, Yamanaki T (1989) Clinical features in anorexia nervosa lasting more than ten years or more. *Psychother Psychosom* **52**(1–3): 140–5

2

Health problems and anorexia nervosa

Sustained anorexia nervosa has the potential to affect a number of body systems, with potentially serious implications. The nourishment which is supplied in the normal daily food intake is utilised by cells and tissues and allows the body to maintain a state of homeostasis.

This state of equilibrium ensures the healthy functioning of tissues and organs, enabling the complex chemical processes involved in achieving equilibrium to continue to work efficiently.

Cardiovascular system — cardiac dysfunction

⌘ Reduced ventricular size.

⌘ Abnormal ECG recordings: cardiac arrhythmia, bradycardia.

Reduced ventricular muscle mass

Moodie and Salcedo (1983) studied a group of young sufferers using non-invasive methods to assess heart function. Chest x-rays demonstrated a small heart size with a reduction in the mass of the left ventricle. The normal mass measurements are estimated to range between 90–360g. Moodie and Salcedo (1983) found evidence of patients with left ventricular mass measurements of less than 100g. In a healthy heart the left ventricle receives blood from the left atrium which is propelled by muscular contraction into the aorta, and from this point the blood is distributed around the body. The left ventricle is responsible for maintaining the circulation throughout the rest of the body, and any deterioration in this function has potentially serious consequences. Any diminution in ventricular muscle mass leads to a reduction in cardiac output and a low blood pressure, which is found on clinical examination. Moodie (1987) found that heart rate and blood pressure response to exercise were also blunted in anorexics, and oxygen consumption and total work performance were similarly diminished.

Cardiac dysfunction affects the body's ability to cope with vigorous exercise which may have serious consequences for those who indulge in such regimes throughout their illness.

Abnormal ECG recordings

ECG recordings have been found to be abnormal in some studies of young adolescent anorexics. Rapid weight loss in the period immediately prior to having this investigation performed brings about an alteration in the expected QRS axis, and an increased dispersion of the QTC interval (Swenne and Larsson, 1999). Abnormal electro-cardiograph findings appear to be more specific to patients with anorexia, but are not so likely to be detected in those with bulimia nervosa or eating disorder not otherwise specified (Panagiotopoulos *et al*, 2000).

Studies among males with anorexia nervosa have identified similar cardiac complications to those found in female sufferers. Elevated heart rates and some degree of heart failure were found in one small study of male anorexics. Siegal *et al* (1995) suggested that the advanced stage of cardiac dysfunction may have been due to a reluctance on the part of these men to seek treatment and possible difficulties in establishing a diagnosis. The effect of these changes on a young heart may have serious implications for health, and sudden death as a result of cardiac arrhythmia is a known possibility.

Bradycardia is a recognised complication of anorexia nervosa, and can be confirmed on ECG. Kollai *et al* (1994) studied the mechanism by which this complication occurs and the related factors involved in its development. They found that cardiac vagal tone was approximately 30% higher in the anorexic group than the control group, with vagal tone values directly related to the amount of weight loss. This sequence of events was found to play a significant part in the bradycardia which subsequently occurred.

Mitral valve prolapse has also been diagnosed in patients with anorexia, although little is understood about this complication. Oka *et al* (1984) reported a prevalence rate of 74% for this complication, although it is not clear whether the mitral valve dysfunction was present before the onset of anorexic symptoms or materialised as a complication of the illness.

The scope of potential damage to the heart is immense and needs careful investigation at the time of detection of the illness if permanent damage is to be prevented.

Central nervous system

- ⌘ Structural abnormalities.
- ⌘ Reduced grey matter.
- ⌘ Cognitive impairment.

Structural abnormalities

Brain abnormalities have been found to be directly related to the degree of starvation (Golden *et al*, 1996) and it would seem likely that these changes will be more severe in those with low body mass indices. The central canal of the neural tube within the brain is expanded into chambers, known as ventricles. In relation to each ventricle there is a choroid plexus which secretes cerebrospinal fluid.

Cerebral ventricular enlargement has been found among anorexics in several studies (Golden *et al*, 1996; Dolan *et al*, 1988) and also occurs in childhood onset schizophrenia (Hendren *et al*, 2000). Studies to evaluate the cause for this repeated finding have been able to identify an inverse relationship between the patient's weight and the severity of this complication. Golden *et al* (1996) found that the lower the patient's body mass index, the greater the degree of ventricular enlargement. A very low body mass index is most likely to transpire in someone who has been anorexic for some time, suggesting that this problem may worsen as the duration of illness lengthens and weight loss persists.

The issue of whether any physiological effects of self-starvation can be reversed with nutritional improvement has been extensively researched. Swayze *et al* (1996) confirmed that cerebral ventricular size remains reduced in the majority of anorexic patients who are able to regain a normal weight after treatment. These abnormalities are referred to as pseudoatrophy, and although more common in anorexia, they can be found in bulimia and suggest a compromised nutritional state with adverse effects on major organ systems (Mitchell *et al*, 1997).

Reduced grey matter

Reduced grey matter has also been identified as a structural brain abnormality (Katzman *et al*, 1996), which occurs when the brain is starved of vital nutrients. The brain is able to metabolise and utilise glucose extracted from nutritional sources, to produce energy for its own requirements. It is able to store only limited quantities of glycogen and requires a continual supply of glucose from the daily diet to meet its need. It seems a logical assumption that anorexics who persistently deny their body of food will suffer ill-effects from their refusal to satisfy this requirement.

Comparisons with healthy controls have confirmed that grey matter volumes are reduced in anorexics, and studies which have followed long-term prognosis have implied that this may persist after weight gain (Lambe *et al,* 1997). These findings may indicate an irreversible sequence of brain changes that occur as a result of self-starvation and the implication that any significant loss of grey matter which occurs during the illness will be a long-term manifestation.

Cognitive impairment

Given the effect of minimal food intake on brain structure, it would seem rational that poor concentration levels may accompany the deprivation of nutrients required to maintain a healthy body and mind.

Difficulties exist in assessing the affect which anorexia nervosa has on cognitive function, partly because of the range of impairment possible in any one individual. Studies have so far produced variable results with a range of cognitive skills analysed, including memory recall, the ability to learn new tasks, and repetition skills.

Detection rates of impairment are affected by the research methods used and particular functions have been found to be impaired in some studies, but normal in others.

Kingston *et al* (1996) identified a pattern among low weight anorexics who performed poorly across a range of cognitive tasks, particularly those designed to measure attention span, psychomotor speed and certain memory related tasks. Low body weight appeared to play the most significant role in poorer performance among these patients. The long-term outcome is worrying with evidence to suggest that even when weight is restored to a healthier level, deficits on memory tasks and on flexibility and inhibition tasks persist despite substantial weight recovery (Lambe *et al*, 1997).

Musculoskeletal system

⌘ Osteoporosis.

⌘ Increased risk of skeletal fractures.

⌘ Reduced muscle mass/neuromuscular dysfunction.

⌘ Stunting of growth.

Osteoporosis

Osteoporosis is a progressive condition commonly associated with the elderly and is a relatively regular finding among this age group. Many elderly patients endure significant pain from this condition which is responsible for considerable morbidity among sufferers.

Bone loss is considered a normal part of the ageing process and is caused by the body's inability to continue to renew the living cells found in bone. The process begins after the age of 35 and is accelerated after the menopause when oestrogen production slows and eventually ceases. Although its production continues for a while after the cessation of menstruation, this eventually diminishes to such a level that plasma oestrogen levels are unable to maintain the function of those tissues dependent on its presence. Oestrogen is known to have a protective effect on the skeleton and the loss of this protective mechanism is reflected in the loss of bone mass which occurs as a result.

Cases of severe anorexia nervosa are associated with diminished bone mass with potentially serious long-term effects. The basis for bone loss within the context of this illness has been attributed to malnutrition, low calcium and vitamin D levels, and deficient oestrogen levels which are sustained during the period of intense dieting and starvation (Brotman and Stern, 1985; Rigotti *et al*, 1984).

The effects on the body of extreme malnutrition result in amenorrhoea, with a subsequent reduction in plasma oestrogen levels. These cumulative factors are thought to play a pivotal role in reducing peak bone mass in patients with anorexia nervosa. The teenage years are a period of rapid growth and it would appear logical that depriving the body of much needed nutrients at this time will cause considerable damage to health.

Bone mass intensifies during the teenage years as the long bones of the skeleton expand in size during the adolescent growth spurt, and it is estimated that this phase reaches its peak at some point late in adolescence or in some cases in early adulthood.

The maturation of the female skeleton at this time must prepare bone structure for the stresses of pregnancy and labour, and girls in particular need to deposit more calcium in their bones during puberty than their male counterparts to prepare the body (Lyritis *et al*, 2000). Thus, the onset of anorexic symptoms in the early teenage years will have a potentially more devastating effect on skeletal development than those cases of later onset (Bachrach *et al*, 1990); two-thirds of the anorexic girls in this study were found to have bone mineral density measurements below the expected levels for their particular age group. Statistics indicate that osteoporosis among children and adolescents is rare, and since 1965 only 100 cases of ideopathic juvenile osteoporosis have been reported (Lyritis *et al*, 2000).

A study to evaluate the clinical course of osteoporosis followed a group of women over a median period of 25 months. During the course of the follow-up period little change was observed in cortical bone density and there was no difference between women who recovered to within 15–20% of their ideal body weight and those who did not (Rigotti *et al*, 1991). These observations were apparent even in those subjects; whose menstrual cycle had returned to a regular pattern, who had made sufficient weight gains, who had reduced their exercise levels to a healthy amount and had taken calcium supplements in an attempt to rectify the situation. Weight gain during the recovery period and its effect on peak bone mass were evaluated.

Evidence to support the effects of malnutrition on bone mineral density in females is considerable, although to date little research has been conducted to determine whether these findings can also be applied to male anorexics. Andersen *et al* (2000) studied records of patients admitted for assessment and treatment at an American clinic over a period of seven years.

Their findings suggested that anorexic men were more deficient in bone mineral density than women with either anorexia or bulimia. A worrying inclusion to this report was that men with bulimia were also found to have reduced bone mineral density, which suggests that both these conditions have a significant impact on skeletal health in male patients, and are not only frequently found in men with eating disorders but are also serious (Andersen *et al*, 2000).

Skeletal fractures

The severity of bone mass deficit in some cases of anorexia nervosa may be sufficient to result in pathological fractures (Brotman and Stern, 1985), and this increased risk occurs irrespective of the patient's age (Grinspoon *et al*, 1999). Rigotti *et al* (1991) found several incidences of fractures at various sites among young girls, including a pelvic stress fracture, a metatarsal fracture, and a vertebral fracture.

Hartman *et al* (2000) identified a potential association between pathological fractures and excessive exercise. The fractures identified within their study occurred during the course of the anorexic illness in subjects who pursued a rigorous exercise regime, hence subjecting the body to intense physical stress.

Treasure *et al* (1987) reported that bone density was reduced in proportion to the duration of illness, with an increased risk of pathological fractures evident in those whose duration of illness was greater than ten years.

Reduced muscle mass

The drastic weight loss which accompanies anorexia leads to a reduction in muscle mass at a range of sites around the body, with an equivalent amount of muscle weakness. McLoughlin *et al* (2000) studied severely malnourished anorexics and found proximal muscular weakness to be present in all subjects examined. Restoration of normal eating patterns and a healthy weight were found to reinstate the body mechanisms associated with muscle metabolism and the subsequent rebuilding of muscle mass: improvement which became apparent as the nutritional status of the individual improved.

Evidence of neuromuscular dysfunction (defined as significant muscle weakness on examination, together with either an abnormal electromyogram, raised creatinine kinase or abnormal muscle biopsy) has also been discovered in a cohort of patients attending for treatment of their illness. All cases with neuromuscular dysfunction had haematological changes associated with severe weight loss (Shur *et al*, 1988).

The need to detect anorexia nervosa among both males and females becomes even greater, given that the evidence clearly indicates that its effects will remain with the individual for an indefinite period unless early detection and intervention is commenced.

Fluid and electrolyte imbalance in anorexia nervosa

Hypokalaemia is the most frequent electrolyte abnormality encountered in clinical practice, the main cause of which is laxative and diuretic misuse (Tsuchiya *et al*, 1995). Hypokalaemia, hyponatraemia, and hypochloraemia have also been found (Hall *et al*, 1989; Brotman *et al*, 1985). Hypercalcaemia is another major electrolyte abnormality (Tsuchiya *et al*, 1995), while hypochloraemia was found to be present in 25% of patients who vomited or purged, and occurred as a direct result of either the frequency of vomiting or diuretic and laxative abuse (Palla and Litt, 1988).

Electrolyte imbalances of prolonged duration are associated with numerous renal manifestations (Tsuchiya *et al*, 1995), and if these abnormalities remain untreated the medical consequences are mainly those of cardiac arrhythmia and sudden death.

Electrolyte	Normal serum value	Symptoms
Potassium Low (hypokalaemia)	3.7–5.7mmol/l	cramps cardiac arrhythmia muscle weakness
Sodium Low (hyponatraemia)	137–150mmol/l	confusion, fits, lethargy
Chlorine Low (hypochloraemia)	97–108mmol/l	hypotension shallow breathing excitability of nerves and muscles
Calcium High (hypercalcaemia)	2.2–2.7mmol/l	nausea vomiting malaise constipation polydipsia polyuria
Phosphate Low (hypophos-phataemia)	0.7–1.40mmol/l	muscle weakness fatigue

Figure 2.1: Fluid and electrolyte imbalance in anorexia nervosa

Renal dysfunction

Excessive laxative abuse has been found to result in renal insufficiency (Copeland, 1994; Herzog *et al*, 1997), and it is suspected that renal abnormalities may occur in as many as 70% of anorexics (Brotman *et al*, 1986).

Copeland (1994) reported a case of severe renal failure, which was found to be linked to profound volume depletion, a potentially life-threatening complication of laxative abuse and laxative associated renal failure.

Reduced glomerular filtration rates have been found in subjects who are severely malnourished and present with a vast decrease in fat and lean body mass (Aperia *et al*, 1978; Brion *et al*, 1989). The dehydrated state which is often found in anorexia nervosa may play a part in the development of renal stones. Silber and Kass (1984) found evidence of this in a patient who had primary anorexia and nephro-lithiasis, although this association remains relatively poorly understood.

Creatinine clearance and urinary creatinine excretion may also be impaired in those subjects who have lost substantial amounts of weight, although with implementation of a refeeding regime and subsequent weight gain these functions return to normal (Boag *et al*, 1985).

Blood: Haematological abnormalities

Anaemia: deficiency in the quantity or quality of red blood cells.
Symptoms: tiredness, breathlessness, pallor, ankle oedema, lethargy.

Leucopenia: Reduced number of white blood cells.
Symptoms: Reduced infections, the mouth, throat, ears, chest and skin are common sites.

Thrombocytopenia: Reduction in the number of platelets in the blood.
Symptoms: prolonged bleeding, purpura.

Mild anaemia, neutropenia, thrombocytopenia with changes in red cell morphology are common findings in anorexia nervosa (Shur *et al*, 1988).

Devuyst *et al* (1993) found evidence of anaemia, low leucocyte counts, and increased prevalence of leucopenia, neutropenia and thrombocytopenia. The presence of these haematological changes render the individual susceptible to low immunity, and an increased likelihood of contracting infections, a problem which may be further compounded by a reduced ability to make a quick recovery. Devuyst *et al* (1993) found evidence of severe infectious complications among 9% of anorexia patients, with no similar findings among the control group, confirming the likelihood that these problems occurred as a complication of the malnourished state.

In a cohort of patients admitted for treatment, all were found to have evidence of haematological abnormalities on admission, however, all abnormalities reverted to normal during the course of weight gain, with the exception of leucopenia which persisted for several weeks despite improved nutritional status (Shur *et al*, 1988).

Metabolic changes

- ⌘ Lipid abnormalities.
- ⌘ Hypoglycaemia.
- ⌘ Impaired temperature regulation.

Lipid abnormalities

The presence of hypercholesteraemia in anorexia nervosa is puzzling, given that the cholesterol intake of anorexics is normally very low (Feillet *et al*, 2000). The relationship is poorly understood, but it appears that there is identified a negative correlation between total cholesterol and LDL cholesterol and body mass index, with initial high cholesterol levels relating to those patients with the worst nutritional status (Feillet *et al*, 2000). Although this relationship remains poorly understood, theories have included the possibility that deficiencies of selected essential fatty acids occur in anorexia (necessary for normal growth and development) which are matched by changes in non-essential fatty acids in an attempt to compensate (Holman *et al*, 1995).

Nestel (1973) indicated that hyperlipidaemia occurs due to a reduced secretion of bile acid, which normally promotes the emulsification of fat.

Hypoglycaemia

Hypoglycaemia occurs when the blood glucose level falls below normal values resulting in altered mood, sweating and hunger. Severe hypoglycaemia is reported to be a rare event, however its consequences are serious. The pathogenesis remains poorly understood, although several mechanisms, including depletion of liver glycogen, defective gluconeogenesis or failure of glucagon secretion have been proposed (Smith, 1988). Ratcliffe and Bevan (1985) reported two cases of hypoglycaemic coma which resulted in death of one of these cases. The major risk factors have been identified as low body weight (below 30kg), a period of fasting and intercurrent infection, with the possibility that excessive exercise may also play a role (Smith, 1988).

Impaired temperature regulation

Palla and Litt (1988) reported a correlation between pulse rate and body temperature, with the lowest recorded values for each occurring during the night, which the authors attributed to the body's need to conserve its meagre energy stores. Marked hypothermia was noted in 52% of strict dieters, and 33% of those who adopted additional weight control practices, with body temperatures as low as 34°C recorded (Palla and Litt, 1988).

Endocrine changes

⌘ Increased growth hormone levels.

⌘ Increased cortisol levels.

⌘ Altered thyroid function.

⌘ Gonadotrophin levels.

⌘ Amenorrhoea.

Growth hormone

Growth hormone is secreted by the anterior pituitary gland, and stimulates the release of insulin-like growth factor 1 which enhances growth by stimulating protein synthesis (Vander *et al*, 1994).

Abnormalities of the growth hormone, insulin, like growth factor axis have been described in patients with anorexia nervosa (Argente *et al*, 1997).

Golden *et al* (1994) compared growth hormone levels of three groups of women, the first were recently hospitalised anorectic patients, the second were partly recovered anorexics, the third were healthy matched control subjects. They concluded that patients from the ill group had diminished growth hormone action, which was positively linked to low body mass index, which explains the growth retardation seen in anorexia nervosa.

Growth retardation

Danziger *et al* (1994) examined a group of young adolescents who were attending treatment, all of whom had been symptomatic for several months prior to their request for help. Stunting of growth was found to be a feature in all cases, and its appearance as a regular clinical finding, prompted Danziger *et al* to suggest that this particular clinical manifestation should be considered as an inclusion in the diagnostic criteria.

A French study of growth and puberty among nineteen children with anorexia noted important individual changes with some patients enduring a prolonged interruption of growth. Seventeen of the nineteen patients exhibited signs of growth retardation, with some hormonal abnormalities found to persist even after resolution of their illness (Kholy *et al*, 1986). Rates of recovery have been reported to vary from patient to patient. Danziger *et al* (1994) reported different degrees of catch-up growth observed in all patients who remained under treatment for a duration of one year or more.

Increased cortisol levels

Hypercortisolaemia has been reported in subjects with anorexia nervosa (Warren and Vande Wiele, 1973; Girardin *et al*, 1991, Gwirtsman *et al*, 1989).

Girardin *et al* (1991) found that in all subjects examined, both total and free plasma cortisol concentrations were higher than in the control subjects as were their urinary free cortisol levels. Similar findings were reported by Gwirtsman *et al* (1989) who found evidence of elevated cortisol levels in the cerebrospinal fluid, raised plasma cortisol levels and increased levels of urinary free cortisol. In common with other studies plasma adrenocorticotrophic hormone levels (ACTH) were found to be normal (Warren and Vande Wiele, 1973; Gwirtsman *et al*, 1989). Excess cortisol production is found in Cushing's syndrome, which shares some of the clinical features of anorexia nervosa.

Cameron and Warne (1997) suggested that despite the over-production of cortisol in these patients, the obesity of Cushing's disease may be overcome by the combination of diet and exercise which anorexics adopt.

Thyroid dysfunction

The symptoms which anorexics commonly experience include susceptibility to cold, constipation and bradycardia, all of which are experienced in hypothyroidism.

Thyroid hormone levels are decreased in anorexic subjects (Bannai *et al*, 1988; Natori *et al*, 1994). Markedly decreased T_3 levels have been found to correlate negatively with total cholesterol levels, which may suggest that the metabolic state of underweight anorexics depends considerably on the serum T_3 concentration (Bannai *et al*, 1988).

Gonadotrophin levels

Two hormones produced by the anterior pituitary gland are follicle-stimulating hormone and leutinising hormone, which are evident in both sexes but achieve different effects. In anorexia nervosa there are low levels of both hormones with a reduction in the normal rate of episodic release (Warren and Vande Wiele, 1973).

Amenorrhoea

Amenorrhoea is a component of the diagnostic criteria for anorexia and has received some attention to identify the physiological reasons for its existence in the context of this illness.

The hormonal interactions which facilitate onset of the menstrual cycle involve a complex series of mechanisms, which are under the control of the hypothalamus.

Even before the onset of puberty, hormones are released from the hypothalamus and transported to the pituitary gland where they are able to promote the synthesis and release of a number of hormones, all of which are required at different sites around the body. The release of gonadotrophic releasing hormone (GNRH) commences in childhood when small quantities of this hormone are released, but as the body reaches puberty the rate of release is altered so that secretion into the bloodstream takes place in a series of surges which continue throughout the day (Vander *et al*, 1994).

Once menstruation commences the production of GNRH continues in this way throughout the reproductive years, although it is combined alongside a number of complex feedback mechanisms which control the release of a follicle each month in the process of ovulation, and the subsequent monthly bleed if the ovum is not fertilised.

During the ripening of the follicles, prior to ovulation, oestrogen is synthesised and released into the bloodstream. Self-starvation and rapid weight loss suppresses the level of oestrogen, hence interfering with the process of menstruation. The ovaries of severely mal-nourished anorexics also reduce in size, a factor which only resolves on refeeding and restoration of normal body weight (Sharp and Freeman, 1993). During the course of the anorexic illness, the combination of low dietary intake and extreme physical exercise regimes is felt to further enhance the state of amenorrhoea (Couzinet *et al*, 1999).

In male subjects the physiological effects are seen as a diminished production of testosterone, which results in a loss of sexual interest and potency (Walsh and Garner, 1997).

Even in those subjects with a milder illness, there is evidence to suggest that those who engage in mild dieting, with a close to normal, but prolonged period of fat restriction, are likely to experience some interference in gonadotrophin secretion. Copeland *et al* (1995) found that patients who lost an average of 5% of their body weight had cessation of menses within one year.

Factors associated with the resumption of menses in young anorexics have also been investigated (Golden *et al*, 1997). Patients were given a target weight to achieve which was approximately 2.5kg more than the weight at which their monthly periods ceased. Of those who were successful in achieving this weight, 86% were found to resume normal monthly periods within a six-month period of regaining the required target; indicating that, in most cases, a relatively small amount of weight regain is sufficient for resumption of a normal menstrual pattern.

Reproductive system

Pregnancy

Despite the implication that many women will become amen-norrhoeic, some will continue to menstruate and may manage to conceive despite maintaining their weight at sub-optimal levels (Treasure and Russell, 1988). When this arises, it is not without problems. Maternal complications have been noted to include hyperemesis and vaginal bleeding; fetal and birth complications have included low birth weight and premature death (Treasure and Russell, 1988).

Observation of a group of anorexic women followed throughout their pregnancies showed weight gain to be well below the recommended amount. Monitoring of fetal growth demonstrated that rate of growth of the abdominal circumference of all babies was diminished during the last trimester, yet accelerated growth was seen in all babies during the first few months of life (Treasure and Russell, 1988).

Gastrointestinal system

The process of self-starvation induces a reduction in gastric capacity so that when the sufferer does eat, they frequently report symptoms of constipation, bloating, and abdominal pains suggestive of abnormal gastrointestinal motility or transit (Kamal *et al*, 1991).

Comparison of healthy controls and anorexic patients has confirmed that gastric emptying was slower in the ill cohort, although liquid emptying appeared to be normal (McCallum *et al*, 1985). In a group of patients hospitalised for treatment, a variety of gastrointestinal problems were evident on admission, including constipation, diarrhoea, and vomiting. All symptoms with the exclusion of belching made significant improvements with refeeding and weight gain (Waldholtz and Anderson, 1990).

Evidence of gastrointestinal bleeding has also been found to occur in association with excessive exercise (Ferron, 1999). Following admission for investigation of a low Hb, the true cause only became apparent when the girl was found running 'on the spot' for prolonged periods each night during her admission. Her haemoglobin status improved with iron supplementation and improved dietary status.

However, the case highlights the need for vigilance and an awareness that there may be a differential diagnosis.

Skin problems

There is evidence to support the presence of dermatological problems which occur as a consequence of malnourishment. Schultz *et al* (1999) noted the existence of xerosis (a condition which renders the conjuctiva dry), hypertrichosis (diffuse growth of hair which can occur on any part of the body), acrocyanosis (cyanosis with coldness of the feet and hands), and brittle nails.

These conditions were diagnosed in anorexic children (aged eight to seventeen) attending a paediatric clinic. The young age of these subjects suggests that these findings may manifest themselves after a relatively short duration of illness in some individuals.

Similar findings have been detected in older female patients. In women aged nineteen to twenty-four, studies have identified the most common dermatological findings to be xerosis, cheilitis (fissures and maceration at the mouth), hypertrichosis, alopecia, dry scalp, acrocyanosis, nail changes and calluses on the dorsum of the hand in those who induced vomiting (Hediger *et al*, 2000). This study was able to determine the importance of weight loss in relation to these changes. A very low body mass index of sixteen and below appeared to be significant in increasing the likelihood that dermatological changes would be present on examination.

Late onset anorexia

Anorexia nervosa which develops after the age of thirty years is thought to be rare, although not unknown. The clinical features seen in women who develop this condition at an older age have been found to be broadly similar to those exhibited by girls who develop the condition in adolescence. In older women the illness can be even more difficult to diagnose, primarily because the mature age at presentation makes the sufferer more likely to hide their obvious weight loss under the possibility of a co-existing medical condition, and may result in a prolonged period of investigation before the true cause becomes apparent. Joughan *et al* (1991) suggested that such patients may be able to conceal the psychological origins of their problems behind the possibility of a primary physical condition such as depression, with the true diagnosis only becoming apparent when treatment regimes fail to rectify the weight loss and the patient continues their pursuit of thinness despite medical intervention.

Psychiatric comorbidity

From the earliest recognition of eating disorders an association has been made with psychiatric illness. The growing interest in these conditions has led to a volume of research concentrating their potential role in the clinical presentation. Specific areas which have been a focus for debate include the issue of whether psychiatric symptoms precede the onset of the eating disorder and are therefore involved in the aetiology, or develop during the course of the illness. Marked personality changes mimicking primary personality disorders stem from prolonged under-nutrition (Garner *et al*, 1997). A comprehensive and thorough picture of a patient's personality features prior to onset of the illness needs to be gathered. Close family may be able to offer a valuable insight into the person's mood and temperament prior to this period.

Personality disorders

Diagnosis of personality disorders is notoriously difficult. The complex nature of these conditions is further complicated by the fact that many sufferers have been found to exhibit features of more than one of these disorders, at any given time, during the course of their illness.

Estimates suggest that as many as 50–70% of eating disordered individuals meet the diagnostic criteria for more than one personality disorder during the course of their illness (Matsunaga and Kiriike, 1997). Gartner *et al* (1989) found that 57% of patients in one study were found to have two or more personality disorders, while a further 17% met the diagnostic criteria for five to seven diagnoses. The possibility of several of these conditions coexisting at the same time makes the picture extremely complicated and presents health professionals with a considerable dilemma in offering the best treatment to deal with the patient's problems. In these particular instances their role in affecting response to treatment and long-term outcome for patients remains unclear. Murakami and Suwaki (1999) studied the clinical course of a group of anorexia nervosa patients. Follow-up evaluation found that readmission occurred as a result of continued abnormal behaviour patterns associated with their co-morbid illness, suggesting inadequate or ineffective treatment. Those with multiple pathologies required readmission for unresolved symptoms which were directly related to the psychopathology of comorbidity (Murakami and Suwacki, 1999), indicating that such a complex scenario may have an influence on long-term prognosis, with a poorer recovery made by those who share a comorbid condition.

Diagnosis is rarely clear-cut, and a number of criteria need to be satisfied to ensure that the diagnosis is accurate before an individual is assigned to a particular personality type, and can be offered appropriate medical help.

For ease of classification conditions are grouped together, conditions listed within each group are known to share some clinical features, and therefore have some overlap in their presentation.

Association of eating disorders and cluster groups

Cluster A	Cluster B	Cluster C
Eccentric	Borderline personality	Avoidant
Schizoid	Emotionally vulnerable	Anxiety state
Paranoid	Histrionic	Compulsive behaviour

Anorexia nervosa has been found to be associated with personality types in cluster C, particularly those of the obsessive compulsive and avoidant personality types.

Co-existence of personality types in cluster A (eccentric, schizoid and paranoid) has been noted among those with anorexia nervosa, although there is recent evidence to suggest that schizophrenia and schizoid personality types can also be displayed in those with bulimia nervosa.

Anxiety disorders

Anxiety disorders are characterised by irritability, difficulty in concentration, restlessness and a poor memory (Gelder *et al*, 1991). Comorbid anxiety disorders are common in anorexia nervosa (Bulik *et al*, 1997a; Fornari *et al*, 1992), with 58% of patients in one study being found to have exhibited symptoms of their disorder approximately five years prior to the onset of their anorexic symptoms. Bulik *et al* (1997a) reported similar findings with 90% of women in their study having anxiety disorders which preceded the onset of their illness, although panic disorder developed at a later date. Anxiety disorders are particularly prevalent among anorexia sufferers (Deep *et al*, 1995), and the early and common onset of childhood anxiety disorders in a substantial percentage of anorexics raises the possibility that these disorders herald the first expression of a biologic vulnerability in some subjects who later develop anorexia nervosa

Avoidant personality disorders

Individuals who have this personality type are described as highly anxious people who do not cope well with life events. They tend to appear nervous and may avoid the stresses of unnecessary responsibility, primarily because they have problems dealing with the associated distress should they fail at the task that they have been given. They appear as a person who is emotionally vulnerable, fears rejection and failure in many areas of life. They are of a sensitive nature and are easily hurt by people and events which occur around them, and therefore take steps to avoid the possibility of emotional rejection.

These individuals fear rebuff and because of these inhibitions they experience problems in social interaction both at work and in family life, and may be seen to have very few close friends as a result. Avoidant personality disorders have been found to coexist in a number of studies of anorexia nervosa (Pryor *et al*, 1996; Gillberg *et al*, 1995). The effect which the presence of these disorders can have on the illness itself when compared to anorexics without comorbid personality problems appears to be substantial. For those who have this dual diagnosis their anorexia is often characterised by chronicity and low levels of functioning (Skodol *et al*, 1993).

Obsessive compulsive disorder

Anorexia nervosa sufferers frequently exhibit signs of compulsive behaviour which may manifest itself in several forms. This is defined as repetitive and seemingly purposeful behaviours performed in a stereotyped way (Gelder *et al*, 1991). Such behaviour patterns tend to become more severe as the condition progresses. Perpetual calorie counting or the adoption of a gruelling daily exercise regime frequently become a part of the person's daily life. The personality of the anorexic has already been mentioned and there are many descriptions of 'rigid, ritualistic, perfectionist and meticulous individuals' (Matsunaga *et al*, 1999), who display these traits prior to the onset of anorexic symptoms.

Such characteristics have also been attributed to obsessive compulsive disorders which are estimated to affect approximately 1% of children and adolescents (Valleni-Basille *et al*, 1994). Children with this condition are described as secretive in nature, often adhering to ritualistic behaviour patterns in their daily lives, which they are often able to conceal from those close to them.

Bolton *et al* (1995) discussed the impact that such conduct might have on the individual lives of these children, and implied that they may be responsible for the impairment of social functioning. The emotional turmoil which such a condition brings may have an impact on the ability to interact and form friendships, which will ultimately have a long-term effect on the individual's ability to function normally in society.

Bolton *et al* (1995) described protracted psychiatric morbidity as well as long-lasting social impairment as factors associated with this condition. The lifetime prevalence of obsessive compulsive disorder among patients with existing anorexia nervosa is estimated to be a component of the illness in approximately 25% of cases (Halmi *et al*, 1991). The issue which has evoked debate is whether obsessive compulsive disorder exists prior to the onset of anorexic symptoms, and is a causative factor, or whether the condition appears as anorexia progresses. Garfinkel and Garner (1982) suggested that the combination of self-starvation and the extreme weight loss which follows, may have a significant role to play in the development of obsessive compulsive traits in anorexics. They discussed the possibility that such personality traits develop as a consequence of the malnourished state rather than as a predisposing factor which was present prior to the onset of the disease.

A recent Japanese study compared the clinical characteristics exhibited by two groups of patients, one with obsessive compulsive disorder, the other with anorexia nervosa. The findings identified some shared characteristics in the symptomology of the two conditions, although many of the anorexia sufferers manifested significant impairment from primary obsessive compulsive disorder symptoms with a similar level of severity to that exhibited by obsessive compulsive disorder patients (Matsunaga *et al*, 1999).

Schizoid personality/schizophrenia

Schizophrenia is characterised by unusual perceptual experiences, social anxiety, inability to make close friendships, eccentric behaviour and social anxiety (Gelder *et al*, 1991). Paranoia may exist and this type of personality has a deep suspicion of everything and everyone around them, believing that others are 'out to get them'.

They often believe that others mean them harm, and because of this deep mistrust they are unable to form normal social relationships with others and are inclined to be socially withdrawn. They may purposely resist social interaction and appear to others to be grossly introverted, often described as 'loners'.

Eccentric personalities differ from the above in that they are seen to behave in an odd manner, and in a way that differs from the perceived norm within their cultural group.

Schizophrenia

The incidence of schizophrenia in eating disorders is estimated to be approximately 1–3% with a far more likely association to be found with anorexia nervosa than bulimia nervosa (Joos and Steinert, 1997). Delusions are evident in this illness, and it is plausible that where such disturbed thoughts centre around food, food avoidance may form a part of their illness. In those who have presented in this manner investigations have been keen to determine at what stage the clinical features of anorexia nervosa develop. Brzozowska *et al* (1998) studied three patients with the condition, and found that in one case, anorexia developed within the context of the schizophrenic illness, while in the other two patients, the psychotic features emerged following recovery from the eating disorder. Lyketsos *et al* (1985) found eating disorders among schizophrenics to be relatively common, with two fifths of participants within their study experiencing eating disorders which were associated with delusions, a further sixth had an eating disorder associated with hallucinations.

Substance abuse

Excessive intake of alcohol tends to develop after the onset of the anorexic illness, and has predominantly been a feature in those subjects who engage in bingeing and purging alongside their anorexia (Deep *et al*, 1995).

Bailly (1993) identified similar high rates of substance abuse in bulimic and bulimic anorexics, with a lower prevalence rate reported among restricting anorexics. Bailly also noted that bulimic anorexics exhibited similar behavioural characteristics to bulimics with a substance abuse problem (greater impulsive behaviour, tendency to steal, suicide attempts and relationship problems).

Prevalence rates for alcohol abuse or dependence range from 0.6% for those subjects with restricting anorexia nervosa, but this statistic rises to approximately 10–28% in the presence of bulimic symptoms (Laessle *et al*, 1987).

Depression

Depression, anxiety and obsessional behaviour are frequently present in the symptoms of underweight malnourished patients (Pollice *et al*, 1997), and the severity of each of these three conditions varies in severity from patient to patient. When patients are found to have symptoms of more than one of these states, it has remained inconclusive which of these (if any) has presented as the dominant illness. Seventy-five of the anorexics in one study qualified for at least one depression diagnosis at some point in their lifetime, while 45% qualified for at least one anxiety diagnosis in their medical history, which indicated that anorexic subjects were significantly more likely to display depressive symptoms than anxiety disorders (Fornari *et al*, 1992). Some of the symptoms of depression, such as poor sleep patterns and inability to concentrate, are shared with those exhibited by eating disordered individuals, and have been thought to occur as a result of the lack of nutritional intake. In the presence of profound calorie depletion patients with anorexia experience restlessness, sleeplessness, total preoccupation with food and the impulse to forage (Crisp, 1997). Evaluation of depressive symptoms at different stages of illness (underweight, short-term weight restored and long-term weight recovered) revealed the scores for depression, anxiety and obsessional behaviour were highest in the underweight state, with milder but nevertheless elevated symptoms found to persist in the weight recovered group when compared to a group of healthy women (Pollice, 1997).

Assessment of 198 female patients with anorexia nervosa, revealed that 43% met the criteria for major depression on examination, which clearly has practical implications for treatment given the problems of treating these conditions, problems which are likely to be greater when they occur together (Kennedy *et al*, 1994).

Laessle *et al* (1987) studied fifty-two women with a long-standing history of anorexia and found that those who were attempting to resolve their illness had lower rates of depression, and that in most cases the onset of the depressive illness post-dated onset of the eating disorder by at least one year.

Depression is often a long-standing illness, and effective treatment is a necessary pathway for recovery from anorexia nervosa once weight has been restored (Crisp, 1997).

Differential diagnosis

The clinical features of anorexia nervosa and bulimia are shared by a number of medical conditions, and any individual who presents with weight loss (with or without anorexia and associated symptoms) requires further investigation to determine the underlying cause. Because of the young age often associated with the development of eating disorders, there may be a reluctance to consider some of the alternative diagnoses, particularly those which are much more common in adulthood. The clinical picture becomes more complicated when the child is found to display psychiatric symptomatology, which makes the diagnosis of an eating disorder seem a more likely possibility. This warrants further investigation and confirmation that anorexia nervosa is not the diagnosis becomes apparent when a full psychological examination fails to clarify the underlying psychiatric disturbance typical of the illness.

Anorexia is defined as 'loss of appetite' and is a feature which accompanies many medical conditions.

Anorexia, nausea, loss of appetite and weight loss can accompany a number of medical conditions, and any patient who presents with such symptoms requires a full medical examination to gain an accurate clinical picture.

Differential diagnosis might include:

* Carcinoma: cranial lesions.

* Tuberculosis.

* Wasting diseases.

* Crohn's disease.

Carcinoma: cranial lesions

Many of the malignant lesions, particularly early in their stages of growth, are associated with vague changes in the person's health indicative of underlying illness, and a number of site specific symptoms which develop as the disease progresses. Young children who are ill may be unable to describe how they feel, or may be uncooperative and reluctant to do so, leaving medical staff reliant on information supplied by parents to point towards a diagnosis.

De Vile *et al* (1995) reported on three cases of children who were diagnosed as anorexic on their clinical symptoms. Following a period of psychiatric treatment, which failed to improve their illness, all were referred for further investigation, and were later found to have an intracranial lesion. Three cases were cited (all male) in which early signs were extremely similar to those of early onset anorexia nervosa. In males and pre-adolescent girls the absence of menstruation as a component of the diagnostic criteria, makes diagnosis more problematic. In each case there were atypical features of anorexia nervosa, and the personal and family histories of these boys further confused the clinical picture, with evidence of a family history of anorexia and a disturbed childhood.

It is fortunate that all three cases were able to make a full recovery following surgical intervention.

A similar study by Chipkevitch (1994) found that anorexia and psychiatric disturbances preceded the neurological signs and/or the correct diagnosis in all of the twenty-one patients within their study. All participants were found to be emaciated, anorexic, and showing signs of psychiatric disturbance, and were diagnosed as having atypical anorexia nervosa. The existence of subthreshold eating disorders (where the patient does not fully meet the diagnostic criteria) bring with them the danger that when an element of doubt exists patients may be assigned to one of these categories, while the underlying cause remains undetected with a potentially fatal outcome.

The site of the tumour may further influence the symptoms exhibited. Chipkevitch (1994) found that lesions of the hypo-thalamus and other sites involved in food regulation, may mimic the features of anorexia nervosa, and that lesions of the germ cell type may be more likely than others to influence the limbic system towards an anorexic syndrome.

Tuberculosis

Tuberculosis (TB) can affect various sites around the body and the symptoms experienced by the patient will reflect this.

In children, symptoms can be mild, and where the site of infection is the lungs, a positive Mantoux test is often the evidence of a previously undetected infection. Mild symptoms may include lethargy, weakness, fever, cough and sputum. Post primary TB occurs when the original infection is reactivated, and this may occur several years later. This is often as a result of a trigger factor, which may be any debilitating condition, diabetes mellitus, malignancy, or steroid therapy.

The features may be confused with those of anorexia nervosa, and organ specific signs may be useful in differentiating the true cause in many cases. TB peritonitis is associated with abdominal pain and gastrointestinal upset, which makes the features of this condition bear a closer resemblance to those of anorexia nervosa.

Wasting diseases

The muscular dystrophys are a group of diseases which share some of the clinical features of eating disorders. They are influenced by genetics and result in a slow deterioration in muscle function.

Duchennes muscular dystrophy is the commonest and onset often occurs at a young age. It is sex linked and is almost always confined to boys (Hope *et al*, 1994). The patient experiences progressive muscular weakness which is associated with weight loss, anorexia and raised serum creatinine kinase levels. The early features of this condition may mimic the signs of early onset anorexia nervosa. Prognosis is poor.

Crohn's disease

Crohn's disease is a debilitating illness which involves a chronic inflammation of the bowels and can affect any part of the gut. The cause is unknown but, if left undetected, the illness can become one of prolonged duration continuing for several years.

The clinical features vary in severity between patients and can include; abdominal pain which may be cramp-like in nature, weight loss, and altered bowel habit (Bradley *et al*, 1994). Where the clinical history is indicative of more than one illness, the skill of diagnosis comes from extracting specific features which are only generally applicable to one condition.

Jenkins *et al* (1988) described four cases of patients who were given a diagnosis of anorexia on initial examination. All were found to exhibit some of the features suggestive of the condition, although the differential which proved vital to the final diagnosis was that none were found to portray any concerns about their weight and none demonstrated a distorted body image.

Irrational and maladaptive thoughts towards eating, shape and weight appears to be an element which is unique to eating disorders. Benjamin (1988) suggested that disturbance of body image and refusal to maintain body weight have much more diagnostic specificity and are not symptomatic of any physical disease or psychiatric condition: their eminence can only indicate anorexia nervosa.

Given the shared features of anorexia nervosa and Crohn's disease, the presence of psychiatric illness in those whose Crohn's disease has not yet been confirmed might be expected to delay the diagnosis further. Rickards *et al* (1994) reported that among children who displayed some degree of psychiatric morbidity, not only did this mask the true illness, but these children also experienced severe growth retardation, which presumably occurred during the delay in diagnosis, suggesting the possibility that the condition may have been present for some time prior to recognition.

In common with other medical conditions there is often a degree of variability in the nature and severity on presentation. Crohn's disease presenting at a very young age is relatively rare, and a child with mild symptoms may confer a confusing clinical picture. Jenkins *et al* (1988) proposed that in many cases school phobia or functional bowel disorders are likely to be considered as differential diagnoses.

Specific investigations (wherever possible), which are unique to the condition under consideration, are needed .

Haematological abnormalities of significance include raised ESR, raised white cell and platelet counts which are likely to be detected in patients with any inflammatory bowel disease, but are not normally present in anorexia nervosa (Harries *et al*, 1983).

It is evident that accurate diagnosis requires thorough investigation with continued co-operation between professional disciplines. Assessment of clinical symptoms may be insufficient to determine whether the true cause of weight loss is psychological or clinical in origin. Where an element of doubt exists in the diagnosis, collaboration between disciplines and referral to a specialist in an alternative field may be needed for successful diagnosis and management.

Suggested further reading

Associated health problems

Devuyst O, Lambert M Rodhain J, Lefebvre C, Coche (1993) Haematological changes and infectious complications in anorexia nervosa: a case control study. *Q J Med* **86**(12): 791–9

Palla B, Litt IF (1988) Medical complications of eating disorders in adolescents. *Paediatrics* **81**(5): 613–23

Sharp CW, Freeman CPL (1993) The medical complications of anorexia nervosa. *Br J Psychiatry* **162**: 452–62

Psychiatric comorbidity

Halmi KA, Eckert E, Marchi P, Sampugnaro V, Apple R, Cohen J (1991) Comorbidity of psychiatric diagnosis in anorexia nervosa. *Arch Gen Psychiatry* **48**: 712–28

Laessle RG, Kittl S, Fichter MM, Wittchen HU, Pirke KM (1987) Major affective disorder in anorexia nervosa and bulimia: A descriptive diagnostic study. *Br J Psychiatry* **151**: 785–9

Differential diagnosis

De Vile CJ, Sufraz R, Lask BD, Stanhope R (1995) Lesson of the week: Occult intracranial tumours masquerading as early onset anorexia nervosa. *Br Med J* **311**: 1359–60

Rickards H, Prendergast M, Booth IW (1994) Psychiatric Presentation of Crohn's disease: Diagnostic delay and increased morbidity. *Br J Psychiatry* **164**: 256–61

3

Treatment and management of anorexia nervosa

Introduction

The aim of treatment is ultimately to restore an acceptable weight and dietary intake, and correct any physiological abnormalities. Equally important, is the need to eradicate any cause, where this can be identified, and address the inappropriate cognition with the ultimate aim of preventing any subsequent relapse.

There are now a number of specialist treatment units for patients with eating disorders, with services for children and adolescents as well as adults.

Some of the most difficult elements during the recovery phase are those which relate to changing the patient's disturbed thinking and related behavioural patterns. The complexity of this task is so great that in many cases input from a variety of sources is required, with liaison and co-operation between those involved, which may require a combination of treatment methods to achieve the most favourable outcome.

There are now a number of options available, although in many cases the treatment of anorexia nervosa remains difficult and controversial (Touyz *et al*, 1984). The initial assessment must take into account the nature of the clinical features and the length of their existence, and the degree of metabolic disturbance so that an appropriate plan of action can be formed in partnership with the patient, and their family. Motivation to be treated is often ambivalent on the part of the individual (Russell *et al*, 1998) and the task of achieving a substantial weight gain which the patient is able to sustain when treatment is completed presents a considerable challenge to the medical profession.

Making a diagnosis and offering help and intervention requires a two-way partnership, with the willingness of the patient to participate in the treatment programme offered. The latter is often a major stumbling block with the patient themselves refusing to believe that there is any need for medical intervention. As a result, programmes are often initiated in response to pressure from other sources, usually friends and family (Scheuble and Dixon, 1987).

Whereas bulimics have been largely found to be willing to accept professional help once their condition is detected, one of the worrying features about anorexia is the often publicised reluctance to accept medical assistance. When help is offered, many react with anger, deception and an increasing level of manipulative behaviour, which later results in a retreat from society (Waller, 1997). Relapse rates and recidivism are so high that the cost of treatment aimed at weight gain has been questioned (Russell *et al*, 1998). The current therapeutic approach relies on a combination of psychological and behavioural techniques, often provided in an inpatient or outpatient setting (American Psychiatric Association, 1993).

The services available range from intensive inpatient therapy (in which sub-specialty general medical consultations are readily available), through to partial hospital and residential programmes, or varying levels of outpatient care from which the patient can receive general medical treatment, nutritional counselling and/or individual, group or family psychotherapy (American Psychiatric Association, 2000).

A multidisciplinary team approach

Specialist input from a variety of professionals, each with their own particular area of expertise, provides shared knowledge which will allow staff to implement a plan of care that is formulated for the needs of the patient. This can then be evaluated and adapted, based on the information provided by the team. Family should become a part of the multidisciplinary team (particularly in younger patients) and need to be involved in the educational process when this is felt to be helpful. They too need to be able to draw on the skills and knowledge of professional staff, particularly when the patient is of a younger age, so that a recurrence of symptoms can be avoided once treatment is completed. For the outcome to be successful, the team needs to be able to function as a cohesive network, adopting a consistent approach with a mutually agreed definition of what an eating disorder is, how the treatment programme is expected to progress and what will constitute a recovery (Garrow, 1980; Willard *et al*, 1983).

Communication skills are vital to the success of this approach with each team member aware of their own limitations and the need to utilise the expertise of other team members when necessary.

Inpatient or outpatient treatment

The decision to treat either on an inpatient or outpatient basis will depend on a number of factors. The selected choice must be based on a full assessment of the severity of physical, psychiatric and behavioural symptoms which will influence the venue and the type of treatment thought to be most likely to produce a successful outcome.

Inpatient care may be necessary in the presence of:

1. Co-existing medical problems which may have potentially serious implications left untreated.
2. The patient exhibits signs of severe psychiatric disturbance. This may manifest itself as obsessive compulsive behaviour, schizophrenia, or suicidal tendencies which suggest that they may be unsafe if left in the community.
3. The patient has undergone a period of rapid weight loss, or presents in a severely emaciated figure.
4. Family environment is such that it might impede rather than promote recovery.

Other criteria necessitating inpatient care are those cases where patient motivation is poor, and where previous attempts to treat have culminated in failure. The primary reason for admission is usually not an acute suicide risk or severe medical abnormalities alone, but the need to reverse the course of a potentially deadly serious progressive illness (Anderson *et al*, 1997). The highly complex nature of this illness often renders it an unsuitable choice for outpatient treatment, largely because of the multifactorial approach required to address each facet of this disease.

Achieving weight gain

The key aims are:

- restoration of an acceptable weight and an adequate nutritional intake
- correction of any physiological problems which have occurred during the starvation process.

Encouraging restoration of a healthy weight, represents a challenging task for all those involved in the recovery process.

Those with low body weights are often extremely difficult to treat because just as the body resists weight loss by making metabolic adjustments, it also resists weight gain (Garner, 1997).

Establishing a target weight for attainment is often fraught with difficulties and requires a sensitive approach. Persistent weight loss over a period of months or even years has been central to the patient's illness, and it is not surprising that many will produce a negative response to any suggested target which is perceived by them to be greater than they wish to achieve. Health professionals in primary care often refer to standardised charts for advice, but for these patients this approach is inappropriate. The main problem with this practice is that it does not take into consideration that weight norms are statistical averages (based on height and weight) and reveal nothing about the natural variability in body weights which occur around these midpoints (Garner, 1997). In an attempt to overcome opposition the agreed target is often lower than recommended by reference guides, with a specified weight range for the patient to adhere to, so that wherever possible emphasis is removed from actual figures.

The rate at which weight gain is achieved is usually slow, with inpatient programmes often able to achieve a 2–3lb gain without compromising the patient's safety (American Psychiatric Association, 2000).

It is important that adequate weight is gained before the patient is transferred to outpatient programmes. Early discharge has been independently researched as it is believed to increase the risk of future recurrence. Baran *et al* (1995) studied the clinical course of a cohort of women with restricting type anorexia who had been transferred to outpatient care. Half of the group had managed to achieve more than 90% of the recommended weight for their height on discharge, the remainder were less than 85% off this target.

The underweight group continued to exhibit greater abnormal eating behaviour, mood disturbance and continued physiological evidence of malnutrition, with 50% of those in the underweight group at discharge requiring re-hospitalisation (Baran *et al*, 1995). Similar findings have been reported from other studies. Howard *et al* (1999) found that those patients who were below 90% of their ideal body mass at the time of transfer to outpatient care, were ten times more likely than someone above 90% of the recommended body weight to either fail to complete treatment or to require readmission to an inpatient unit (Howard *et al*, 1999).

A return to a normal pattern of menstruation is regarded as an indicative measure of adequate weight gain, although in premenstrual adolescents and male subjects this criteria is obviously not applicable. In these cases, a return of normal physical and sexual growth, and in males, normal sexual drive and hormone levels are regarded as acceptable treatment goals (American Psychiatric Association, 2000).

Parental nutrition

Croner *et al* (1985) reported on a cohort of women who were between 25–50% below the recommended weight at the time of commencement of treatment.

They were admitted to hospital and given intravenous nutrition via a controlled regime, which was closely monitored. The regime allowed each patient to receive approximately 55kcal per kg of body weight over a 24-hour period. Close monitoring was adhered to and after a period of three to eight weeks (dependent on individual progress), oral intake was substantially improved and it was felt safe to discontinue total parenteral nutrition.

Despite successful weight gain and normalisation of electrolyte disturbances (Croner *et al*, 1985), although there was some improvement in psychological functioning, it is unlikely that this would be sustained after completion of treatment without appropriate intervention to change the underlying psychopathology.

Problems encountered during the refeeding process

Continuous monitoring of psychological and physical symptoms is required if adverse effects are to be avoided during this stage of the patient's recovery.

Hypophosphataemia has been found to occur during the refeeding stage of recovery in those who were severely emaciated at the start of treatment, and has developed secondary to oral re-feeding in severe anorexia nervosa, with values returning to normal with caloric restriction and replenishment with phosphorous supplementation (Fisher, 2000).

There is also some evidence to suggest that hypophosphataemia may be a contributory factor in the development of cardiac arrhythmia during the refeeding process. Heart failure, secondary to hypophosphataemia, has been reported despite oral phosphate supplementation

(Birmingham *et al*, 1996). Cardiac arrhythmia and hypophos-phataemia developed while patients were receiving intravenous saline and potassium to correct low potassium levels (Beumont and Large, 1992).

For those patients who have regularly abused laxatives and diuretics as part of their illness, abrupt cessation of these practices is associated with several problems. Fluid retention, oedema and bloating have been reported, which are thought to be due to salt and water retention (American Psychiatric Association, 2000). Such manifestations have resulted in death, highlighting the potential dangers for some patients and the need for constant vigilance.

Diaphragmatic function and respiratory function, which has been severely impaired in the malnourished state, may be subjected to further stress during the refeeding process. Assessment over thirty days found that vital capacity and FEV1 improved dramatically by the thirtieth day, while diaphragmatic contractility remained depressed, but returned to normal as nutritional status improved (Murciano *et al*, 1994).

Nutritional counselling

Food avoidance has been an integral part of the anorexic illness and nutritional counselling may be useful in educating the patient towards a better knowledge of food and management of their own intake. The goals of treatment are not only to restore normal eating patterns and dietary constituents, but also to relate eating behaviour to mood, and to increase the confidence of the subject so that she/he can remain in control as she gains weight (Hall and Crisp, 1987). During the course of their illness anorexics display a great interest in food and nutrition, and might give the impression that their knowledge is excellent. Unfortunately, much of this information proves to be misguided and may be specifically tailored towards particular issues such as low calorie or low fat diets, which they have incorporated into their meagre diet.

Because research and experience has indicated that many of the physical, psychological and social problems associated with the condition are secondary to the disturbance of nutrition (Beumont *et al*, 1997), rectifying abnormal thoughts and feelings towards food and nutrition are of paramount importance if improvements are to be sustained.

Such improvements are regarded as a long-term goal: the

complexity of the issues to be addressed is such that a considerable duration of treatment is needed. The patient has subjected themselves to months, and even years of bizarre eating practices, accompanied by distorted perceptions relating to diet, and even when progress is made in terms of weight gain, this alone is not necessarily matched by psychological recovery, without interventions geared towards their abatement (Touyz and Beumont, 1993).

Of all eating disordered groups, anorexics would appear to be the most difficult to influence because of their reluctance to acknowledge the seriousness of their condition and physical health.

Comparison of dietary advice and psychotherapy found that the dietary advice group made modest weight gains which they had sustained at follow-up, and were also more likely to seek out alternative treatment elsewhere (Hall and Crisp, 1987) which would indicate that sufficient progress had been made to keep them wanting to sustain their health. This study highlighted the need for prolonged follow-up in some cases, particularly where there is considerable work needed to improve psychological dysfunction.

Family therapy

Family therapy involves one or both parents and the affected child, or it may be used for couples, and its aim is to deal with some of the emotional problems surrounding the illness. In many cases there are problems in identifying specific factors deemed to have been influential in the onset of the condition, and it is important to avoid conflict within the family which might severely jeopardise the sufferers motivation to co-operate. This type of therapy has been deemed to be more helpful, in that it attempts to shift the blame away from the family and enables them to consider themselves as a resource for effective treatment (Waller, 1997).

Research into its success has suggested its use to be more suitable for younger anorexics, particularly where family conflicts are evident. Patients with anorexia of an early age at onset (younger than eighteen years of age), and a short duration of illness have been found to have a significantly better outcome after family therapy than those treated individually (Eisler *et al*, 1997). Intervention is guided by the nature of difficulties within the family. Sessions will be organised and conducted with the patient themselves and the person or persons from within the family group with whom conflict exists. As treatment progresses it is hoped that this approach will bring about change and effect an improvement in both communication and social functioning.

Russell *et al* (1987) suggest that for anorexia nervosa sufferers who have children of their own, family therapy should incorporate additional input relating to advice on parenting skills so that the risk of an eating disorder in their children can be avoided. Recent research has indicated that there may be problem in some anorexic mothers whose abnormal perception of their own body size is in some way transmitted to their children. Russell *et al* (1998) found evidence of anorexic mothers who grossly underfed their children during the course of their illness, which in some cases was reflected in low body weight and stunted growth. Intervention in these cases included a combination of family therapy and hospital admissions to rectify the problems of poor nutritional intake in those children concerned.

Psychoeducation

Psychoeducation is used to correct faulty ideas about the effects of dieting, vomiting, laxative and diuretic abuse and inappropriate beliefs on weight and shape. It provides specific information on several areas that are particularly important in the process of recovery (Garner *et al*, 1985). A Canadian study compared the effectiveness of family group psychoeducation with that of family therapy. After four months of inpatient treatment both groups made weight gains, reaching 91–96% of their ideal weight on completion of the programme, and both were able to acknowledge dysfunctional attitudes within the family (Geist *et al*, 2000). This type of therapy provides an equally effective method of providing family orientated treatment to newly diagnosed, medically compromised anorexia patients and their families, and may be a less expensive form of treatment (Geist *et al*, 2000).

Individual therapy

Individual psychotherapy offers one-to-one support, and has been found to be particularly effective for anorexia sufferers who are older (eighteen or above) at the onset of their condition with a short duration of illness, but has been less successful in treating those with bulimia nervosa and anorexics of adolescent onset, or those who have had a prolonged duration of illness prior to commencement of therapy (Eisler *et al*, 1997).

During the acute phase of refeeding and while weight gain is occurring, it is essential to provide patients with individual psycotherapeutic management that is psychodynamically sensitive and informed, providing empathetic understanding, explanations, praise for positive efforts, coaching, support, encouragement and other positive behavioural reinforcement (American Psychiatric Association, 2000).

In some cases a combination of family therapy and individual therapy may be considered more appropriate. This dual approach allows for specific issues to be tackled either on a one-to-one basis, or via family therapy, giving the therapist the opportunity to tailor therapy to individual situations and need.

Brief psychotherapy

Psychotherapy is used in the treatment of a number of conditions and can be appropriately applied to a variety of settings either on an individual basis or in group settings.

The aim of psychotherapy within the context of anorexia nervosa is to remove the emphasis away from the subject of weight gain and concentrate on dealing with emotional problems which will help to restore morale and self-confidence.

The number of sessions required will vary from patient to patient, and may span over many months in some cases.

The benefits of brief psychotherapy (comprising a total of twelve sessions of combined individual and family psychotherapy) was studied by Hall and Crisp in 1987. During the course of their therapy, short-term intervention yielded benefits in terms of weight gain but, unfortunately, not all were able to sustain this improvement after completion and, in three of the cases discussed, the relapse was described as serious.

Greater success has been assigned to this treatment method when the approach of the therapist has been supportive, and has adopted an honest, caring, sensitive approach, giving the patient an assurance that they are genuinely interested and understand the client's condition (Lambert *et al*, 1978).

The relationship between client and therapist encompasses the skills of listening and expressing; requiring an element of empathy on the part of the therapist if the client is to feel that their personal difficulties are understood. The nature of this relationship and its potential effect on the outcome of treatment has been the subject of a number of papers. Arguably, the ability to fully understand and empathise with the feelings of the anorexic requires a thorough knowledge of the complexity of the condition, and an appreciation of such knowledge has been cited by anorexics themselves as beneficial to their recovery (Yager *et al*, 1989).

Cognitive behaviour therapy

This type of therapy involves a two-way interaction between client and therapist, and aims to involve the client in a process of self-analysis.

Research has found its use more effective in the treatment of bulimia nervosa and its application for this illness will be discussed in more detail in the next section. The client is encouraged to recognise and evaluate the thought processes which have led to, and underlie, their current behaviour patterns.

The length of treatment for anorexia nervosa is generally much longer than that required for bulimia, primarily because the longer duration is required to overcome motivational obstacles, achieve appropriate weight gain, and occasionally implement inpatient or partial hospitalisation (Garner and Needleman, 1997).

Programme content is largely similar in both anorexia and bulimia, with certain modifications to address specific elements which are only pertinent to anorexia sufferers.

The treatment is staged as follows:

1. Establishing a trusting relationship between client and therapist.
2. Changing ideas and beliefs relating to food and eating behaviour.
3. Treatment conclusion where preventing relapse is the primary focus.

Considerable skill and experience is needed to encourage the client to 'open up' and, again, the therapeutic relationship is vital to the final outcome.

The danger exists that if the patient feels threatened in any way, or is distrustful of the therapist, they may become unco-operative, and will attempt to withhold information vital to solving the underlying problems. If these factors culminate in a client resorting to deceptive methods, perhaps resorting to giving false and inaccurate information, then the effectiveness of any therapy will be limited.

A successful relationship between the two parties will enable the client to acknowledge disordered thought processes and it is hoped that by getting them to accept why change is needed, this interaction can bring about a gradual reduction in dysfunctional thought processes and the associated behaviour patterns which accompany the anorexic illness.

These particular improvements are fundamental to the success of this therapy as it is acknowledged that continued abnormal behaviour and thought processes are instrumental in retaining the behavioural, psychological and physical processes that make up the disease.

The second stage moves towards patient recognition that recovery is possible and, more importantly, that the patient wishes this to occur. The enormity of this task cannot be underestimated given the earlier dogmatic refusal to recognise either the need or the importance of medical help.

As the patient advances towards a restoration of physical and emotional health, termination of treatment becomes a consideration. Sessions may be reduced as the time approaches when the patient is considered well enough to function independently. It is accepted that among those patients whose illness has been further complicated by multiple pathologies, even in the event of a recovery, there will be a percentage of patients who will continue to display these features (Casper, 1990). Before treatment is completely terminated the patient should be fully aware of potential warning signs (declining weight and a return to a preoccupation with shape, weight and food intake) which herald the need for urgent reinitiation of treatment.

Pharmacotherapy

For many years a range of pharmacological interventions have been tested in the search for a suitable effective oral therapy for anorexia. The complex nature of the condition has made this a difficult task.

For many patients, drug side-effects may deter them from completing the full course of treatment, while their reluctance to accept help in the first instance makes monitoring and supervision of a subject's drug administration an additional problem.

Drugs have been used in an attempt to promote restoration to health in a number of key components of the illness, ie: food intake and weight gain; associated psychiatric disturbances; and the medical complications associated with the starvation itself (Kennedy and Goldbloom, 1991).

Antidepressants

The presence of depressive symptoms would suggest that antidepressant medication might be a useful addition to the treatment regime. In previous studies serotonin uptake inhibitors (SSRIs) have provided some benefits in the treatment of obsessive compulsive disorder (Piggott, 1996; Baumgarten and Grozdanovic, 1998). These act by blocking the uptake of serotonin which is effective in increasing neurotransmission, because it allows for increased amounts of neurotransmitter to be present at the central synapse.

Serotonin may play a role in the pathophysiology of obsessive compulsive disorder because of the anti-obsessional effect of selective serotonin reuptake inhibitors (SSRIs) (Baumgarten and Grozdanovic, 1998).

A randomised control trial studied the effectiveness of fluoxetine against a placebo in anorexic women. Results confirmed that there were no significant differences in the outcome between those receiving active medication or placebo (Attia *et al*, 1998). Current recommendations suggest that the role of antidepressants is best assessed following weight gain when the psychological effects of malnutrition are resolved (American Psychiatric Association, 2000).

Zinc supplementation

The use of zinc supplementation has been found to have some benefits in achieving weight gain. When compared to placebo, patients receiving the active treatment managed to achieve a weight increase of 10%. The rate of weight increase in those who had received the zinc supplement was found to be twice that of the placebo group (Birmingham *et al*, 1994).

Naltrexone

This is an opioid antagonist and is normally given to detoxified patients who were formerly opioid dependent. Trials of naltrexone have been found to be useful in reducing binge-purge symptomatology in anorexics who also have bulimic tendencies (Marrazzi *et al*, 1995).

Naloxone

This is used as an antidote to opioids and it is administered intra-venously. It has a short duration of action and requires close monitoring of subjects during administration. Moore and Mills (1991) reported the usefulness of naloxone in achieving weight gain in severely emaciated patients and there is some evidence to suggest that it can reverse amenorrhoea (Palla and Litt, 1988).

Long-term outcome

Anorexia nervosa, because of its eminence in the late 1980s, has been the subject of numerous research papers for many years, and it would seem plausible to assume that more recent papers may be able to determine whether the long-term prognosis has improved or not. There are a number of factors which influence the findings and these include: the sample size (more recent studies tend to report greater sample sizes, drop-out rates from follow-up studies, and the willingness of patients to be continually monitored in follow-up studies (Steinhausen *et al*, 1991). The latter are highly variable with relatively short periods before review takes place, where others may be of much longer duration (ten years or more).

Prognostic indicators

There is still an element of controversy surrounding the relative importance of some of the factors below and the degree to which they influence outcome.

Age at onset

Younger age of onset of the illness has been found to be indicative of good recovery in some studies (Ratnasuriya, 1991). In this study patients who were aged eighteen or above when their symptoms commenced, were found to follow a more prolonged course, with only two making progress towards recovery.

Other studies have attached less relevance to this. Hawley (1985) studied the outcome of twenty-one children, all of whom were under the age of thirteen when they developed anorexia and the age when dieting commenced was as young as seven in some cases, with a mean age given as eleven and a half. At follow-up eight years later, 67% were classed as having made a good recovery, and were within 15% of their recommended weight. Sixty per cent had reverted to a pattern of normal regular monthly bleeding with a further 20% reporting the presence of menstrual bleeding but not at regular intervals. However, 36% of subjects admitted to the continued presence of extreme dieting, interspersed with a disturbed pattern of eating and half of these were using laxatives or vomiting as a further adjunct to weight control. Cases of anorexia involving both early and late onset have raised concerns that opposite ends of the age spectrum may influence the outcome.

Age alone might be insufficient to act as a marker for poor long-term outcome but its influence is thought to be confounded by other factors. A more severe initial clinical picture, a longer length of in-patient treatment, and co-morbidity of mood and personality disorders have been cited as the most relevant negative prognostic indicators (Saccomani *et al*, 1998).

Continued symptoms and recovery

If patients continue to display any degree of symptoms after dis-charge it suggests that cognitive impairment and psychological disturbance have not been dealt with adequately.

Assessment of seventy women who had attended treatment programmes approximately twelve years previously revealed that, although the majority of patients no longer met the diagnostic criteria in terms of weight loss and cessation of monthly periods, there was still evidence to suggest that the persistent concern with body image and weight had not subsided (Sullivan *et al*, 1998). It is accepted that distorted attitudes about shape and weight are least likely to change, and that excessive exercise may be one of the last of the behaviours associated with the condition to abate (American Psychiatric Association, 2000). In those women who retain these features despite intensive therapy, the potential exists to develop a chronic illness with periods of remission and relapse, or alternatively, with those whose symptoms are less severe after treatment, they may continue to exhibit features of a subthreshold disorder.

Sullivan *et al* (1998a) reported that twelve years after initial assessment and referral for treatment, approximately 10% continued to meet the diagnostic criteria for anorexia nervosa with a further

10% showing the signs of a subthreshold disorder.

Parental influences

The impact of parental control and rearing practices have been discussed for their effect and potential influence in the aetiology of eating disorders (*Chapter 1*). The relationship between adolescents and their mothers has been investigated with particular emphasis on measures relating to life events and family functioning, both at the initial assessment and again two years later. Childhood experiences within the family vary widely and each sibling may give a different account of parental upbringing. Strober (1997) described cases which have involved abuse, gross neglect and hostile criticism.

Subjects with a good perception of their upbringing in terms of relationships between family members were more likely to demonstrate a good outcome at one year's duration, as were those who could recall a distressing life event in the year preceding onset of the illness (North *et al*, 1997).

Personality traits

The features of perfectionism, ritualistic behaviour and a tendency towards meticulous habits have been cited as evident within the anorexic psychopathology (Srinivasagam *et al*, 1995; Lilenfield *et al*, 1998; Walters and Kendler, 1995). Previous studies have devoted time to determining their existence prior to the onset of the illness, or whether these traits develop during the progression of the illness or are exaggerated by it (Garner and Garfinkel, 1980).

Assessment of a group of recovered anorexics who had remained symptom free for twelve months or more found that women who had long-term recovery from their illness continued to show behaviour that could be characterised as an obsessive need for exactness and order (Srinivasagam *et al*, 1995). There are problems in determining which personality variables were already present before onset of the condition, making the contribution of the personality difficult to establish since there is little opportunity to study children prior to development of the disorder (Casper, 1990).

Bastiani *et al* (1995) suggested that such perfectionism may contribute to the vulnerability of some individuals who develop anorexia nervosa, and may play some part in resistance to treatment, and the potential for relapse.

Psychiatric comorbidity

The issue of whether obsessional traits persist after recovery has to date remained unclear. Seventy-three recovered anorexics were assessed to determine attitudes towards their current weight status, eating behaviour and the continued presence of psychiatric symptoms. Results identified that nearly three-quarters of those studied had made a full recovery, which included eradication of any psychiatric problems. One quarter appeared to continue to display a variety of psychiatric symptoms along with weight preoccupation and some restriction in their eating pattern, which when compared to the control group revealed a greater degree of self-control and more conventional and pedantic thinking patterns (Casper, 1990). This suggests that for many subjects, physical recovery may not be matched by emotional and psychological recovery.

Longer term evaluation, seven years after treatment for anorexia nervosa, identified that 50% were found to have made a recovery, while the majority of those whose symptoms persisted had become more restrictive in their eating habits. Psychiatric comorbidity was found to be present in 62% of subjects, with patients who exhibited a poor outcome showing significantly more problems in psychosocial functioning than those in the good outcome group (Herpetz-Dahlmann 1998/1999). Even those who were felt to have made a satisfactory recovery from their illness continued to display more psychosexual difficulties than controls.

Long-term physiological effects (bone health)

The effect of self-starvation on bone health has been extensively researched (Rigotti *et al*, 1984; Treasure *et al*, 1987) and recent evidence suggests that even in the event of a full recovery, bone mineral density may not return to its normal levels (Hartman *et al*, 2000). After twenty-one years free of their illness, bone mineral density was reported as considerably less among those in the recovered group than the control group, with two subjects having sustained fractures during the course of their illness. Although fractures following recovery and during middle life was not a significant problem, recovery from anorexia nervosa did not correlate with the establishment of normal bone density (Hartman *et al*, 2000).

Compulsory treatment

The treatment of patients with anorexia nervosa must be constantly reviewed to ensure that it accords with the five ethical principles of beneficence, autonomy, non-maleficience, justice and utility (Russell, 1995).

A patient's refusal to accept treatment is distressing both for friends and family, and remains a subject surrounded by controversy.

The wishes of the ill person may differ considerably from those of the professional, which further challenges the ethics of compulsory treatment. One of the concerns in anorexia nervosa is that given the known effects of starvation on the brain it may be unethical to act in accordance with the patient's apparent decision to reject treatment, when this decision may have been made in a severely emaciated state with severe cognitive impairment (Tiller *et al*, 1993).

Ramsey and Treasure (1996) explored the attitudes of psychiatrists towards palliative care for these patients. Terminal care and the use of hospices was generally considered acceptable for other conditions, but this consensus of agreement was not reflected in their opinions towards the use of treatment in anorexia nervosa, many refusing to accept that this illness should be regarded as an incurable disease. Symptoms of depression, common in very underweight patients may also occur in close family members, making them underestimate any previous positive interventions and times of relative improvement (Williams *et al*, 1998). Williams *et al* (1988) also suggest that there are important issues to be raised when considering the ability of patients who reach a very low weight to withhold consent for treatment, a decision which may have been made in a state of impaired mental reasoning. The effects of imposing treatment under these circumstances has widespread consequences for all those involved, including clinical staff who are expected to administer care under the most difficult of circumstances.

Any patient's reluctance to participate in the treatment offered may be associated with a worse outlook (Tiller *et al*, 1993) and this is reflected in mortality statistics, which represent the worst outcome for the patient and their family. Death rates among detained patients are higher than among those who accept help voluntarily (Ramsey *et al*, 1999), with a greater probability that their history will contain a higher number of admissions for treatment, hence a high failure rate.

Crossover from anorexia nervosa to bulimia nervosa

The transmission from anorexia nervosa to bulimia has been previously reported (Hsu, 1982), which suggests that the eating disorder has taken a different course, and may continue as a full or partial syndrome.

Sullivan *et al* (1998a) reported that over half of the former anorexic group met the criteria for lifetime bulimia nervosa at follow-up (twelve years after their initial presentation for treatment), 15% met the criteria for a subthreshold condition, and one individual exhibited some features of both anorexia and bulimia.

In a longer term study conducted twenty years after treatment, 15% of patients had progressed to the full syndrome of bulimia nervosa at follow-up. At five years post-treatment, a small percentage of these patients appeared to be making a good recovery, which suggests that deterioration and transition to bulimia may have taken place after an initial period of improvement.

The younger age of anorexics and the older age of bulimics might indicate that more crossover will be found after a longer duration of follow-up (van der Ham *et al*, 1994), suggesting that a disordered eating pattern continues and takes on a chronic course although with different clinical features.

Mortality in anorexia nervosa

Crude mortality (or the proportion of subjects who were dead at follow-up) produces variable statistics, with results ranging between zero to over 20% in many studies when all causes of death are taken into account (Sullivan, 1995). All causes of deaths include those which may be totally unrelated to the anorexia nervosa, and the greater the follow-up period, the more deaths would be expected over longer periods of time (Sullivan *et al*, 1995). The greater risk of death occurring among subjects who are unwilling to participate in treatment programmes has been established (Ramsey *et al*, 1999) but the circumstances which accompany this are highly variable. Ramsey *et al* (1999) reported that 54% died as a direct result of complications of the eating disorder, 27% committed suicide, and a further 19% were the result of other causes.

Causes of sudden death are most commonly reported as:

- suicide
- cardiac arrhythmia.

Suicide has been cited as the commonest cause of death among anorexia nervosa subjects, and is often associated with misuse of drugs or alcohol (Patton, 1988). Osona Rodriguez *et al* (2000) reported high rates of attempted suicide although many of these were unsuccessful resulting in hospitalisation, rather than death. In this study, 70% of those who had attempted to end their life were found to have a psychiatric condition alongside their anorexic illness.

Cardiac arrhythmias detectable on ECG have been discussed, and statistics suggest that they may be evident in as many as 87% of subjects (Sharp and Freeman, 1993). Deaths from ventricular dysrhythmia have been reported, with prolonged QT interval detected on ECG in the days prior to death (Isner *et al*, 1985). Unfortunately, the risk of such a devastating event is of concern both during the acute phase of the illness and continues during the recovery phase (Powers, 1982). Unfortunately, the risk of mortality is substantial, and for those whose illness becomes one of chronicity, anorexia nervosa has the highest mortality rate of any psychiatric condition (Sullivan, 1995).

The most gloomy figures relating to prognosis suggest that in the hundred or so years since its recognition, recovery rates have worsened, with most patients having less than a 50% chance of recovery within ten years and a 6.6–15% risk of dying ten to twenty years after the onset of the disorder (Bergh and Sodersten, 1998). Other studies have presented more optimistic findings.

Steinhausen (1997) reported that as many as 52% of patients in this study were able to make a full recovery, with only 19% continuing to exhibit features which led to a chronic illness and a further 29% making a moderate improvement.

Ratnasuriya *et al* (1991) reported that approximately 40% of patients continued to be gravely ill or had died; however some patients had managed to recover even after a prolonged duration of illness of fifteen years or more. Unfortunately, with increasing length of illness the probability of recovery is gradually diminished and reduces sharply after fifteen to twenty years, although Ratnasuriya (1991) indicated that a later age of onset appeared to be a marker for poor prognosis.

This information is supported by Norring and Sohlberg (1993) who identified significant differences at follow-up in those who were still ill (or had died) and those who had made a full recovery. They found that those who were perceived to have made a good recovery were younger, had a shorter duration of illness, and a better capacity for work or further education and study, while the poor outcome group had received substantial treatment input over a longer time period.

Suggested further reading

Treatment and management

Beumont PJV, Russell JD, Touyz SW (1993) Treatment of anorexia nervosa. *Lancet* **341**: 1635–40

Parenteral nutrition

Croner S, Larrson J, Schildt B, Symreng T (1985) Severe anorexia nervosa treated with parenteral nutrition: Clinical course and influence on clinical chemical analyses. *Acta Paediatr Scand* **74**(2): 230–60

Nutritional counselling

Huse DM, Lucas AR (1983) Dietary treatment of anorexia nervosa. *J Am Diet Assoc* **83**(6): 687–90

Family therapy

Crisp AH, Norton K, Gowers S, Halek C, Bowyer C, Yeldham D, Levett G, Bhat A (1991) A controlled study of the effect of therapies aimed at adolescent and family pathology in anorexia nervosa. *Br J Psychiatry* **159**: 325–33

Psychoeducation

Geist R, Heinmaa M, Stephens D, Davis R, Katzman DK (2000) Comparisons of family therapy and family group psychoeducation in adolescents with anorexia nervosa. *Can J Psychiatry* **45**(2): 173–8

Individual therapy

Eisler I, Dare C, Russell GFM, Szmuckler G, Le Grange D, Dodge E (1997) Family and individual therapy in anorexia: a 5-year follow-up study. *Arch Gen Psychiatry* **54**(11): 1025–30

Psychotherapy

Brodaty H, Andrews G (1983) Brief psychotherapy in family practice. A controlled prospective intervention trial. *Br J Psychiatry* **143**: 11–19

Cognitive behaviour therapy

Channon S, de Silva P, Hemsley D, Perkins R (1989) A controlled trial of cognitive behavioural and behavioural treatment of anorexia nervosa. *Behav Res Ther* **27**(5): 529–35

Pharmacotherapy

Kennedy SH, Goldbloom DS (1991) Current perspectives on drug therapies for anorexia nervosa and bulimia nervosa. *Drugs* **41**(3): 367–77

Outcome

Ratnasuriya RH, Eisler I, Szmuckler GI, Russell GF (1991) Anorexia nervosa: outcome and prognostic factors after 20 years. *Br J Psychiatry* **158**: 495–502

Herzog W, Deter HC Fiehn W, Petzold E (1997) Medical findings and predictors of long term physical outcome in anorexia nervosa: a prospective, 12-year follow-up study. *Psychol Med* **27**(2): 269–79

Eckert E, Halmi K, Marchi P, Grove W (1995) Ten-year follow-up of anorexia nervosa: clinical course and outcome. *Psychol Med* **25**(1): 143–56

Sullivan PF (1995) Mortality in anorexia nervosa. *Am J Psychiatry* **152**(7): 1073–4

Section II: Bulimia nervosa

4

Bulimia nervosa

Epidemiology of bulimia nervosa

The true prevalence of bulimia is extremely difficult to estimate, largely because of the secretive nature of the disease. Like anorexia, the condition is generally regarded as a disease of western nations, and current statistics indicate that the incidence of recorded cases has been steadily rising in recent years. Given the preference to conceal their illness it is highly likely that a hidden cohort of sufferers remain undetected. Several studies have implied that for this reason statistics probably do not accurately reflect the true prevalence of bulimia, or eating disorders in general (Hoek, 1991; Whitehouse *et al*, 1992), as there is considerable evidence to suggest that the number of diagnosed cases is probably only a fraction of those with symptoms (Abraham and Jones, 1984).

In 1989, the number of patients with a confirmed diagnosis rose from 2.8 per 100,000 females in 1980 to 10.1 per 100,000 in 1989 (Lacey, 1992). Recent projections estimate the lifetime prevalence rates for bulimia nervosa to range between 1.1% and 4.2% (Garfinkel *et al*, 1995), although these figures vary from community to community. Of most concern is the indication that there has been a threefold increase in the recording of bulimia nervosa cases between 1988 and 1993 (Turnbull *et al*, 1996) with a greater affinity for certain geographical locations.

Hoek (1991) found the incidence of bulimia nervosa to be three times higher in larger cities than in smaller urbanised or rural areas. Many of the large scale studies involving 100,000 or more individuals have been conducted in cities to enable the required number of subjects to be recruited. Further research in 1995, confirmed that the incidence of bulimia nervosa was lowest in rural areas, intermediate in urbanised areas and highest in large cities (6.6, 19.9, and 37.9 respectively per 100,000 females each year (Hoek *et al*, 1995). This pattern was not replicated in the statistics for anorexia nervosa, with urbanisation not found to influence prevalence rates in epidemiological studies conducted in these populated areas.

Over the five-year study period, urbanisation was cited as a potential risk factor for the development of bulimia nervosa but not for anorexia (Hoek *et al*, 1995).

Eating disorders have been found to be a common problem among female high school and college students (American Psychiatric Association, 2000). Cooper and Fairburn (1983) estimated that approximately 4% regularly induce vomiting to control shape and weight. Jones *et al* (1986) reported that despite the existence of a group of students who admitted to episodes of frequent bingeing, many did not consider this to be a problem, and did not feel that they suffered from an eating disorder. The findings from these studies have not been without criticism, particularly as many such studies have been conducted on college campuses where the population under consideration has consisted of mainly white students of higher socio-economic status with little inclusion of minority ethnic groups, (Yanovski, 2000). Such studies would also exclude those of a lower educational ability.

Like anorexia nervosa there is some indication that partial syndromes of bulimia nervosa may also be relatively common. King (1989) reported that patients identified in a London GP practice with partial symptoms outnumbered those who fully met the diagnostic criteria by two to one.

Aetiology of bulimia nervosa

Like anorexia nervosa the factors which surround the onset of bulimia nervosa are multifactorial, and differ widely from patient to patient. Halmi (1997) suggests that antecedant conditions include genetic and physiological vulnerability, and psychological predispositions that are often affected by the family and societal influences.

Factors linked to the onset of bulimia:

⌘ Peer pressure/media influence.

⌘ Family background, genetic factors.

⌘ Adverse life events preceding the onset.

⌘ History of sexual abuse.

⌘ Tendency towards obesity prior to onset.

⌘ Possession of certain personality traits.

Peer pressure

Many teenagers hold a high regard for the opinions and attitudes of peers and are anxious to be seen as popular among fellow school-children. The desire to be loved and popular has been found to be sufficiently strong enough in some adolescents to persuade them to change their own attitudes and opinions to suit those of their closest friends. Field *et al* (1999) found that 6% of teenagers in one study admitted to changing their eating patterns frequently or always to suit their peers, a further 4% reported that thinness was important to their peers, and became important to them.

Cruel jibes from peers about weight and appearance can have a long lasting and often detrimental effect on the confidence and self-esteem of the individual concerned. The cycle of low self-esteem is further reinforced when accompanied by adverse comments from family members, which can only serve to increase the despondency and despair which the child is feeling.

Low self-esteem in particular has been found to be a predictive factor, and evident in the personalities of those girls who went on to later develop bulimic symptoms (Button *et al*, 1996; Williams *et al*, 1993), with the greater the influence of peers in persuading girls to change their eating habits, the more likely they were to begin purging within the next year (Field *et al*, 1999).

Media influence

The influence which media images have on adolescents has been the subject of debate for several years. Extensive interest in establishing a clear link has been well researched, and it is widely accepted that the role models, such as actresses, television personalities and pop stars, which many teenagers aspire to, have a considerable impact on their perception of an acceptable and desirable weight and shape. There is concern about the growing number of fashion magazines, many of which have a heavy focus on 'looking good', beauty and physical fitness. Alongside the ever increasing number of women's journals there are also a similar number of magazines aimed specifically at a teenage market. The influence which the media can have on vulnerable teenagers appears to be significant, with recent statistics revealing that approximately 6% of girls interviewed in one particular study reported making considerable effort to look like females on television, in movies or magazines, with further evidence to suggest that the more effort that was made to accomplish this, the greater the risk of beginning to use laxatives or some means of purging to achieve weight control (Field *et al*, 1999). Even if the desired weight is reached, many have considerable difficulty in maintaining it. This results in several failed attempts to achieve what, for many, is an unattainable goal and increases the effect which low self-esteem and low self-confidence can have, with potentially devastating long-term effects.

Family background

Problems in childhood, and the long-term emotional damage which a troubled upbringing can cause in vulnerable personalities, has been studied as a possible predisposing factor in the onset of bulimia nervosa.

Bulimic subjects who have been asked to describe their childhood have reported a past history of life events which appear to indicate a chaotic lifestyle (Shisslak *et al*, 1990). This took the form of high levels of violent clashes and conflict within the family, accompanied by a lack of parental warmth and care, which was described as leaving the child feeling confused and unloved. Similar findings are supported by Schmidt *et al* (1993) who found that 65% of bulimics in one particular study were able to recall having experienced two or more adverse life events during their early years. Difficulties exist in collecting data for these types of study because of the variable perceptions of upbringing styles among both children and adults, with any data collected subject to the effect of memory bias and personal opinion. Parental recollections of their style of upbringing will invariably differ from those of their child, and there is some suggestion that the child's perception of parental behaviour may well be more relevant to personality characteristics or pathology than the real nature of this parental behaviour (Castro *et al*, 2000). Webster and Palmer (2000) suggested that bulimia sufferers appeared to have been exposed to dieting behaviour among family members, which was frequently accompanied by critical comments about weight and shape in the family. This particular finding was more evident among bulimics than any other eating disordered group, and was in fact a feature which distinguished them from sufferers of other eating disorders.

Much has been written about childhood abuse, and it is widely accepted that it can take several forms. Research has proved that the effects of abuse (whether this has been physical, sexual or mental) can remain with the person into their adult life with resulting long lasting psychological damage. Fairburn *et al* (1997) found that among bulimia nervosa sufferers there was a distinctive trend towards a history of negative comments from family members about their eating habits, appearance or weight.

The level of parental intrusion during the adolescent years has also been debated for its possible effect on the child's sense of independence. Overconcern on the part of parents is often perceived by the child as overprotective and restrictive and where it is seen by the child to be excessive it may evoke a period of rebellion. Rorty *et al* (2000) described higher levels of maternal invasion during the adolescent years, limited privacy, parental intrusiveness, maternal jealousy and competition, and over-concern with their daughter's shape and weight.

Genetic factors

Genetic influences are known to be a predictive factor in a number of illnesses so it would appear plausible that this could also be applicable to eating disorders. Findings conducted using sets of identical and non-identical twins have identified higher rates of bulimia among monozygotic twins than dizygotic twins (Hudson *et al*, 1987; Hsu *et al*, 1990), suggesting that genetic factors may be at least in part responsible. Kendler *et al* (1991) studied 2163 female twins and found similar aetiological risk factors existed between this group and other bulimia nervosa sufferers. Proband wise concordance for narrowly defined bulimia was 22.9% in monozygotic twins and 8.7% in dizygotic twins with the indication that familial aggregation was due solely to the influence of genetic factors (Kendler *et al*, 1991).

A study of Caucasian female twins taken from the Virginia twin registry found that heritability played a significant role, with a high degree of genetic correlation, which the authors felt might occur as a result of substantially overlapping genetic aetiological factors (Kendler *et al*,1991).

When compared to a comparison group who were non-eating disordered, Strober *et al* (2000) found evidence of both full and partial syndromes of bulimia nervosa in the female relatives of the ill group, which comprised of both anorexic and bulimic subjects. There were no similar cases among the relatives of the non-eating disordered group which indicates that bulimia may have the same tendency for cross-transmission in families with a similar common or shared family diathesis to that of anorexia nervosa (Strober *et al*, 2000).

Familial factors may be important in the aetiology of bingeing and vomiting but may exert their influence only in concert with an individual's genetic make-up (Sullivan *et al*, 1998b).

Adverse life events

A traumatic event which occurs at any age can seriously disturb the emotional well being of any person. The fact that particularly distressing situations may be instrumental in precipitating the onset of an eating disorder in some people would seem to be a plausible concept. Attempts to clarify such an association have been difficult, primarily because of the suspected time lapse between the initial onset of symptoms and detection of the disorder. This time period may be several years, making recall and analysis of events surrounding the earlier stages of the illness and the months preceding the appearance of symptoms difficult to establish and hence unreliable. There are also problems in defining what would constitute a significant life event, and it is unclear why any particular trauma might have a greater effect on the mental health of some individuals than on others. The dilemma of assessing when symptoms commenced is further confounded by the fact that most individuals with bulimia have experienced a period of disordered eating prior to the onset of the full syndrome (Welch *et al*, 1997).

The coping mechanisms adopted by individuals vary widely, and it would appear that if life events are an aetiological factor then personality traits must play some part in making some people more vulnerable and less able to cope than others. Stress and its potential consequences have received considerable attention in recent years, and it is widely reported that bereavement of a close family member is thought to be highest in terms of its effect on the individual.

Binge eating is often triggered by a variety of events, including specific thought, negative emotions and interpersonal stressors (Wilson *et al*, 1997).

Welch *et al* (1997) found that circumstances such as death of a relative, or a serious illness were less likely to have occurred in bulimics in the year preceding onset of the disease, but that more generalised disruptions such as break-up within a family, relationship problems or a house move were likely to have taken place. Assessment of younger adolescents identified that bullying in the school environment might potentiate the development of abnormal eating behaviour among vulnerable individuals (Kaltiala-Heino *et al*, 1999).

When compared to anorexics, Schmidt *et al* (1997) noted significant differences between incidences which had occurred in the year before onset. Although the nature of events did not differ from those encountered in other eating disordered groups, what did differ was the personal involvement of the individual. Where relationship problems were the stressor, the patient themselves appeared to be directly involved in the conflict prior to the onset of bulimic symptoms.

History of sexual abuse

In recent years sexual abuse has been recognised as a problem which has far reaching consequences. The possibility that a history of childhood sexual abuse might influence the vulnerability to develop an eating disorder has produced a quantity of research designed to establish whether a relationship exists between these two entities.

Welch *et al* (1994) compared fifty community-based bulimic subjects with a hundred community-based non-eating disordered subjects, and fifty community-based subjects with psychiatric illness. Incidences of sexual abuse (including subcategories of abuse such as rape and deliberate harm by a relative) were found to be just as common among the women with a psychiatric illness as they were among those with bulimia nervosa.

Another study (Pope and Hudson, 1992) revealed higher rates of sexual abuse among the psychiatric group than among the eating disordered group, and identified that 80% of subjects with multiple personality disorder reported a history of sexual abuse. They suggested that some studies may have failed to reveal an association with bulimia nervosa because the control groups used may have been comprised of psychiatric patients.

The rising incidence of eating disorders in Japan has led to a volume of research from this country. A recent study looked at the history of physical and sexual abuse in eating disordered Japanese patients, and found that rates of sexual abuse were higher among the control group, with histories of physical punishment more universal among the eating disordered group (Daniels *et al*, 1999).

Obesity

Parental obesity has been found to be more prevalent among children who later develop bulimia nervosa and may suggest that these children have had a greater exposure to dieting vulnerability (Fairburn *et al*, 1999). Studies of bulimic subjects have also incorporated a history of the sufferers previous weight, and particularly whether they have encountered problems themselves in the past in controlling their own weight.

Fairburn and Cooper (1984) found that a high proportion of subjects had a past history of a weight problem, with 42.9% revealing that the extent of their obesity had been as much as 120% heavier than that recommended. The use of purging, particularly vomiting after eating, allows the bulimic to continue to consume large quantities of food, often of the type which would not be permitted on a weight reducing diet, without the added fear of weight gain, which such eating habits would normally bring. Overweight children often bear the brunt of teasing and cruel remarks which may leave the child feeling extremely self-conscious. In adulthood excess weight is the focus of health promotion activity in primary care and subjects who require routine surgery are often asked to reduce their weight prior to the procedure. The adverse effects of excessive weight are not only medical, but are also emotional and psychological, with evidence to suggest that in Western societies, negative attitudes towards obesity are prevalent as a whole (Devlin *et al*, 2000).

Obesity has been cited as a risk factor for the development of anorexia nervosa (Fairburn *et al*, 1999) and it is interesting that Fairburn and Cooper (1984) found that a quarter of subjects in a sample of bulimia sufferers had previously fulfilled the diagnostic criteria for anorexia nervosa, with a self-induced weight loss of below 75% of the matched population mean weight.

Personality traits

The fact that bulimia nervosa develops in only a few of those individuals who are subjected to the above influences suggests that the personality of the sufferer may play a role in the aetiology of its onset. Some of the personality traits are:

- being a perfectionist
- low self-esteem
- being histrionic.

Depressive, anxious and impulsive are also terms which have been used to describe the personalities of those who develop bulimic symptoms (American Psychiatric Association, 2000). In recent years a greater emphasis has been placed on bulimia nervosa as a distinct condition, and when compared to anorexia nervosa it appears that different personality types can be assigned to each of these conditions (Halmi, 1995).

Histrionic personality types are generally characterised by an ability to over-dramatise in any given situation. Schmidt *et al* (1993) suggested that where the sufferer has a histrionic personality there may be a tendency to exaggerate or over-report family problems, thereby influencing data related to these issues.

It is also true that incidences which occurred in childhood are subject to a degree of memory recall and consideration should be given to the fact that long-term memory is not always accurate, and may have been tarnished by subsequent events which have taken place in the period between onset of symptoms and recognition or detection of the illness.

There is some evidence to suggest that it may be possible to detect early warning signs which occur prior to puberty and may indicate a predisposition towards the later development of abnormal eating behaviour (Corcos *et al*, 2000). Evaluation of behavioural and emotional changes, and their significance as early psycho-pathological signs have suggested that those who develop bulimia have previously expressed attitudes of withdrawal and social isolation when compared to controls, as well as declaring concerns with their body image and weight (which might appear to close family members as a personality change, and part of the transition from adolescence to adulthood).

Role of serotonin

Serotonin acts as a vasoconstrictor and is found in high concentrations in some parts of the central nervous system, blood platelets and the intestine. It is derived from the amino acid trypto-phan which is itself one of the essential amino acids within the body. It has an action which inhibits gastric secretions, but stimulates smooth muscle. Serotonin has been found to have an effect on the moderation of satiety and food intake regulation, and dieting itself has been shown to affect serotonin levels in women (Waller, 1997). Intensive effort to reduce weight is thought to reduce synthesis of serotonin, and there is some suggestion that there may be an association between decreased central nervous system serotonergic responsiveness and abnormal eating patterns in patients with bulimia nervosa (Jimerson *et al*, 1997).

Kendler *et al* (1991) suggested that serotonin may be involved in increasing the level of satiety after eating, rather than to decrease appetite, and its role in the pathophysiology of psychiatric disorders has been investigated (Fairburn *et al*, 1999). They deliberately lowered the level of serotonin neurotransmission by reducing plasma levels of tryptophan which, when released, acts as a precursor in the synthesis of serotonin in the brain. The findings indicated that these mechanisms are potentially capable of inducing some of the clinical features of bulimia nervosa in those individuals who are vulnerable to develop this condition. Whether this physiological mechanism alone is sufficient to precipitate onset of the condition or whether it is just one of several factors working in combination is a matter that remains unanswered.

The effect of reduced tryptophan levels is particularly important in the aetiology of bulimia, because there is reason to believe that periods of moderate or sustained dieting induce a similar effect (Walsh *et al*, 1995), and may be potentially influential in setting the scene for the development of this illness.

Diagnosis of bulimia nervosa

Diagnostic criteria for bulimia (DSM-IV, 1994)

1. A similar dread of weight gain to that exhibited by anorexics and an associated preoccupation with body shape.
2. Episodes of bingeing behaviour, consuming large quantities of food in a relatively short period of time.
3. Feelings of guilt are dealt with by purging to rid the body as quickly as possible of the food consumed. The person may adopt a combination of methods or choose a single one, (laxatives, diuretics, or vomiting).

The criteria suggest that these binge-purge episodes should occur approximately twice a week or more and continue over a period of at least three months.

Subthreshold disorders

As already mentioned, eating disorder not otherwise specified is used to encompass those patients who present with a vague clinical picture, but do not meet the criteria for any other eating disorder. The history will often reveal an over zealous exercise pattern with intermittent severe dieting. Bingeing and purging may be less frequent than in bulimics and bulimic anorexics. There may also be periods of relatively normal eating, interspersed with the abnormal eating pattern.

Diagnostic criteria for eating disorders not specified (American Psychiatric Association, 1994)

1. The individual meets all of the diagnostic criteria for bulimia nervosa, but does not perceive themselves to be worried about their weight or express any concerns when questioned about potential weight gain.
2. The individual meets the diagnostic criteria for bulimia, engaging in regular episodes of binge-purge behaviour which must take place at least once per week over a time span of approximately three months or more prior to diagnosis.
3. The individual may actively avoid the act of swallowing food by chewing and spitting out any food taken into the mouth.
4. Using compensatory weight loss methods even though only a small amount of food has been consumed.

Additional tools to confirm the diagnosis include:

❖ The Eating Attitudes Test (Garner and Garfinkel, 1979), which can establish the severity of a number of features associated with eating disorders, including dread of weight gain and dieting behaviour patterns.

❖ The Binge Eating Scale: This can be used for evaluation of binge-eating disorder and bulimia nervosa. It can differentiate between the obese who binge and those who do not, and also between bulimics and controls (Marcus, 1993).

❖ Bulimic Investigatory Test Edinburgh (BITE) (Henderson and Freeman, 1987) has measures of both symptoms and their severity, but is particularly useful because it can be used to assess response to treatment.

Difficulties in making a diagnosis

Despite the existence of the diagnostic and statistical manual of mental disorders (DSM-IV) devised by the American Psychiatric Association there is evidence to suggest that inaccurate and missed diagnoses of eating disorders continue to be a problem, although it is accepted that in many cases a patient may choose to withhold any information that they do not wish to divulge.

Bulimia sufferers are able to adopt a secretive behaviour pattern to conceal their illness and in many cases will exhibit few outward signs of ill health. Many are of normal weight (Blades, 1997) and do not show the drastic weight loss which is seen in anorexia and is regarded as a crucial sign. Whereas anorexics refuse to accept that they have a problem, bulimics are fully aware but often find it difficult to admit to and to ask for help (Stangler and Printz, 1980).

The problems faced by primary care staff in detecting this elusive condition have been demonstrated in several studies.

Research conducted in three Cambridge practices found that half of the patients identified as having had an eating disorder had not been diagnosed by their GP (Whitehouse *et al*, 1992). A number of these patients had consulted their doctor on numerous occasions, for treatment of a condition that was later found to be secondary to the eating disorder. Two cases were diagnosed following referral to a consultant for a problem that was later found to be a direct result of the underlying condition. Other studies have confirmed that this scenario is not unique. A cohort of patients selected across four inner city London GP practices over a twelve- to eighteen-month period were screened, and those with an eating disorder were identified and followed for the duration of the study. The GPs involved remained unaware of the underlying diagnosis and had failed to offer significant intervention, despite being consulted by the patient on several occasions.

Similar findings from a Dutch study showed that bulimia nervosa in the community remained poorly diagnosed with very few (approximately 11%) receiving a firm diagnosis, which resulted in a very small minority being referred for specialist intervention.

Problems with diagnosis in the GP setting are not unique to this environment and may also exist in the hospital environment. A recent study of obstetricians and gynaecologists revealed that a number of those interviewed did not feel confident in making an eating disorder diagnosis, and several of those who took part provided factually incorrect responses to some questions.

Only a fifth of those interviewed felt entirely satisfied with their ability to make a diagnosis. Seventy-nine per cent of those questioned underestimated amenorrhoea in anorexia nervosa by 25%, and 85% believed that regular menstrual periods were characteristic of bulimia nervosa in normal weight sufferers (Morgan, 1999).

The fact that it is possible for the eating disorder to remain undetected even after referral to a consultant for a condition secondary to the eating disorder suggests that there is a need for a simpler screening questionnaire for use by non-specialists (Morgan, 1999).

The implication that there may be substantial numbers of ill people who choose never to seek treatment raises suspicion that those who do present for investigation may differ in some way to those who remain undetected.

Fairburn *et al* (1996) predicted that cases seen in clinic settings might consist of individuals with a more severe form of illness, possibly of longer duration, who are more likely to have a history of anorexia nervosa.

This proposal has been confirmed in a comparison study of community subjects and those attending a clinic for treatment, which identified that the latter were more likely to have a history of anorexia nervosa (41% compared to 26%), and were of lower weight and, as suspected, had a more severe eating disorder with a greater frequency of bingeing and vomiting and had experienced more associated symptomatology than community subjects.

Partial syndromes

The prevalence of partial eating syndromes has aroused some interest among the medical profession. Assessment of 534 high school students used a combination of criteria, including a questionnaire which focused on their normal eating behaviour, presence of obsessional behaviour and depressive symptoms. Maladaptive patterns of behaviour were found in 18% of subjects, 20.8% were found to have partial anorexia nervosa and 11.3% were found to have partial bulimia nervosa (Stein *et al*, 1997). Other studies have identified similarly high rates of subclinical eating disorders with statistics that range from between 1.3–15% in young adolescent women (Patton *et al*, 1990; Buddeberg-Fischer *et al*, 1996). Partial syndromes were significantly related to a number of risk factors which were felt to place those individuals in high risk categories for the future transition to a full blown eating disorder.

These included; weight fluctuations, dieting behaviour, irregular menstrual cycle, depressive symptoms, obsessional behaviour and a preoccupation with eating in the family, with partial bulimics faring worst on most of these parameters than partial anorexics (Stein *et al*, 1997) .

Onset of bulimia nervosa and its clinical features

Table 4.1: Features of bulimia nervosa		
Behavioural	**Psychological**	**Physical**
Secrecy	Morbid fear of fat	Tiredness
Consumption of vast amounts of food	Mood swings	Lethargy
	Irritability	Thirst
Vomiting after meals	Body image disturbance	Swollen glands
Use of laxatives/ diuretics		Sore mouth

Behavioural symptoms

Episodes of binge eating take place (often in secret) where the person is able to consume large quantities of food in a relatively short space of time, often selecting several types of food during any one binge. Typical choices for consumption are often those which the individual would normally deny themselves during periods of dieting (pies, pastries, cakes, biscuits etc). The frequency and duration of binges will vary from person to person, but the one feature which unites all bulimia sufferers is the need to keep these episodes secret. The condition is accompanied by feelings of shame and secrecy (Fairburn and Cooper, 1982), and the guilt which follows is superseded by the need to purge the body of the vast quantity of food which the individual has ingested. This may be by the use of laxatives, diuretics or by vomiting, and in some individuals a combination of these methods may be used. The binge is associated with feelings of extreme loss of self-control and only ends through physical discomfort, social interruption, or ending of supplies (Freeman and Newton, 1995). In an effort to regain some measure of self-control, a period of fasting may follow in the immediate period following an episode of bingeing. An alternate regime might be adoption of a very low calorie diet accompanied by exercise in a desperate attempt to compensate for earlier behaviour. Once the illness comes to the attention of medical staff extracting an accurate history, particularly relating to past behaviour, is often difficult.

Inability to recall accurately episodes of bingeing and purging presents problems in assessing the true duration of illness.

A sample of university men and women were assessed for eating habits, attitudes, presence of bulimic symptoms and dieting history. Ten years later all subjects who had responded to the first assessment were contacted again to assess the accuracy of their ability to recall the history of their symptoms, and to document any changes. At ten-year follow-up, the percentage number who reported ever having binged or purged was less than at the initial assessment with some denial of ever having had a problem, which indicates that the ability to accurately recall past bingeing and purging episodes may be only modest (Field *et al*, 1996).

Patients who choose vomiting as a means of purging have been found to be more reluctant to reveal their condition (possibly because of the associated shame and disgust that they feel), while those who abuse laxatives are generally older and have a longer duration of illness (Fairburn and Cooper, 1984).

Some bulimia sufferers have admitted to rumination as a feature of their condition. Those who engage in this behaviour are often reluctant to admit to its existence, and little explanation or understanding of its place within the condition has been found to date. Fairburn and Cooper (1984) found this phenomenon was only discovered following intense questioning of the subject.

Comparisons have been made between the clinical features of bulimia nervosa and those of seasonal affective disorder, mainly fuelled by the fact that sufferers of both conditions appear to have an increased appetite and a particular liking for foods high in carbohydrate content (Rosenthal *et al*, 1984).

The extraction of some shared features has led to some interest in the possibility that bulimia sufferers might have some seasonal variation to the nature and severity of their symptoms, similar to those seen in sufferers of seasonal affective disorder.

Assessment of thirty-one bulimic patients (who were not involved in any treatment programme at the time of recruitment to the study) questioned subjects on a number of factors related to their symptoms. Patients were asked to describe months of the year when they felt that their symptoms might be worse, when they perceived changes in food choices, experienced seasonal weight loss or weight gain and sleep disturbance. The findings suggested that binge eating and bulimic behaviour exhibited marked seasonal patterns, with binge eating being more frequent during seasons characterised by low levels of light (Blouin e*t al*, 1992).

Psychological symptoms

In common with anorexia sufferers, bulimics display a characteristic set of disturbed attitudes often referred to as 'a morbid fear of fatness' (Fairburn *et al*, 1991), with some studies reporting high rates of such disturbances. Fairburn and Cooper (1984) found these symptoms to be present among 85.7% of the sample within their study. Dissatisfaction with personal appearance is synonymous with both anorexia and bulimia.

Bulimics cannot pursue the levels of food restriction which anorexics are capable of, and their pursuit of the ideal body image culminates in despair and disillusionment. Blundell (1990) viewed the development of bulimic illness as an escape from any further need to continue dieting.

Mood swings and temperamental behaviour are frequently associated with adolescence and the changes which this period of life brings. Erratic alterations in mood are found in the clinical features of this condition, but such behaviour is often thought by friends and relatives to be an integral part of the hormonal changes which accompany puberty, when many youngsters rebel against authority as they strive for independence. Bulik *et al* (1996) studied the impact of mood and anxiety disorders on the presentation of bulimia nervosa and found that disorders of mood were the most frequently occurring psychiatric disorder (75%), a further 64% also exhibited features of an anxiety disorder. The study was able to establish that in many cases, the latter had preceded the onset of both the mood swings and the commencement of bulimic symptoms. Psychological symptoms further confound the clinical picture and have been noted as poor impulse control, depression, lack of assertiveness and the need to always seek approval, as well as problems with interpersonal relationships (Rosch *et al*, 1992).

Physical symptoms

Some of the physical symptoms overlap with those exhibited by the anorexic. Tiredness and lethargy are common because of the reduced energy intake.

Following an episode of vomiting after a binge the bulimic may experience a period of extreme thirst caused by the loss of fluid. Sore mouth and throat may be regular occurrences, with inflammation of the gums possibly being the feature that takes the individual to see their GP.

Suggested further reading

Epidemiology

Whitehouse AM, Cooper PJ, Vize CV, Hill C, Vogel L (1992) Prevalence of eating disorders in three Cambridge general practices: hidden and conspicuous mortality. *Br J Gen Pract* **42**: 57–60

Fairburn CG, Beglin SJ (1990) Studies of the epidemiology of bulimia nervosa. *Am J Psychiatry* **147**: 401–8

Aetiology

Schmidt U, Tiller J, Treasure J (1993) Setting the scene for eating disorders: childhood care, classification and course of illness. *Psychol Med* **23**(3): 663–72

Strober M (1981) The significance of bulimia in juvenile anorexia nervosa: an exploration of possible aetiological factors. *Int J Eat Disord* **1**: 28–43

Diagnosis

Cooper Z, Fairburn CG (1987) A semi-structured interview for the assessment of the specific psychopathology of eating disorders. *Int J Eat Disord* **6**: 61–8

Mann AH, Wakeling A, Wood K, Monck E, Dobbs R, Szmuckler G (1983) Screening for abnormal eating attitudes and psychiatric comorbidity in an unselected population of fifteen year old schoolgirls. *Psychol Med* **13**(3): 573–80

Onset and clinical features

Cooper PJ, Cooper Z (1987) The nature of bulimia nervosa. *Paediatric Reviews & Communications* **1**(3): 217–37

Troop NA, Treasure JL (1997) Psychosocial factors in the onset of eating disorders: responses to life events and difficulties. *Br J Med Psychol* **70**(pt 4): 373–85

Russell GFM (1979) Bulimia nervosa: an ominous variant of anorexia nervosa. *Psychol Med* **9**: 429–48

5

Health problems and bulimia nervosa

Cardiovascular system

Cardiomyopathy

Bulimics and bulimic anorexics may purchase emetic agents over the counter as an adjunct to induce vomiting. Ipecac is readily available over the counter in America, and there is evidence to suggest that abuse of this substance may affect cardiac function. Excessive use of this drug has been found to be associated with a number of related health problems, some of which are potentially serious, inducing a toxic effect if ingested in large quantities. Ho *et al* (1998) reported evidence of cardiac toxicity with resulting ventricular dysfunction. In other studies serious and sometimes fatal myopathies have been attributed to the use of ipecac (Palmer and Guay, 1985). It is not known whether long-term overuse will lead to eventual irreversible damage, however, in short-term studies cardiomyopathy appears to be fully reversed after a short period of withholding the drug (Ho *et al*, 1998).

Musculoskeletal problems

Several studies of anorexia nervosa have made an association between self-starvation, duration of illness and reduced bone mineral density (Bachrach *et al*, 1990; Rigotti *et al*, 1991; Lacey et *al*, 1979), and there are many reports of musculoskeletal problems in which reduced bone mineral density and pathological fractures have been described. Newton *et al* (1993) compared a group of twenty women who met the diagnostic criteria for bulimia nervosa with sixteen control subjects. Eight of the ill subjects had a past history of anorexia nervosa. Several of those in the bulimia group reported irregular monthly periods, while a further four patients had cessation of menstruation. The results identified that bulimics with a past history of anorexia nervosa, a duration of amenorrhoea and low body mass index, accounted for those subjects found to have reduced bone density, which the authors suggested might reflect the nature of the irreversible damage to bone health which occurs during anorexic illness.

Renal system

Renal failure

In severe cases, where vomiting and laxative abuse are frequent, kidney function may be severely compromised to such a degree that renal abnormalities develop. Palla and Litt (1988) studied the medical records of a number of both anorexics and bulimics and found pyuria, haematuria and proteinuria evident among the clinical findings. Prolonged laxative abuse may induce both hypokalaemia and volume depletion leading to renal insufficiency, although in many cases this is not severe enough to require haemodialysis (Copeland, 1994).

Fluid and electrolyte imbalances

⌘ Dehydration (as a result of excessive vomiting/laxative abuse).

⌘ Hypokalaemia (low potassium levels).

⌘ Hyponatraemia (low sodium levels).

⌘ Hypocalcaemia (low calcium levels).

The nature of weight control practices adopted by bulimics may upset the normal balance of electrolytes within the body. Overuse of laxatives and/or diuretics with or without vomiting is associated with various abnormalities which can be detected by laboratory investigations. Specific electrolyte imbalances are dependent on the method of purging adopted by the patient, vomiting is associated with metabolic alkalosis, whereas metabolic acidosis is found in those who misuse purgatives (Fairburn, 1990).

Metabolic alkalosis occurs as a result of an increase in the alkali reserves in the bloodstream, metabolic acidosis is indicative of a decrease in the alkali content which may result in disturbance of the normal pH levels of body fluids.

Laxative abuse results in low levels of potassium and

bicarbonate, both of which are lost from the bowel during the episodes of diarrhoea. Their loss is therefore greater when misuse of these products is evident.

Frequent vomiting is associated with low chloride and potassium levels. The depletion of these elements is associated with fatigue, muscle weakness, constipation and dysphoria (Thompson, 1993).

The level of volume depletion directly influences the pattern of electrolyte imbalance. These abnormalities are not specific to bulimics and are likely to be found in anorexics who also adopt binge-purge methods as an additional means of weight loss between periods of self-induced starvation. One study identified that 32% of bulimic anorexics had medical problems associated with laxative abuse (Turner *et al*, 2000), 48% of bulimics have been found to have electrolyte imbalances, the most common of which was elevated serum bicarbonate levels (Mitchell *et al*, 1983).

Hypokalaemia

The most important electrolyte imbalance is hypokalaemia which, if severe enough, can result in cardiac arrhythmia, muscle cramps, muscle weakness and tetany. Statistics from studies demonstrating the prevalence of this complication in eating disorders are variable and many projects have been able to demonstrate normal values even when the patient is severely ill or emaciated, a factor largely due to the fact that the compensatory mechanisms within the body are remarkable and laboratory abnormalities may not be observed until the illness is far advanced (Greenfield *et al*, 1995). It is well documented that the body often attempts to regulate and correct a number of physical problems.

Biebl and Kinzl (1996) demonstrated an association between the method of purging and the electrolyte imbalance detected, with hypokalaemic subjects more likely to purge using laxatives, while those subjects with hyperamylasia are more likely to use vomiting. They studied the serum electrolyte values of 106 outpatients with eating disorders, and found hypokalaemia to be present in 9% of anorexics and 18% of bulimic subjects, with bulimic subjects also found to have raised serum amylase levels. The variable prevalence rates of electrolyte imbalance has lead to some concern for their reliability as a diagnostic tool in the detection of eating disorders. Greenfield *et al* (1995) indicated that although hypokalaemia is virtually certain evidence that the patient is purging at least once daily, because of its relatively low incidence it is not a reliable diagnostic test.

Haematological changes

Palla and Litt (1988) reported several haematological changes in bulimic subjects. Six per cent were found to have low white cell counts, a further 6% also had low haemoglobin levels, although these changes were rectified with improved nutritional status and weight gain.

Endocrine changes

Thyroid dysfunction

The function of the thyroid gland is controlled by the thyroid stimulating hormone (thyrotropin), produced by the anterior pituitary gland. This hormone stimulates the thyroid gland to secrete the thyroid hormones, thyroxine (T_4) and triiodothyronine(T_3), which control the metabolic rate.

Prolonged alteration in the eating pattern of an individual is thought to reduce their metabolic rate, although the precise effect of grossly abnormal eating behaviour remains poorly understood.

Spalter *et al* (1993) studied bulimic patients during a period of hospital admission, when all subjects included were experiencing a period of abstinence from their binge-purge behaviour. Blood levels taken at the end of a three-week period of abstinence established a decrease in T_3 and T_4 levels and an increase in thyroid stimulating hormone. This would appear to suggest that metabolic rate actually rises during episodes of bingeing and purging. Spalter *et al* (1993) suggested that decreases in T_3 levels may occur as a result of significantly reduced calorie intake which would happen during a period when calorific intake is normalised. These findings have been repeated in more recent research. Altemus *et al* (1996) studied thyroid stimulating hormone levels and thyroid hormone levels both during a period of active bingeing and vomiting and again following a seven-week period of abstinence. Similar findings to those of Spalter *et al* were found with reductions in T_3 and T_4 levels evident in samples taken at the end of the period of abstinence. Altemus *et al*

(1996) reported a positive correlation between increased calorific intake in the bingeing phase of the illness and TSH values, suggesting that the body attempts to deal with the vast intake of food consumed during a binge episode by increasing the level of thyroid activity, and hence attempting to metabolise the increased calorific intake.

Reproductive system

⌘ Menstrual irregularities.

⌘ Possible infertility.

Bulimia sufferers frequently display few outward signs of ill health and the sudden onset of menstrual irregularities may cause the individual to consult their GP for this problem, or may induce close family members to insist that the patient seeks medical advice. In some cases this results in further investigations and referral to a gynaecologist.

The reproductive histories of forty-eight women who had recovered, or were recovering from bulimia nervosa identified that despite the fact that 74% were considered to be recovered, 63% were still without menstrual periods, and had been for a period of twelve months or more (Abraham, 1998).

Where patients experience cessation or irregularity of their periods, they may present requesting help for fertility problems, leaving the true diagnosis undiscovered. Stewart *et al* (1990) identified rates of 7.6% of subjects attending an infertility clinic to be suffering from either anorexia nervosa or bulimia nervosa, which rose to a total of 16.7% when eating disorders not otherwise specified were also taken into account.

Low body mass index is associated with absence of menstruation, hence its more common appearance in anorexia nervosa where weight loss is often substantially greater than that seen in bulimia. Although it is rare for periods to cease completely in bulimia, a disruption to the normal pattern is likely. The presence of a regular menstrual pattern has been detected in those with a body mass index of nineteen or more, who were no longer using additional weight control practices (Abraham 1998).

In those bulimics who do conceive, pregnancy appears to produce a variable impact on their illness. In a retrospective study of 113 women, all of whom had been assessed at an eating disorder unit between 1988 and 1994, bulimic symptoms appeared to improve during the pregnancy, with 34% of women considered to be symptom free after delivery (Morgan *et al*, 1999), which the authors felt might be influenced by the willingness of the pregnant mother to take care of her unborn child. However, 57% were reported as having worse symptoms after the delivery than they had experienced prior to conception. Unfortunately, in approximately two thirds of those whose condition improves during the course of their pregnancy a return of symptoms takes place after the delivery (Lacey and Smith, 1987). Problems during pregnancy include miscarriage, hyperemesis gravidarum, and postnatal depression, the incidence of which are reported to be greater among women who had not recovered from their eating disorder at the time of their pregnancy (Abraham, 1998). After delivery, postnatal depression has been identified in a third of subjects, all of whom had active bulimia nervosa at the time when conception occurred (Morgan *et al*, 1999).

Gastrointestinal system

Some research papers have identified gastrointestinal problems, particularly in those who regularly induce vomiting. Frequent episodes of heartburn can be troublesome and this is thought to occur as a result of gastric acid reflux. These symptoms may mask the underlying cause which is discussed in more detail in the section relating to differential diagnoses in bulimia nervosa.

Dental caries and mouth problems

Toothache is common and the person may complain of frequent sore throats and gums. Dental erosion may be detected at routine dental appointments. The erosion of tooth enamel is believed to be accelerated when the individual cleans their teeth immediately after vomiting.

Enlargement of the parotid and salivary glands is a common finding which gives the appearance of a swollen bloated face (Levin *et al*, 1980).

Erosion of the dental enamel and subsequent decaying of the teeth occurs as a result of the persistent contact of the oral cavity with the acid contents of the stomach which occurs during repeated episodes of vomiting. This particular complication is found in bulimics and anorexics who use this as a means of purging the body of food; in some instances this practice may have been used for several years. These signs are evident in the majority of bulimics who have engaged in bulimic behaviour for at least four years and are one of the best diagnostic indicators for the presence of the underlying illness (Mitchell *et al*, 1997).

There are several procedures which the patient can utilise in an attempt to try and prevent such problems. Roberts and Tylenda (1989) suggest the use of gastric acid neutralising antacid rinses and the daily application of topical fluorides, although they argue that extensive oral care should be postponed until the underlying psychiatric problems have been dealt with. The long-term effects of bulimia on oral health have prompted the need for more research, because loss of tooth tissue remains even if the eating disorder itself disappears (Rytomaa, 1998).

Skin

Russell's sign

Some patients who are able to induce vomiting by inserting the fingers into the throat are prone to develop dorsal lesions (Russell's sign). The repeated contact of the incisors to the skin of the hand can result in abrasions of the skin, small lacerations, and callosities on the dorsum of the hand, overlying the metacarpophalangeal and interphalangeal joints (Daluiski *et al*, 1997).

These lesions may be the only outward physical sign, prompting health professionals to maintain a high level of suspicion and to suspect the possibility of an underlying cause if their presence is detected.

Early onset bulimia nervosa

Early onset bulimia nervosa is reported to be rare, although because it does occur, there is interest into its aetiology and whether it differs in any way from cases which occur at a more typical age of onset.

There is some debate surrounding this subject, since the true age at which symptoms originally commenced may be several years prior to detection of the illness.

Interest in nutrition and dieting is believed to be commencing at an earlier age than ever before, with children as young as five years of age expressing an interest in the avoidance of obesity (Edelman, 1982). Those who develop bulimia at a typical age of onset have a number of factors thought to influence their condition and these have been discussed. Schmidt *et al* (1992) suggested that younger subjects may have experienced a higher loading on risk factors: genetic or environmental, as is the case in coronary heart disease or Alzheimer's type dementia.

This would suggest that their illness might be precipitated by an unusually high level of aetiological factors which will have occurred in a shorter time span. The study by Schmidt *et al* found greater levels of inadequate parental control, and more cultural stress as a result of family migration had clearly resulted in emotional distress sufficient to cause bulimia nervosa in those who possess additional vulnerability factors.

The finding that the prevalence of bulimia among young people may be more common than originally thought is perhaps the most worrying implication. A Finnish study conducted among adolescents aged between fourteen and sixteen years of age found the prevalence of bulimia among girls was 1.8% and among boys 0.3%, with subclinical bulimic behaviour evident in 14% of the sample (Kaltiala-Heino *et al*, 1999). These rates are similar to those identified in other studies with Kendler *et al* (1991) suggesting a lifetime prevalence of 1.1–4.2% for bulimia in women, and Carlat *et al* (1997) reporting an approximate 0.2% prevalence rate for young males.

A retrospective study of children attending a child and adolescent psychiatry department found a number of cases of atypical bulimia in prepubertal patients with subjects exhibiting some, but not all, of the symptoms needed for diagnosis, the youngest being under the age of thirteen (Le Heuzey, 1999).

Psychiatric comorbidity

Personality disorders

Bulimia nervosa is more commonly associated with personality types from cluster B and C, particularly borderline personality disorder and avoidant personality types (see *p.36*) (Skodol *et al*, 1993).

Borderline personality

Considerable research has been conducted into this condition and the complex range of traits which accompany its presence. Borderline personality disorder is associated with a complex set of behaviour patterns which cause considerable distress for those who share the person's life, and present a considerable challenge for health professionals who come into contact with individuals who exhibit features of this personality trait. There is now sufficient evidence to confirm that approximately one in three bulimics or anorexics who engage in bingeing behaviour have some degree of comorbid borderline pathology (Dennis and Sansone, 1997). Pazzagli and Monti (2000) describe dysphoria, anger and aloneness as the three main characteristics which are found in those who possess this disorder. Dysphoria suggests an uneasy emotional state which renders the individual prone to angry outbursts. People who demonstrate such characteristics are often described as histrionic personality types. They are prone to emotional outbursts and are able to use these to benefit themselves when the need arises, and may be seen as manipulative and striving to get their own way. Aloneness would suggest a person who has few friends and feels a sense of isolation.

In certain circumstances the individual is capable of using extreme behaviour in order to achieve what they feel to be the desired result. There is a restless search for new experiences, coupled with short-lived enthusiasm, readiness to boredom, and a craving for novelty (Gelder *et al*, 1991).

The aetiological factors which have been attributed to the onset of bulimia include a brief description of the personality traits which have been most commonly found among sufferers. These traits make the individual liable to angry outbursts and erratic changes in temperament which can lead to distress in personal relationships.

The potential impact which parental upbringing can have on a child has been discussed in *Chapter 1*. Bulimic individuals who have comorbid borderline personality disorder have been found to describe feelings of rejection in their childhood (Wonderlich *et al*, 1994), citing the relationship with their parents and other siblings in the family as very relevant to the way they were treated within the family unit during their early years. Wonderlich *et al* (1994) found that among bulimics with this dual diagnosis, many recalled their fathers as showing them less affection than those in the control group, while at the same time the sufferer believed that their father exercised greater control over their behaviour than that of their siblings.

Those who possess this personality type appear to experience a more complicated clinical course during their illness, which is associated with a greater number of suicide attempts, more depressive symptoms, and more frequent anxious and obsessive symptoms (Matsunaga and Kiriiki, 1997).

Where symptoms are severe these patients will require a greater level of professional input and a more intensive treatment programme if their long-term outcome is to prove successful.

Affective personality disorders

These personality types are associated with mood disturbances which can occur with varying degrees of severity.

Low mood and mildly depressive symptoms are relatively common and experienced by many at some time in their life, however, affective personality types will experience more pronounced problems with mood regulation over a number of years.

Schizophrenia

Although schizophrenia and schizoid personality types have been more commonly associated with anorexia nervosa recent research has suggested a possible correlation with bulimia nervosa. The existence of abnormal eating patterns among schizophrenics is thought to be a common finding (Lyketsos *et al*, 1985), although the comorbidity of bulimia and schizophrenia remains a complex association and has until recently been little researched. Deckelman *et al* (1997) discussed an interaction between psychotic and bulimic behaviour. One case of bulimia developed after the onset of the schizophrenia, other cases were found to exhibit characteristics of bulimia, and shared similar risk factors, although the symptoms shown by these sufferers did not match the expected profile which would normally be associated with that of bulimia nervosa. This suggests that some cases of schizophrenia experience a disordered eating pattern, which is able to correlate with their psychiatric symptoms to present a complex clinical picture.

Substance abuse

Substance abuse has received a significant amount of interest in recent years because of the detrimental effects which its existence brings to those societies where it is most prevalent. In Russell's early description of bulimia published in 1979, reference was made to the fact that eating disordered individuals frequently abused alcohol and drugs. The risk of indulging in substance abuse appears to be greater among bulimia sufferers and anorexics who engage in bulimic behaviour, with a much lower incidence reported among restrictive anorexics (Holderness et al, 1994; Kennedy and Garfinkel, 1992). This greater prevalence was also linked to a higher distribution of impulsive behaviours (ie. stealing, self-mutilation and attempted suicide) (Bailly, 1993). Awareness of this association has led to incorporated criteria to detect substance abuse as part of the assessment of patients attending for treatment of eating disorders. Statistical variations exist in the figures which have been put forward, but several studies have produced findings to support alcohol abuse as being particularly a problem among bulimics. Mitchell et al (1985) and Garfinkel et al (1980) found that between a quarter and a half of ill patients admitted to drinking alcohol at least once a week, but in some cases this was found to be more frequent, amounting to several times weekly. Other studies have suggested that in many cases, alcohol abuse may be more serious, with several studies able to support the existence of alcohol addiction. Bulik (1987) and Newman and Gold (1992) estimated that between 14% and 50% of bulimic individuals met the diagnostic criteria for alcohol dependence. One other significant point concerns the patient's age, with one study reporting that among older bulimic women as many as 50% were found to have an alcohol problem (Beary et al, 1986).

The association between substance abuse and bulimia suggests that professionals who work in treatment centres for addictions require additional skills, given that they may be dealing with a complex array of problems hidden beneath the one presenting condition.

Some studies have identified high rates of substance abuse among relatives of bulimics, with first degree relatives most likely to have this problem (Lilenfield et al, 1997; Bailly, 1993). The reasons for the latter association are poorly understood and remain subjects for future research.

It is unclear whether the abuse of drugs and/or alcohol develops alongside the features of the eating disorder, or is a manifestation of the personality disorder which often accompanies the condition itself. Bulik *et al* (1994) compared the characteristics of two groups of bulimic women, one of which abused alcohol, the other did not. The two groups shared many characteristics, and did not show significant differences in the nature of their bulimic illness, depressive symptoms, or associated psychiatric illness. The only significant finding was that the alcohol abuse group had been heavier in terms of their highest ever body weight. Bailly (1993) suggested that the relationship between alcohol and substance abuse within the context of eating disorders is that the eating disorder develops alongside these conditions as part of a behaviour pattern of multiple addictions. Where comorbidity exists there are even greater problems with detection and treatment which may mask the true underlying illness. Peveler and Fairburn (1990) suggested that such multiple pathology may potentially lessen the effect of medical intervention. Where a dual diagnosis exists it is generally accepted that treatment of the substance abuse problem is required separately, prior to treatment of the eating disorder, primarily because commitment and co-operation is severely impaired if the patient continues to misuse drugs or alcohol.

Depression

The prevalence of depression among patients in the primary care setting has been extensively studied, and unfortunately, is a condition which affects many people at some time or other.

A study in 1986 conducted among a cohort of college students, found depression to be closely linked with mood swings among those who admitted to episodes of bingeing and purging (Jones *et al*, 1986).

Fornari *et al* (1992) found bulimic anorexics the most likely group to exhibit depressive symptoms, with 72% of those studied found to have major depressive disorder at presentation. The clinical picture is difficult to establish where the symptoms exhibited by the patient mimic those of depression. There have been few studies into starvation-induced physical, endocrine, or psychological changes which mimic the symptoms of depression (Casper, 1998), and where vomiting is persistent, the lethargy and weakness which follow may be misinterpreted as depressive symptoms.

There is some suggestion that in certain cases depressive symptoms may not require direct treatment, but will ameliorate alongside a balanced nutritional intake improvement in bulimic behaviour (Laessle *et al*, 1991).

Differential diagnosis

Because of the apparent lack of any outward signs of physical illness and the secrecy surrounding this condition, the health professional may have no reason to suspect bulimia nervosa as the true cause for the patient's complaint. The patient is often clever enough to mask their illness and has been proved capable of doing so for many years in some cases.

Alternative diagnoses include:

- gastrointestinal symptoms
- Addison's disease.

Gastrointestinal symptoms

It would seem logical to expect some adverse gastrointestinal events in bulimics (and bulimic anorexics) who regularly use vomiting as a means of purging the body of food. Patient complaints may include feeling bloated, particularly after a meal, constipation, and generalised problems associated with a disturbance in the normal process of gastric emptying (Kamal *et al*, 1991; McClain *et al*, 1993).

Endoscopic examination of the gastric mucosa has confirmed the presence of gastritis and hiatus hernia (Kiss *et al*, 1989). Abnormal findings were not linked to the duration or the severity of the illness, although it is wise to consider that any data collected relating to these issues relies on the willingness of the individual to impart such information. Symptomatology among patients who regularly vomit as part of their illness appears to be variable. Cuellar *et al* (1988) reported evidence of gastrointestinal problems in almost half of the subjects examined. Delayed gastric emptying, oesophagitis, gastric and duodenal ulcers were all reported. Mitchell (1982) reported rare instances of gastric dilatation and gross enlargement of the stomach caused by the vast amounts of food consumed during a binge.

Palla and Litt (1988) found that patients who regularly vomited sometimes complained of involuntary regurgitation which on further questioning was thought to occur as a consequence of severe reflux of gastric contents into the oral pharynx.

Heightened awareness of the possibility of an alternative diagnosis is required for identification and referral of the eating disorder, while at the same time the underlying gastrointestinal pathology requires separate investigation. Intervention in these cases requires a significant level of clinical expertise.

Addison's disease

The insidious onset of this condition is marked by complaints of generalised weakness, weight loss, irregular periods, anorexia, lethargy and abdominal pain, and the cause remains unknown. The presenting clinical features make the diagnosis of Addison's disease a believable possibility given their similarity to those of eating disordered individuals. The use of laxatives and/or diuretics has an effect on the normal electrolyte balance (Sharp and Freeman, 1993). Excessive vomiting results in low plasma potassium levels, while repeated episodes of diarrhoea caused by laxative abuse has the same effect (Palla and Litt, 1988). The resulting volume depletion induces secondary hyperaldosteronism, leading to retention of sodium ions, through renal tubular exchange for hydrogen and potassium ions (Greenfield et al, 1995).

Clinical analysis of the underlying cause requires expert diagnostic skills particularly when the illness is cleverly masked by vague symptoms which may lead the patient through a range of investigations.

Suggested further reading

Associated health problems

Mitchell JE, Pyle RE, Eckert ED, Hatsukami D, Lentz R (1983) Electrolyte and other physiological abnormalities in patients with bulimia. *Psychol Med* **13**(2): 273–8

Kiss A, Wiesnagrotzki S, Abatzi TA, Meryn S, Haubenstock A, Base W (1989) Upper gastrointestinal endoscopy findings in patients with long-standing bulimia nervosa. *Gastrointest Endosc* **35**(6): 516

Howat PM, Varner ML, Hegsted M, Bruer MM, Mills GQ (1989) The effects of bulimia on diet, body fat, bone density and blood components. *J Am Diet Assoc* **89**: 929–34

Psychiatric comorbidity

Matsunaga H, Kiriike N (1997) Personality disorders in patients with treatment resistant eating disorders. *Jpn J Psychosomatic Med* **37**(1): 61–8

Gartner AF, Marcus RN, Halmi K, Loranger AW (1989) DSM-111R Personality disorders in patients with eating disorders. *Am J Psychiatry* **146**(12): 1585–91

Caspar RC (1998) Depression and eating disorders. *Depression Anxiety* **8** (Supplement 1): 86–104

Differential diagnosis

Kiss A, Wiesagrotski S, Abatzi TA, Meryn S, Haubenstock A, Base W (1989) Upper gastrointestinal endoscopy findings in patients with long-standing bulimia nervosa. *Gastrointest Endosc* **35**(6): 516–18

Newton JR, Freeman CP, Hannan WJ, Cowen S (1993) Osteoporosis and normal weight bulimia nervosa — which patients are at risk? *J Psychosom Res* **37**(3): 239–47

6

Treatment and management of bulimia nervosa

Introduction

Since its recognition, bulimia nervosa has been the subject of extensive research in an attempt to find an effective treatment which will enable sufferers to rectify their illness, and to sustain improvements made during active treatment in the long-term.

Russell (1979) suggested that the treatment of this condition presented problems, in that it appeared to be resistant to interventions, and was associated with a poorer prognosis than anorexia nervosa. Improvement and expansion of the range of therapeutic options has been matched by a greater likelihood that the condition can respond to certain interventions, although the difficulty appears to lie in the patient's ability to sustain this. Modern treatments have resulted in greater than 50% reductions in the severity of depression ratings, or in the frequency of binge-eating episodes, which may support the efficacy of an intervention, yet the patient remains clinically ill (Goldbloom and Olmsted, 1993). For a full recovery to be made, treatment must address all pathological elements of the patient's condition, to ensure that physical, social and psychological health have been restored. There is still debate concerning combinations of treatment options and the duration of follow-up required to ensure that relapse does not occur. The fact that many sufferers require more than one attempt at recovery (Herzog *et al*, 1991) indicates that the illness has the potential for high rates of chronicity, relapse, recurrence and psychosocial morbidity, suggesting that long-term eradication of symptoms represents an enormous achievement for all those who have been involved in the patient's illness (Keller *et al*, 1992).

Recent interest in the treatment of eating disorders has focused on a stepped care approach, where logically derived interventions are graded into levels or steps based on level of intensity, cost and the probability of success (Garner and Needleman, 1997). This particular strategy follows adoption of criteria for intervention, where the patient commences their programme at the lowest level thought to be suitable, and moves through the steps until a successful outcome is reached.

Inpatient or outpatient treatment

The majority of patients with bulimia nervosa can be treated on an outpatient basis. There are certain circumstances which might necessitate hospitalisation, including; poor response to previous therapy, serious concurrent medical problems (eg. metabolic abnormalities, severe vomiting, abnormal vital signs), suicidal tendencies, psychiatric disturbance or severe drug or alcohol abuse (American Psychiatric Association, 2000).

Self-help strategies

Self-help strategies can take many forms, including videotapes, audiotapes, books, educational leaflets, booklets and support groups and have been found to be successful in the treatment of a number of conditions, and their use may be particularly appropriate for those patients whose symptoms are relatively mild.

Treasure *et al* (1994) devised a self-help manual which adopted a problem-solving approach to bulimia. The educational approach which formed the basis of its content included self-monitoring, goal setting, assertiveness training, cognitive restructuring, and advice on preventing future relapse.

Forty-one patients were given the self-help manual, a further twenty-one patients followed a course of cognitive behaviour therapy (sixteen sessions) and a further nineteen subjects joined a waiting list. The findings suggested that the use of the self-help manual alone did produce some improvement, and although its use was not as effective as the cognitive behaviour therapy, the improvement in the former group was greater than that seen by those on the waiting list who received no intervention. Some patients expressed difficulty in coping with the amount of information given to them in one go, which led to non-compliance in those who were put off by this, suggesting that this form of treatment may be inappropriate for some subjects.

A German study allocated half the chosen sample to receive a self-help manual alongside eight sessions of cognitive behavioural therapy, the remaining half received sixteen sessions of cognitive behaviour therapy, with all being patients seen on an outpatient basis. The content of the cognitive behavioural sessions varied between the two groups with those following the self-help manual receiving less educational input (it was felt that this particular area was dealt with in the content of the manual itself).

The latter was felt to be useful in guiding the therapist sessions, allowing areas of difficulty to be discussed and resolved. Results showed that both treatments led to significant improvements in bingeing, vomiting, dietary constraint, shape and weight concerns, although those who had received additional educational input via the self-help manual had a better knowledge of their condition and a higher self-esteem at follow-up (Thiels *et al*, 1998). These improvements were still apparent when patients were followed-up at approximately forty-three weeks after completion of their treatment programme.

Dietary counselling and nutritional advice

Dietary counselling has an important role to play in the rehabilitation of all eating-disordered patients, and has probable relevance in achieving modification of eating behaviour and eating attitudes (Thompson, 1993). Potentially achievable benefits include:

❖ Educating the patient so that they feel confident in maintaining a healthy weight without the need for bingeing and purging.

❖ Helping the patient overcome their fear of eating in public.

For all eating disorders, whether food intake has occurred in secret or has been refused altogether, helping the patient to accept meals in social situations is an integral part of the recovery process. Indicators of emotional or psychological recovery are when the person (American Dietetic, Association, 1988):

- is able to eat with others without calling attention to themselves through abnormal eating
- is flexible enough to eat with others without controlling what is eaten, when meals are served or where meals are eaten
- no longer focuses on food as a way to deal with anxiety about interpersonal situations.

For many bulimics who have endured their illness for several years, achieving this target is a major accomplishment. Restoration of a healthy eating pattern which encourages a range of foods is implemented under the guidance and support of a dietician.

Nutritional management using assessment of food diaries has been utilised to provide information and discussion on metabolic processes, energy requirements, determinants of body weight, and the biological and psychological effects of starvation (Laessle *et al*, 1991). Therapist intervention in this study enabled the focus to change throughout the three-month programme of intervention, with the final sessions geared towards prevention of relapse. One of the concerns expressed by bulimics is their fear of weight gain which they believe will be inevitable when a return to normal eating patterns occurs. This has been proved unlikely, with the resumption of normal meals and cessation of purging thought to result in minimal weight gain (often as little as 1–3kg), much of which is believed to be attributable to the process of rehydration (Beumont *et al*, 1997).

The risk of relapse once contact with specialist services has ceased also needs to be addressed. A strategy to deal with this should be built into the final stages of the programme so that in the unfortunate event that it should occur the patient has immediate access to help and advice.

Stress management

Laessle *et al* (1991) described bulimia as a maladaptive coping strategy to manage stressful situations or personal problems. Eighty per cent of patients in one study cited stress as an important factor in precipitating relapse (Olmsted *et al*, 1994).

Evaluation of the effectiveness of stress management compared to nutritional counselling assigned half of those recruited to each of these programmes. The stress management group focused more on developing problem-solving skills and short-term action plans to alleviate the potential effects of adverse events; the nutritional advice group utilised food diaries, with a greater emphasis on nutritional requirements and eating behaviour.

Both forms of treatment achieved some measure of symptom relief, although there were specific differences in the nature of the improvement seen between the two groups.

Nutritional management achieved more success in bringing about abstinence from bingeing and purging, with 36% of subjects abstinent after three weeks, while stress management proved beneficial in helping patients deal with feelings of interpersonal distrust and anxiety (Laessle *et al*, 1991).

Behavioural therapy

This approach is designed to increase the patient's control over eating, eliminating food avoidance and changing maladaptive attitudes (Thompson, 1993).

The ultimate aim is to enable the individual to adopt a more normal pattern of dietary intake and ensure that they no longer feel the need to continue with their former approach to eating. Eradication of dietary restraint is important because this aspect is thought to promote abnormal eating behaviour among this group of patients (Fairburn *et al*, 1991).

One of the problems with this type of therapy is its need for the patient to maintain their motivation towards recovery, which some individuals may find difficult given that it adopts a self-monitoring approach. The impact of stressful life events and their potential to induce bulimic behaviour may render the individual susceptible to relapse, or make it particularly difficult for some individuals to maintain a consistent level of motivation which, if recovery is to be sustained, needs to continue long after treatment has finished.

Behaviour therapy has been studied alongside other forms of psychological intervention, and although its use can promote early improvements, its effects have been shown to be relatively short-lived. Fairburn *et al* (1995) found that when compared to other treatment methods (interpersonal psychotherapy and cognitive behaviour therapy), subjects who had received behaviour therapy fared worst, with 86% of those who had received this type of treatment still experiencing symptoms of an eating disorder at follow-up (bulimia nervosa in the majority of cases).

Cognitive behavioural therapy

Cognitive behaviour therapy is used in the treatment of a number of conditions and has been modified for use in eating-disordered individuals.

The adaptability of its use is based on the premise that cognitive and behavioural factors are relevant to all human experience and in successful cognitive behaviour therapy, a primary change in cognition will be followed by a secondary change in behaviour (Gelder *et al*, 1991).

Its use in the treatment of bulimia nervosa has received encouraging results and several studies have found it to be more effective than other forms of therapy (Whittal *et al*, 1999).

The programme is undertaken in three phases:

1) Self-monitoring of eating behaviour: Patients are encouraged to keep records of their daily food intake, including any episodes of abnormal eating and the thoughts, feelings and events which may accompany these relapses. The patient may be able to recognise specific situations which they find pre-empt their eating behaviour.

2) Educational phase: The patient is taught a greater understanding of their condition. This involves helping the patient identify and thereby achieve a greater understanding of those factors which may be instrumental in continuing the pattern of abnormal eating behaviour.

3) Sustaining improvement: Strategies to prevent relapse are fundamental to the successful outcome.

When compared to other therapies, cognitive behaviour therapy had an overall advantage in that it achieved its effect in a shorter time span (Fairburn *et al*, 1993). A marked reduction was seen in overeating, the use of vomiting as an adjunct to weight control, psychiatric symptoms and social adjustment (Fairburn *et al*, 1991). Abnormal perceptions relating to shape and weight are difficult to change, but were found to respond to this type of therapeutic intervention.

Although all the therapies under evaluation achieved some success, cognitive behaviour therapy was found to have had the greatest all-round effect.

The stages of the programme take the patient through a process of self-examination and analysis. This begins with the patient being asked to document all episodes of bingeing and purging, including details of specific events or thoughts which surrounded these occasions. The educational element involves increasing the person's understanding of the potentially harmful effects of purging. A focus on normalisation of eating is then implemented, although no suggestion is made of what this food should be and choice is largely the domain of the patient.

The second stage moves towards widening the range of foods consumed and increasing the amount of food eaten at each meal. Because this stage involves incorporating foods which would previously only have been consumed during or prior to a binge, this represents an enormous step for the patient. They are supported with self-control strategies and self-coping mechanisms.

One of the major concerns for professionals involved in the treatment of eating disorders is whether improvements made during the course of therapy will be sustained once treatment has finished.

Studies of the long-term effect of cognitive behaviour therapy have found that not only were its benefits substantial to the health of the patient in the short-term, but they were well maintained with continued improvement seen at follow-up (Fairburn *et al*, 1993).

Interpersonal psychotherapy

This therapy has its origins in the treatment of depression.

It differs from cognitive behaviour therapy in that it places no emphasis on weight or weight gain, or on the patient's perception of their own shape and weight; nor does the treatment contain any of the specific behavioural or cognitive procedures that characterise cognitive behaviour therapy (Agras *et al*, 2000).

In a similar manner to cognitive behaviour therapy, interpersonal psychotherapy follows a staged approach with identification of personal difficulties which might be instrumental in perpetuating the disease identified early in the programme. It is believed that such personal problems, although common in bulimia nervosa, are often not recognised by the patient because of the distracting influence of their preoccupation with thoughts about eating, shape and weight (Fairburn, 1997).

The second stage largely follows the same strategy that would be implemented for those patients receiving this treatment for depression, with the final stages concerned with maintenance of recovery and prevention of relapse.

Studies have shown this therapy to be effective in reducing the frequency of overeating, with these improvements sustained at follow-up assessment (Fairburn *et al*, 1993). Comparison studies with cognitive behaviour therapy have identified problems with its effect on cognitive dysfunction. While improvements were made in psychiatric symptoms, interpersonal psychotherapy was less efficient in modifying the patients' disturbed attitudes towards their shape and weight, their attitudes towards diet, and their use of vomiting as an adjunct to weight control (Fairburn *et al*, 1991). The success of any treatment is dependent to a large extent on the determination and the desire of the individual to overcome their illness, and many clinicians feel that continued dysfunctional thoughts will affect the long-term outcome, with a greater chance of relapse in those patients who continue to exhibit abnormal attitudes towards shape and weight after completion of their treatment. Because of its lesser effect on certain highly important facets of the illness, interpersonal psychotherapy is generally regarded as less successful in the treatment of bulimia nervous (Fairburn *et al*, 1991). One of the most encouraging features of interpersonal psycho-therapy is its association with a number of positive events. The study by Fairburn *et al* (1993) observed patients making changes in their personal relationships, which were instrumental in promoting a series of further lifestyle alterations.

These positive benefits might need to be taken into account when considering the patient's individual circumstances and formulating a treatment plan appropriate to their needs.

Light therapy

The possibility that some individuals may experience worsening bulimic symptoms during the winter months has been previously mentioned (*pp. 83–84*). Lam *et al* (1994) conducted a trial of light therapy in seventeen patients, half of whom reported a deterioration of their condition during winter and were treated with bright white light for thirty-minute periods each day for a two-week period. Once completed the same regime was adopted for a further two weeks, substituting dim red light as an alternative light source. Subjects were asked to self-monitor and record binge/purge episodes, but were assessed by a psychiatrist for mood patterns and depressive symptoms.

Those with confirmed seasonal variation to their illness were found to benefit greatly while receiving the white light treatment, however a return of symptoms occurred during therapy with dim red light. Exposure to bright white light not only significantly reduced the depressive symptoms, but also curtailed the cardinal symptoms of bulimia nervosa, namely binge eating and purge episodes (Lam *et al*, 1994). Such were the benefits perceived by these subjects, that over a third of those included purchased a light for personal use after completion of the study.

Pharmacotherapy

Pharmacological intervention for the treatment of bulimia nervosa has followed a number of routes. Kennedy and Goldbloom (1991) describe two lines of enquiry; the first relating to the anxiety and mood disorders which are frequently allied to the condition, and the second relating to the regulation of the appetite.

Fluoxetine

The use of antidepressants in the management of bulimia nervosa has been found to be effective in helping to reduce some of the symptoms of bulimia nervosa and particularly the frequency of overeating (Agras and McCann, 1987).

This is in contrast to the reported lack of effect in the treatment of anorexia nervosa (Halmi *et al*, 1986).

A collaborative study (Bulimia Nervosa Collaborative Study Group, 1992) divided subjects into three study groups, treated as follows:

- group one received a placebo
- group two received a 20mg daily dose of fluoxetine
- group three received a higher daily dose of 60mg daily.

Fluoxetine at 60mg proved significantly superior to placebo, 20mg proved modestly but not always significantly superior to placebo, but the major concern is that antidepressant therapy cannot address the additional features of abnormal perceptions of shape or disturbed attitudes towards dieting which, if left unresolved, may affect long-term outcome (Mitchell, 1989). The use of this drug is the preferred choice of antidepressant therapy and it can probably be used as an adjunct to psychotherapy in many cases not responding to a course of adequate psychological treatment (Garner and Needleman, 1997).

Phenelzine

Phenelzine belongs to the classification monoamine-oxidase inhibitors, and is associated with a number of drug and dietary interactions (which make it a less favourable choice than some of the alternative options). There are a long list of potential side-effects which may affect compliance and make it an unpopular choice with patients.

The use of these drugs demands careful adherence to a dietary regimen to avoid a hyperadrenergic crisis: a possible difficulty for patients who experience a lack of control of food intake (Kennedy and Goldbloom, 1991).

Desipramine

The efficacy of this drug in reducing the frequency of binge eating has produced short-term benefits with a rapid relapse once treatment is completed, which might have implications for the duration of pharmacological intervention.

Trials of the drug when compared to placebo have found that its use during the active phase of therapy was associated with significant reductions in the behavioural and psychological disturbances characteristic of bulimia nervosa (Walsh *et al*, 1991), but a third of those who reached the final stage of the trial relapsed within the following four months.

Lithium carbonate

A controlled trial of lithium carbonate in bulimic outpatients achieved significant reductions in bulimic episodes after eight weeks of therapy (Hsu *et al*, 1991). This improvement was achieved at higher plasma levels (at low plasma levels its effects were no better than placebo). Its use is impeded because of the associated side-effects, which include gastrointestinal problems, polyuria, polydypsia, weight gain and oedema, which are dose-related (*British National Formulary [BNF]*, 1999).

The possibility of weight gain would make this an unsuitable choice in bulimic individuals where avoidance of weight gain is a key component of their illness.

Combination treatments

The swift relapse following discontinuation of oral therapies has lead to an interest in their use in combination with psychotherapy. Several studies (Walsh *et al*, 1995; Agras *et al*, 1992) have shown that psychotherapy produced better improvements than medication alone but, in combination with antidepressants (either fluoxetine or desipramine), patient improvement was considered to be greater.

Long-term outcome

Bulimia nervosa

The later inclusion of bulimia to the spectrum of eating disorders has meant that long-term outcome studies remain relatively few in number when compared to the vast array of material related to anorexia nervosa.

Topics that have been investigated are similar to those thought to influence prognosis in anorexia nervosa, and include age at onset and severity of symptoms (Keel and Mitchell, 1997; Keel *et al*, 1999), comorbid psychopathology (Keel *et al*, 1999), social factors (Johnson-Sabine *et al*, 1992), and past history of anorexia nervosa (Collings and King, 1994).

Age at onset

Follow-up conducted ten years after their initial presentation, established that age of onset appeared to be unrelated to outcome, but duration of symptoms at baseline (measured as the difference between age at onset and the age at presentation) was significantly correlated with long-term prognosis. Those with the longest duration of illness prior to detection were most likely to signify a worse eating disorder outcome (Keel *et al*, 1999).

Duration of follow-up

Johnson-Sabine *et al* (1992) reported that at five-year follow-up 25% of subjects were found to have continued symptoms, and still met the diagnostic criteria for bulimia nervosa. Only 31% were felt to have made a substantial recovery, the remainder still had some binge-eating symptomatology but of a less severe nature. Ten-year assessment of the same subjects found that over half of those included were fully recovered, indicating improved outcome with longer duration of follow-up. Data concerning periods of remission are often not available and it is difficult to see whether a specific pattern precedes recovery or alternatively relapse. Such information might be useful in helping patients to recognise vulnerable periods and formulating a strategy to help them stay in remission and prevent a recurrence of symptoms.

Comorbid psychiatric symptoms

Those patients who drop out of treatment programmes are often lost to the system and do not respond to follow-up invitations. Keel *et al* (1999) reported that 20% of subjects who were potentially suitable for follow-up did not participate and half of these could not be traced. Those who fail to complete treatment programmes are more likely to have a past history of depression and poorer social adjustment than those who complete (Agras *et al*, 2000). Johnson-Sabine *et al* (1992) identified a third of patients assessed five years after treatment who reported continued psychiatric disturbance (other than mood disturbance); although for patients as a whole there appeared to be a generalised reduction in anxiety and depressive symptoms during the follow-up period.

Collings and King (1994) suggested that those patients who had failed to make a recovery at longer duration following treatment completion, were more likely to continue to experience a range of psychological difficulties and abnormal eating patterns.

Personality disorders

Not all individuals who develop an eating disorder have comorbid personality disorders but several studies have identified high rates among bulimia sufferers (Bulik *et al*, 1997a; Bulik *et al*, 1996, Vaz and Penas, 1998). Those with personality disorders tend to be more often hospitalised (Matsunaga and Kiriike, 1997), which might reflect a cycle of improvement and deterioration in these patients. The issue of whether the existence of personality disturbances has an influence on response to treatment or can have an impact on long-term recovery has received some interest. Assessment of a cohort of bulimic women following treatment of their illness with cognitive behaviour therapy found that personality disorders were still evident in 39% of subjects, a further 19% were considered to have personality difficulties, and 28% were found to have more than one personality disorder with histrionic and anxiety disorders most prevalent (Fahy *et al*, 1993). Those who continued to demonstrate continued symptoms related to their personality disorders were found to have a poorer response to treatment (in terms of a reduction in bulimic behaviour). On initial assessment, personality disordered individuals were found to weigh less and exhibit features of depression. The addition of these two factors were found to make treatment more difficult than in those individuals with personality disturbance as a single entity (Fahy *et al*,

1993). The importance of low weight in anorexia has been recognised, and the combination of depression, low weight and personality disorders might signify the need for a more intensive approach to treatment and have an impact on the duration of treatment required to make a significant improvement.

Social factors

The treatment of eating disorders attempts to improve social functioning and interpersonal difficulties, and since it is common for bulimic episodes to be precipitated by interpersonal events (Fairburn *et al*, 1997) it seems logical to assume that those who continue to experience problems in their personal life will have a poorer prognosis. Assessment five years post-treatment confirmed that subjects who achieved a good outcome with no evidence of bulimic symptoms reported fewer social problems, while those with a less favourable outcome reported difficulties in their relationships with either their husband or partner, problems with relatives or financial difficulties (Johnson-Sabine *et al*, 1992). Lack of a stable relationship has been noted as an influential factor in other studies. Collings and King (1994) established that none of the subjects who were not fully recovered at follow-up had ever been married, or lived with a partner, and lack of such a relationship was associated with greater psychiatric disturbance. Social class was also relevant with subjects from higher social classes being more likely to make a full recovery than those from lower social classes.

History of anorexia nervosa

Research evidence suggests that transmission of symptoms from anorexia nervosa to bulimia is more commonly found than the reverse, although little is known about the extent to which this affects long-term outcome (Keel and Mitchell, 1997). Norring and Sohlberg (1993) found eating disorder not otherwise specified to be the most common diagnosis at follow-up, six years after presentation.

Keel *et al* (2000) suggested that the delay in recognising bulimia nervosa may be partially attributable to the observed cross-over of patients from anorexia to bulimia.

History of substance abuse

Whether a history of substance abuse has an impact on long-term recovery from bulimia nervosa remains unclear. It would seem logical to predict that a dual diagnosis of this nature would impede recovery, and this was found to be true in one study which found that a quarter of the sample at follow-up were found to be drinking excessively, with one male patient having received treatment for alcohol dependency (Johnson-Sabine *et al*, 1992). All of these patients fell into the category labelled as 'poor outcome'.

Relapse in bulimia nervosa

There have been a number of investigative studies estimating the rates of relapse, with figures suggesting that for many the risk of symptom recurrence is quite high.

Statistics vary widely and are difficult to compare because of the different criteria used to assess what is considered to constitute either recovery, or relapse. Keel and Mitchell (1997) suggested that studies which assess women five or more years after treatment rely on sharply decreasing numbers of women (342 women followed for five to six years compared with sixty-eight women for nine to ten years). The follow-up of women ten years after treatment experienced similar problems; 20% of women potentially suitable for follow-up assessment did not participate and half of these women could not be located (Keel *et al*, 1999). The secrecy which surrounds the presence of bulimic symptoms may have some influence on statistics produced because it is possible that those who have relapsed will not want to undergo further investigation.

Little work to date has focused on specific factors that might pre-empt this relapse.

Figures produced two years after completion of treatment, indicated that 16.7% of those assessed met the criteria for relapse quite quickly (within three months of leaving their treatment programme). By the end of a six-month period 25% of subjects had suffered a relapse, a figure which increased to 31% by two years (Olmsted *et al*, 1994).

A comparison of those who relapsed and those who did not revealed a number of variables thought to be influential, some of which related to the patient's illness prior to treatment, others to factors which occurred post treatment.

Pre-treatment variables were recorded as vomiting frequency, post-treatment variables were noted as vomiting frequency and the level of interpersonal distrust (Olmsted *et al*, 1994).

Following an initial improvement Pyle *et al* (1990) reported outcome after a six-month period. During the treatment phase patients were assigned to one of four programmes, and received either psychotherapy alone, psychotherapy combined with anti-depressants, antidepressants alone or a placebo substance.

On completion of the therapy a number of follow-up support mechanisms were implemented and a follow-up assessment was made at six months post-treatment completion. The most influential factor in preventing relapse in those who had made an early response to treatment was group psychotherapy, and this was regardless of any maintenance treatment received (Pyle *et al*, 1990).

The commitment of the individual, and their desire to eliminate bulimic behaviour has been cited as relevant to the success of treatment, particularly in those receiving cognitive behaviour therapy. Mussell *et al* (2000) found these two factors predictive of treatment outcome, while symptom remission at the end of treatment and one-month follow-up was predictive of longer term outcome.

Long-term outlook

Five-year outcome of bulimia nervosa has been associated with a relatively poor outlook (Fairburn *et al*, 2000), although Keel *et al* (1999) suggest that its long-term prognosis may be more favourable than that of anorexia nervosa. Several papers have confirmed the continued presence of bulimic symptoms at variable stages of follow-up (Keel *et al*, 1999; Keel *et al*, 2000), and in some instances eating disorder not otherwise specified has been identified as the commonest eating disorder diagnosis at follow-up (Fairburn *et al*, 2000; Keel *et al*, 1999), which suggests that in those who have failed to make a full recovery, a partial version of the illness may continue.

There are few long-term outcome studies conducted to date, although one study conducted several years ago suggested that illness which had persisted for a period of six years or more was indicative of a poor outcome (Theander, 1985).

Given that treatment strategies have altered since this time their is a need for further research to determine current predictors of outcome.

Suggested further reading

Nutritional management

Story M (1986) Nutrition management and the dietary treatment of bulimia. *J Am Diet Assoc* **86**: 517–9

Stress management

Laessle RG, Beumont PJV, Butow W, Lennerts W, O'Connor M, Pirke KM, Touyz SW, Waadt S (1991) A comparison of nutritional management in the treatment of bulimia nervosa. *Br J Psychiatry* **159**: 250–61

Cognitive behaviour therapy

Wilson GT, Eldredge KL, Smith D, Niles B (1991) Cognitive-behavioral treatment with and without response prevention for bulimia. *Behav Res Ther* **29**(6): 575–83

Garner DM, Rockert W, Davis R, Garner MV, Olmsted MP, Eagle M, (1993) Comparison of cognitive-behavioral and supportive-expressive therapy for bulimia nervosa. *Am J Psychiatry* **150**(1): 37–46

Interpersonal therapy

Agras WS, Walsh T, Fairburn CG, Wilson GT, Kraemer HC (2000) A multicenter comparison of cognitive-behavioral therapy and interpersonal psychotherapy for bulimia nervosa. *Arch Gen Psychiatry* **57**(5): 459–66

Self-help

Treasure J, Schmidt U, Troop N, Tiller J, Todd G, Keilen M, Dodge E (1994) First step in managing bulimia nervosa: controlled trial of a therapeutic manual. *Br Med J* **308**: 686–9

Light therapy

Lam RW, Elliot M, Goldner MD, Solyom L, Remick RA (1994) A controlled study of light therapy for bulimia nervosa. *Am J Psychiatry* **151**(5): 744–50

Avery DH, Khan A, Dager SR, Cox GB, Dunner DL (1990) Bright light treatment of winter depression: morning versus evening light. *Acta Psychiatr Scand* **82**(5): 335–8

Pharmacotherapy

Kennedy SH, Goldbloom DS (1991) Current perspectives on drug therapies for anorexia nervosa and bulimia nervosa. *Drugs* **41**(3): 367–77

Goldbloom DS, Olmsted MP (1993) Pharmacotherapy of bulimia nervosa with fluoxetine: assessment of clinically significant attitudinal change. *Am J Psychiatry* **150**(5): 770–4

Outcome

Fichter MM, Quadflieg N, Rief W (1994) Longer term course (6-year) of bulimia nervosa. *Neuropsychopharmacology* **10**(772S)

Fahy TA, Russell GFM (1993) Outcome and prognostic variables in bulimia nervosa. *Int J Eat Disord* **14**: 135–45

Section III:
Binge-eating disorder

7

Binge-eating disorder

Epidemiology of binge-eating disorder

The prevalence rates for this disorder are still not known, however its relatively recent recognition has been matched by a growing amount of interest among the medical profession. The condition is reported to have first appeared in the medical literature in the early 1950s and since this time, research projects have identified it as an eating disorder whose sufferers are likely to be obese (Spitzer *et al*, 1993). Many of the prevalence studies have used subjects from communities which are likely to have high numbers of obese subjects.

Recent research suggests that, like anorexia nervosa and bulimia nervosa, female dominance of binge-eating disorder may not be the case. Substantial numbers of men have been found to suffer from this condition, with a suggested ratio of three females affected to every two males (Spitzer *et al*, 1992). Kinzl *et al* (1999) found a prevalence rate of 0.8 % among men who met the full diagnostic criteria for binge-eating disorder, a further 4.2% had some degree of symptoms and were categorised as having a partial binge-eating syndrome.

Male sufferers identified in Kinzl's study were also overweight or obese, however this finding applied more to those who met the full diagnostic criteria for binge-eating disorder, rather than to those with a less severe version.

Statistics confirm a similar prevalence of binge eating among African American, non-Hispanic white, and Hispanic women with the latter group found to have the greatest severity of symptoms (Fitzgibbon *et al*, 1998) which confirms that race may be no barrier to this condition.

A recent American study compared a community sample of white women with a similar community sample of black women, aged between sixteen to fifty years. Black women were found to be as likely to report binge eating as their white counterparts, with the indication that this condition poses a significant health problem for this group of women, with potentially serious long-term physical and mental health problems if left untreated (Striegel-Moore *et al*, 2000).

Aetiology

Factors linked to the onset of binge-eating disorder:

- ⌘ Personality traits.
- ⌘ Childhood obesity.
- ⌘ Exposure to risk factors for psychiatric disorder.
- ⌘ Genetic factors.
- ⌘ Stressful events.

Although investigative studies are increasing in number, an element of uncertainty still surrounds its possible association with the later onset of other eating disorders, particularly bulimia nervosa with which it is believed to share the greatest similarity (Fairburn *et al*, 1993; Hay *et al*, 1996). Because binge eating is a relatively new addition to the list of eating disorders, it remains poorly understood and requires further research to establish a greater understanding of its aetiology and clinical features.

Fairburn *et al* (1993) have studied the aetiological factors involved in the onset of anorexia, bulimia and binge-eating disorder. Because of the shared similarity in clinical features to those exhibited by patients with bulimia nervosa, an association between these two separate conditions has been the subject of investigation, to determine whether the latter condition in some way precedes or is influential in bringing about the onset of bulimic symptoms. Marcus (1997) indicated that there is, indeed, a greater risk of transmission to bulimia nervosa in those who display specific personality types.

Personality traits

In common with bulimia sufferers, binge eaters have been found to have low personal self-esteem, to be of a quiet shy nature, with a tendency towards perfectionism. Negative self-evaluation and a vulnerability to obesity are particular characteristics of those who possess a premorbid perfectionism and subsequently develop bulimia nervosa (Fairburn *et al*, 1997).

This passing from one condition to another may be fuelled by the weight gain which follows in many who indulge in persistent binge eating, given that body image disturbance and preoccupation with size has been found to be greater among the obese who adopt abnormal eating patterns (Mussell *et al*, 1996b).

Childhood obesity

Current problems with weight control or a past history of weight problems, has been cited as an aetiological factor for both bulimia nervosa (Fairburn *et al*, 1997) and binge-eating disorder (Spitzer *et al*, 1993). There are variable statistics surrounding the actual age at which the patient's weight became a significant problem, although a general estimate is reported to be approximately fifteen years of age; data indicates that this is slightly younger than in the obese who do not indulge in binge episodes (Spitzer *et al*, 1993).

When compared with healthy controls, negative self-evaluation, and unpleasant comments about shape and weight were cited as risk factors implicated in the development of eating disorders in general, while comparisons with psychiatric controls have cited similar high levels of negative comments from family members and a greater history of childhood obesity among those who developed binge-eating disorder (Fairburn *et al*, 1998). Obese children often the bear the brunt of jibes from their peers; and teasing which commences at an early age may have an impact on eating behaviour and body dissatisfaction in future years (Thompson *et al*, 1995).

The relationship between onset of obesity, eating disorder psychopathology, and overall levels of body dissatisfaction appear to be directly influenced by the amount of tormenting the young person has endured. Jackson (2000) noted that those subjects whose obesity developed at a young age reported a history of more teasing about their weight and size than those whose weight problem developed in adulthood. This study indicated that teasing about general appearance (but not weight and size) was significantly associated with greater levels of binge eating frequency in the obese women and more severe dietary restraint in non-obese women.

Exposure to risk factors for psychiatric disorders

Fairburn *et al* (1998) concluded that there are a wider range of risk factors associated with bulimia nervosa, while binge-eating disorder sufferers appeared to have been exposed to specific elements which predispose the individual to psychiatric disorder and to obesity. Incidents thought to be relevant included a history of psychiatric illness among the parents, and possible physical abuse, with the impact of these elements directly correlated to the level of exposure which the individual has endured: the greater the exposure, the higher the risk of developing binge-eating disorder.

Genetic factors

The belief that obesity stems from greed and a lack of will power has now been discarded on the evidence from twin studies, studies of familial aggregation, adoption and animal models of obesity; all of which indicate that obesity is a result of both genetic and environmental factors (Friedman and Halaas, 1998). The tendency to gain an excessive amount of weight in certain individuals has evoked considerable interest, particularly in the light of the statistics which support the rising prevalence of this condition in society as a whole.

Adoption, twin and family studies have consistently supported the view that obesity is strongly linked to a heritable component with data suggesting that approximately 30–70% of individual variability in body weight is attributable to genetic influences (Allison *et al*, 1996).

Because of the similarities shared with bulimia nervosa it would seem plausible that there is the similar possibility of a genetic influence in binge-eating disorder, and the potential for transition to bulimia nervosa. A study of women from a population-based twin registry assessed a number of variables (including demographic factors, current symptoms, psychiatric symptoms, both current and lifetime) and a number of genetic and environmental factors which might influence the condition.

Overlap was found to exist between the genetic risk factors for the development of binge-eating disorder, and the genetic risk factors for the transition from this condition to bulimia nervosa, although non-shared environmental factors may be more important in increasing the risk for bulimia once binge eating is initiated (Wade *et al*, 2000).

Stressful events

In vulnerable individuals food intake and eating behaviour can be affected during times of personal crisis and has been described as 'emotional eating' (Telch *et al*, 1994). Women have been found to report abnormal eating patterns as a response to negative emotions, particularly anger, frustration, anxiety and depression (Tanofsky *et al*, 1997)

The possible role of serotonin in the aetiology of bulimia nervosa has already been mentioned, and its release is involved in many functions, including sleep onset, pain sensitivity, blood pressure regulation and control of mood (Wurtman and Wurtman, 1995). Ingestion of carbohydrate rich foodstuffs is instrumental in increasing the amount of serotonin released in the body, which when consumed in large quantities acts as a mood enhancer. This tendency to use certain foods as though they were drugs is a frequent cause of weight gain and may be seen when an individual is exposed to stress, during premenstrual syndrome, and in those exposed to 'winter depression' (Wurtman and Wurtman, 1995).

A comparison study between women who binged regularly and those who did not showed that in the former group, binge episodes were associated with troublesome or stressful events which had occurred prior to their loss of control on binge days (Wolff *et al*, 2000). The actual nature of incidences did not differ between days when binge episodes occurred and those when they did not, but the deciding influence appeared to be reaction of the individual to such events on any particular day, which would suggest that the individual's ability to cope with such situations was in some way impaired. Wolff *et al* (2000) proposed that binge eaters used the same number of adaptive coping responses as normal eaters but, in addition, used maladaptive coping responses (such as smoking, excessive eating and drinking) and generally reported a more negative mood on days when a binge episode occurred.

Sexual abuse as an aetiological factor

Sexual abuse in childhood has long-lasting psychological repercussions which can affect the quality of life for many years following the event. The detrimental effect on a young child has been linked to the later onset of a number of distressing conditions, including problems with personal relationships, confidence in sexual relationships and low self-esteem (Browne and Finkelhor, 1986). Sexual abuse was thought to be an aetiological factor because those who have experienced such abuse exhibit similar characteristics to those found in eating-disordered subjects, eg. shame, low self-esteem and a negative attitude towards their bodies (Welch and Fairburn, 1994).

The association has been difficult to prove resulting in variable statistics, with controversial and inconclusive evidence. Prevalence rates are affected by a multitude of factors, including the assessment method used and the criteria adopted by the researcher to determine what constitutes a definite occurrence of sexual abuse. The inclusion of incidences which do not include any physical contact has led to a high rate of sexual abuse in eating disorders in some studies (Welch and Fairburn, 1994). Information provided by the person relies on the willingness of the individual to provide personal details and, if the event occurred many years ago, its recall is subject to the accuracy of the person's memory which may have been tarnished by subsequent events in adult life. There may be a reluctance among some subjects to remember such events because of the shame and distress which such a recollection may bring. Abuse can occur in different forms and can range from a relatively minor incident to one of a much more serious nature.

A study of more serious incidents of abuse that had taken place prior to the onset of the eating disorder was undertaken to determine whether a direct association could be made (Welch and Fairburn, 1994). This study found that rates of sexual abuse were just as prevalent among those with a psychiatric condition. Vize and Cooper (1995) found that a history of sexual abuse had an association with impulsive behaviour and the overall level of personality disturbance, concluding that childhood abuse is a vulnerability factor for psychiatric disorder but not eating disorders in particular. However, there is some evidence to indicate that a history of sexual abuse is associated with greater levels of psychiatric comorbidity in those who do develop an eating disorder later in life (Rorty *et al*, 1994).

Diagnosis of binge-eating disorder

1. Large quantities of food consumed in a relatively short period of time, not fuelled by hunger.
2. The patient is unable to restrain the quantity of food ingested during a binge and may feel that they have 'lost control'.

For further clarification, the criteria suggest three or more of the following are also adopted during a binge:

❖ Eating in isolation so that the amount of food consumed remains secret.

❖ Continual eating until unable to eat any more.

❖ The amount of food eaten does not relate to any degree of hunger and is usually far more than would normally be eaten at a meal.

❖ Feelings of extreme distress often accompanied by disgust.

The criteria suggest that binge episodes should have taken place at least twice each week for a minimum six-month period.

Difficulties in making a diagnosis

The diagnosis of this condition is based on information supplied by the patient and needs to adopt a uniform understanding of the definition of binge episodes, and a clear interpretation of the questions asked if misdiagnosis and misinterpretation of the information supplied are to be actively avoided. Beglin and Fairburn (1992) attempted to find out how young women apply the use of the term 'binge eating' to their own eating behaviour and secondly, to establish what these women understand the term to mean. Nineteen per cent reported episodes of objective overeating, and 13% reported subjective overeating, although when examined against the diagnostic criteria, few episodes of objective or subjective overeating could be classified as true 'binges'.

The second part of the study found that women were clearly more concerned about the apparent inability to control the episodes of binge eating. The findings indicated that on self-report questionnaires the response of many will refer to episodes of perceived overeating (Beglin and Fairburn, 1992), rather than to episodes of binge eating which correlate to the criteria for a diagnosis of binge-eating disorder.

Onset and clinical features

The exact age of onset of binge-eating behaviour is difficult to determine, although when compared to bulimic subjects, obese binge eaters appear to be significantly older (De Zwaan *et al*, 1994). The majority of cases identified to date have been in subjects aged over forty years of age (Castonguay *et al*, 1995). The older age at diagnosis, together with their apparent struggle with a weight problem would appear to clarify the suspicion that this pattern of eating may have been present for several years.

Table 7.1: Features of binge-eating behaviour		
Behavioural	**Psychological**	**Physical**
Consumption of large quantities of food	Emotional stress	Obesity
	Depression	Leading disordered life
Eating pattern		Hypertension
Episodes of binge eating		Diabetes
		Hyperlipidaemia
May include night eating		

Behavioural

The fact that many eat alone is often attributed to the embarrassment that they feel at the quantity of food they have eaten.

Recurrent binge eating is described as the persistent pattern of eating a large amount of food, which is often much more than would be comfortable for the individual. Many sufferers express feelings of inadequacy and anguish, particularly at the fact that they feel unable to restrain or restrict the quantity of food consumed during any one episode. This description emphasises the association with the clinical features of bulimia nervosa, with one major exception: the absence of binge-purge behaviour to rid the body of the grossly abnormal amounts of food eaten. There is little data to clarify how much food the individual may consume for these episodes to be classified as a binge (De Zwaan *et al*, 1994), similarly the duration of such events is highly variable with some reports suggesting that bingeing may continue for several hours with a vast amount of calories being consumed, although this will vary widely from person to person. It is particularly difficult to classify where each binge ends, specifically because there is no definable end point which can be regarded as a marker for termination of these episodes.

Differences between the obese who indulge in this behaviour and those who do not have shown that those in the former group regain lost weight more rapidly in behavioural programmes, and have a greater attrition during treatment than subjects without binge-eating disorder (Marcus *et al*, 1988).

Binge eaters have consistently been shown to have a higher body mass index than their non-binge-eating obese counterparts (Telch, 1988), and there is suspicion that the battle with obesity often persists for many years with periods of dieting and weight loss, often superseded by further weight gain and distress at the inability to sustain their weight reduction. Fluctuations in weight and the tendency to enter a cycle of dieting and weight gain has been found to be a feature of obese binge eaters, and is termed weight cycling in the medical literature. Failed attempts at weight loss frequently result in considerable despondency, with a history of numerous unsuccessful attempts to lose weight. Patients often adhere to a set diet with variable success, only to relapse with a return to former eating habits, and in many cases a greater weight gain ensues.

Adami *et al* (1995) suggested that the more subjects attempt to diet or restrict their food intake in order to lose weight, the more they are prone to loss of control over food intake and to binge eating, which further exacerbates the problem. Self-esteem is often low and many feel guilty when their will power fails them and they indulge in foodstuffs which are normally forbidden in the active phase of dieting.

Night-eating syndrome

This relatively recently recognised eating disorder has been described as a differential diagnosis for sleep-related eating disorders, binge-eating disorder and bulimia nervosa with night time eating (Yager 1999). Binge-eating disorder does not have episodes of night eating as part of the diagnostic criteria (Brewerton, 1999), but their are several similarities between these two conditions. The syndrome is little understood and remains under professional scrutiny, although research to date has identified that, although the non-obese can be affected, the prevalence of night-eating syndrome is said to increase with increasing adiposity (Birketvedt *et al*, 1999).

It is characterised by an abnormal pattern of eating, where the individual indulges in late night consumption of food which may occur prior to the onset of sleep and often extends into the early hours. The presence of these symptoms is nearly always accompanied by little desire to eat during the day, with hunger abated until the evening.

Epidemiological studies have estimated a prevalence rate of approximately 1.5% in the general population, although this statistic is reported to be higher among populations where the number of obese individuals is greater. One study found the number of subjects with night-eating syndrome in an obesity clinic to be nearly four times greater than the expected prevalence rate (Stunkard *et al*, 1996).

Psychological symptoms

Striegel-Moore *et al* (1998) found that the behavioural patterns shown by those with binge-eating disorder were associated with an impairment of psychological adjustment, although this association has to date been associated with binge eating among white women. The relationship with obesity suggests the possibility that a degree of psychiatric disturbance may occur as a result of the grossly obese body shape (Mussell *et al*, 1996a), rather than existing prior to the development of their weight problem. Fichter *et al* (1993) attempted to clarify the level of psychiatric disturbance and found that the obese who frequently binged scored higher than those obese patients who did not, but their overall level of psychopathology was closer to those with bulimia nervosa.

Many studies have been able to describe feelings of extreme distress both during and after episodes of bingeing (Beglin and Fairburn, 1992; American Psychiatric Association, 1994). Patients' recollections of these feelings have been described as an abject sense of lack of control which has been of more concern to the patient themselves than the vast quantities of food consumed during a binge episode (Beglin and Fairburn, 1992).

Cargill *et al* (1999) studied 159 subjects attending a weight loss programme where increased perceptions of poor body image and depressive symptoms were found to be significantly related to loss of control over food intake. The patients reported more disturbance in body dissatisfaction and size perception than non-binge eaters (Mussell *et al*, 1996a), and this sense of shame and concern at their public persona is believed to have the strongest relationship with binge eating across all factors (Cargill *et al*, 1999).

Depression

In most comparison studies obese binge eaters have exhibited higher scores for depression than their non-binge-eating counterparts and on further questioning are more likely to have a past history of this condition (De Zwaan *et al*, 1994).

Yanovski *et al* (1993) also found that these patients were likely to have had previous contact with mental health problems at some time in their lives and received psychotherapy or counselling, which would appear to suggest that their problem may be long-standing. In an earlier study, Yanovski *et al* (1992) reported rates of a lifetime history of major depression at 51% in binge eaters. Bouts of depression are frequently seen to affect weight and may result in weight gain (with loss of appetite) or weight loss. There are difficulties in establishing the severity of depression, and changes in weight status are mentioned in the diagnostic criteria for major depressive disorder (American Psychiatric Association, 1994).

Kolotkin *et al* (1987) identified a relationship between the severity of binge-eating symptoms and the degree of depression. They suggested that the greater the binge-eating severity, the greater the depression felt by the individual, with similarly increased levels of anxiety, social isolation, impulsive behaviour and anger.

One of the controversial issues is the age of onset of binge-eating behaviour and the fact that this is often a considerable time before the appearance of depressive symptoms (Mussell *et al*, 1995). Two possible theories might explain this. The first is that as the child reaches adulthood they become more aware of the negative attitudes which society has towards them. The second is that as the person's age increases so does their weight, so that in the long term, the level of depression and the degree of body dissatisfaction felt by the sufferer are positively correlated (Jackson *et al*, 2000).

Physical symptoms

Obesity is the primary physical symptom and poses a considerable problem for health professionals because it is affiliated with a number of chronic conditions, many of which are the cause of morbidity and ill health.

There are varying levels of obesity:

- overweight is defined as a body mass index of 25
- obesity is a body mass index of thirty or over.

Body mass index is calculated by dividing the person's weight in kilograms by their height in metres squared.

The incidence in the Western world is said to be rising and current statistics estimate that approximately ten million of the adult population are clinically obese with alarming projections that this figure will rise to fifteen million within ten years (Legge, 2000). Statistics in America suggest a similar concern with the number of overweight individuals not confined to the adult population: childhood and adolescent obesity have become the most prevalent nutritional diseases in the United States (Caprio and Tamborlane, 1999).

It is accepted that both genetic and environmental factors may influence the potential to develop obesity, although in many cases the excess adipose tissue occurs when the amount of food taken in greatly exceeds that used in energy, which is the scenario seen in binge-eating disorder. In contrast to bulimia nervosa patients, those with this illness are unable to exercise calorie restriction (Marcus *et al*, 1992), and appear to have little awareness of the number of calories they consume in a day.

Obese people do not show markedly different attitudes or personality characteristics to thin people, except for the feelings of rejection which society imposes on them (Thompson, 1993). Body disparagement and self-consciousness are enhanced by the attitudes of those around them, with evidence to suggest that obese individuals are treated differently from those of normal weight, and encounter more problems in everyday situations. Concerns that obesity affects the psychological status of the individual has been accompanied by reports that obese females have a lower quality of life, and the severity of the obesity interferes with physical functioning more than it does with psychological or social adjustment (Mannucci *et al*, 1999).

Suggested further reading

Epidemiology

Wilson GT, Nonas CA, Rosenblum GD (1993) Assessment of binge eating in obese patients. *Int J Eat Disord* **13**: 25–33

Kinzl JF, Traweger C, Trefalt E Mangweth B. Biebl W (1999) Binge-eating disorder in males: a population based investigation. *Eating Weight Disord* **4**(4): 169–74

Striegel-Moore RH, Wilfley DE, Pike KM, Dohm FA, Fairburn CG (2000) Recurrent binge eating in black American women. *Arch Fam Med* **9**(1): 83–7

Birketvedt GS, Florholmen J, Sundsfjord J, Osterud B, Dinges D, Biler W, Stunkard A (1999) Behavioural and neuroendocrine characteristics of the night eating syndrome. *JAMA* **282**(7): 657–63

Aetiology

Fairburn CG, Doll HA Welch SL, Hay PJ Davies BA, O'Connor ME (1998) Risk factors for binge-eating disorder: a community based case control study. *Arch Gen Psychiatry* **55**: 425–32

Wade TD, Bulik CM, Sullivan PF, Meale MC, Kendler KS (2000) The relationship between risk factors for binge eating and bulimia nervosa: a population based female twin study. *Health Psychol* **19**(2): 115–23

Heatherton TF, Baumaster RF (1991) Binge eating as an escape from self-awareness. *Psychol Bull* **110**(1): 86–108

Diagnosis

De Zwaan M, Mitchell JE, Specker SM, Pyle RL, Mussell MP, Seim HC (1993) Diagnosing binge-eating disorder: Level of agreement between self report and expert rating. *Int J Eat Disord* **13**(3): 289–95

Goldfein JA, Walsh BT, LeChaussee JL, Kisselheff HR, Devlin MJ (1993) Eating behaviour in binge-eating disorder. *Int J Eat Disord* **14**(4): 427–31

Wilfley DE, Schwartz MB, Spurrell EB, Fairburn CG (1997) Assessing the specific psychopathology of binge-eating disorder patients: interview or self-report? *Behav Res Ther* **35**(12): 1151–9

Gormally J, Black S, Daston S, Rardin D (1982) The assessment of binge eating severity among obese persons. *Addict Behav* **7**(1): 47–55

Ricca V, Mannucci E, Moretti S, Di Bernardo M, Zucchi T, Cabras PL, Rotello CM (2000) Screening for binge-eating disorder in obese outpatients. *Compr Psychiatry* **41**(2): 111–5

Onset and clinical features

Mussell MP, Mitchell JE, Weller CL, Raymond NC, Crow SJ, Crosby RD (1995) Onset of binge eating, dieting, obesity and mood disorders among subjects seeking treatment for binge-eating disorder. *Int J Eat Disord* **17**: 395–401

Yanovski S (1993) Binge-eating disorder: current knowledge and future directions. *Obesity Res* **1**: 306–24

Goldfein JA, Walsh BT, LaChaussee JL, Kisselheff HR, Devlin MJ (1993) Eating behaviour in binge-eating disorder. *Int J Eat Disord* **14**: 289–95

8

Health problems and binge-eating disorder

Many of the health risks associated with binge-eating disorder, occur as a result of the obesity rather than the disordered eating pattern which sufferers adopt.

Obesity is associated with:

⌘ Increased cardiovascular risk.

⌘ Hypertension.

⌘ Raised cholesterol/triglyceride levels.

⌘ Type 2 diabetes.

⌘ Joint problems.

⌘ Menstrual disturbances.

Cardiovascular risk

The Framingham study confirmed obesity as an independent risk factor for the development of coronary heart disease (Hubert *et al*, 1983). In women alone, the risk of myocardial infarction is increased threefold in those who have a body mass index greater than twenty-nine, when compared to women of recommended weight (Manson *et al*, 1990). During the eight-year study period, 605 first coronary events occurred (eighty-three of which were fatal) which were directly correlated to increasing weight status.

Recent research has focused on whether waist/hip ratio has a more significant impact on health than body mass index and total fat distribution alone. A large scale study conducted in Iowa found that waist hip/ratio was the best anthrometric predictor of total mortality, and was significantly correlated with increased mortality from cardiovascular causes, diabetes and hypertension (Folsom *et al*, 2000).

Hypertension

The association between obesity and hypertension has long been recognised. A large scale study of obese American adults using 16,884 subjects identified that for both men and women, high blood pressure was the most common overweight and obesity-related problem (Must *et al*, 1999). They identified a direct correlation between the level of hypertension and increasing body mass index, suggesting that the greater the degree of overweight the more hypertensive the person was found to be. This finding was of particular concern because hypertension was equally as prominent in young overweight subjects as it was among older subjects. The risk for moderately obese 45–54-year-old men, is roughly two-fold higher than for their non-obese peers of the same age (Thompson *et al*, 1999).

The value of weight reduction as a non pharmacological measure in reducing blood pressure is well documented. Weight loss achieved by reduced calorie intake is one of the lifestyle modifications suggested by the British Hypertension Society, which proposes that achievement of the ideal body weight may obviate the need for drug treatment or at least reduce the dose or number of drugs required (Ramsey *et al*, 1999). The effect of weight loss on both systolic and diastolic blood pressure has been well researched, a reduction in weight of 3kg produces an estimated fall in blood pressure of 7/4mmHg, while a weight loss of 12kg produces a fall of 21/13mmHg (O'Brien *et al*, 1995).

Raised cholesterol levels

Fifty per cent of hypertensive patients have hyperlipidaemia, and the cardiovascular risk is particularly increased with higher plasma cholesterol concentrations and low HDL levels (O'Brien *et al*, 1995). The Framingham study looked at the long-term epidemiological prediction of heart disease and suggested that hypertension, hyper-lipidaemia or diabetes act as independent cardiovascular risks. In addition, lack of exercise can independently affect the risk associated with any of the atherogenic traits (Kannel and Larson, 1993). This confirms the close relationship between these entities and their ability, in combination to culminate in poor health.

Must *et al* (1999) found that high blood cholesterol values were a feature in all of the obese subjects in their study.

Type 2 diabetes

The risk for the development of type 2 diabetes in the overweight is almost three-fold higher than in the non-obese population (Thompson *et al*, 1999) and those individuals who later develop this condition frequently have upper body adiposity, increased triglycerides, decreased HDL cholesterol and high blood pressure, and are at an increased risk of cardiovascular disease (Haffner, 2000). An increased amount of abdominal fat has been associated with greater risk of insulin resistance (Tai *et al*, 2000; McClain *et al*, 2000), while insulin resistance is associated with type 2 diabetes (McClain *et al*, 2000).

The clinical picture in newly diagnosed middle-aged diabetes is often one of multiple health problems, and as many as 50% of newly diagnosed patients are found to have hypertension at the time of presentation (Kobrin, 1999). The rising incidence of obesity around the world is matched by a predicted similar rise in the incidence of diabetes. Recent changes to the diagnostic criteria for this condition are set to increase the numbers of new cases further, with individuals previously classed as borderline now included in the statistics.

Seidell (2000) suggested that the number of people with the condition around the world will increase from approximately 135 million in 1995 to 300 million in 2025, attributing the rising levels of both obesity and type 2 diabetes to increasingly sedentary lifestyles and the high energy density of diets.

An American study conducted over a five-year period, analysed the relationship between weight gain, fat distribution and the level of obesity, and the risk of developing type 2 diabetes in a group of males. Weight gain had occurred as a gradual process during the adult years. Early obesity, increasing body mass throughout adulthood, and waste circumference were found to be good predictors for the development of diabetes, but the most dominant risk factor was found to be the highest attained BMI (Chan *et al*, 1994). A longer term study conducted over a ten-year period identified that the risk of diabetes in US adults increased with weight gains as little as 5kg (Ford *et al*, 1997).

Sedentary lifestyle

Physical inactivity carries its own risk and is regarded as an important contributory factor in obesity and associated medical conditions. A study of overweight men found a graded association between rising body mass index and the risk of diabetes in middle-aged men, with this risk reduced by more than 50% among men who took moderate exercise (Perry *et al*, 1995). The benefits of regular physical activity are widely accepted, although until recently it has been unclear whether greatest health improvement is achieved by increasing overall level of exercise or whether bouts of rigorous exercise are more effective.

Wareham *et al* (2000) studied the effects of a range of physical activities and found that increasing the total level of energy expenditure achieved the greatest health benefits.

Joint problems

Excessive weight puts considerable strain on joints, and is associated with poor mobility, reduced quality of life and ill health.

Joint problems are a considerable cause of morbidity and are one of the commonest reasons for early retirement in the obese patient (Burden, 1995). It would seem logical to assume that the greater the level of obesity, the greater the strain on weight bearing joints. Must *et al* (1999) found that the prevalence of osteoarthritis increased sharply among both overweight and obese men and women, and that this increase corresponded with increasing weight categories.

Menstrual disturbances

Reports suggest that obese women are more prone to experience heavy menstrual periods, which may be the cause of emotional distress. Severe menorrhagia may be capable of interfering with daily living activities. Women themselves may have short-term concerns regarding their cycle control, but in the long term they are at an increased risk for endometrial hyperplasia and cancer (Slupik, 1999). A study of 107 obese patients confirmed that eating disorder symptoms worsened during the pre-menstrual phase, disturbances which were not matched in the non-obese control group (Zucchi *et al*, 2000)

Psychiatric comorbidity

Binge-eating disorder

Variable prevalence rates have been obtained in studies of psychiatric co-morbidity in this condition. These have been influenced to some degree by the nature of the samples used for comparison, some studies have used bulimics, others have used obese non-binge eaters, or normal weight, non-eating disordered subjects.

High rates of borderline personality disorder, and avoidant

personality disorder have been reported, although these patients do not appear to display any association with substance abuse, or anxiety disorders (Yanovski *et al*, 1993). Subthreshold binge-eating disorder has also been evaluated, with no evidence to support the prevalence of psychiatric comorbidity among obese individuals who did not meet the full diagnostic criteria for binge-eating disorder (Yanovski *et al*, 1993).

Differential diagnosis

Binge-eating disorder

Those with binge-eating disorder share the same reluctance to reveal their abnormal pattern of eating when questioned.

There are some medical conditions where obesity is a feature and obese patients will need investigation to eliminate these diseases from the clinical picture. These are:

- hypothyroidism
- Cushing's syndrome
- Prader Willi syndrome.

Hypothyroidism

This condition occurs as a result of undersecretion of thyroxine. It has a slow, insidious onset with progressive weight gain. The reduced metabolic rate which ensues is accompanied by cognitive impairment and mental slowness. Patients complain of constipation, dry hair and dry skin and menorrhagia. The latter may be the most troublesome symptom for the female patient, and be the reason that they seek medical advice.

Weeks (2000) suggested that hypothyroidism may be greatly under-diagnosed as a cause of this menorrhagia. The association between obesity and heavier menstrual periods has already been mentioned, and although clinical guidelines do not advise routine testing of thyroid levels, it is necessary to eliminate the presence of hypothyroidism as a cause of obesity, when the symptoms and medical history indicate that there may be a need to do so.

Cushing's syndrome

Cushing's syndrome occurs as a result of excess production of cortico-steroid hormones. The hypothalamus secretes corticotrophin releasing factor which, in turn, stimulates the secretion of adrenocorticotrophin from the pituitary gland. This then acts on the adrenal cortex.

Hormones secreted by the cortex of the adrenal glands are:

cortisol corticosterone	}	Influence the metabolism of glucose and other nutrients
aldosteron		Influences how sodium, potassium and hydrogen ions are dealt with by the kidneys
androsterone		This is converted to testosterone by an enzyme within the cells of each testes

Cushing's syndrome can be caused by a tumour of the adrenal cortex (benign or malignant) or may occur as a result of prolonged or excessive use of steroids which leads to excessive secretion of adenocorticotrophic hormone (ACTH). The excess production of this hormone results in obesity, with fat deposits predominantly seen across the back of the neck and the shoulder area. There may be wasting of body tissues, hypertension, water retention, hyperglycaemia and osteoporosis.

Rossi *et al* (2000) studied the clinical and hormonal features of sixty-five patients who were found to have adrenal adenomas on investigation. Although all were described as clinically silent 48% were hypertensive, 24% had type 2 diabetes, 12% had glucose intolerance, 28% had lipid abnormalities, and 36% were diffusely obese and in all cases the underlying adenomas were discovered by chance.

The complex interaction of these problems indicates that there is a need for careful evaluation of these patients particularly when they appear to be relatively symptom-free, and obesity may be the only outward sign.

Prader Willi syndrome

This condition occurs as a result of a chromosomal defect which affects chromosome 15, and is the most frequent form of syndromal obesity (Eiholzer *et al*, 2000). The symptoms manifest themselves in infanthood with delayed developmental progress, both physical and mental. Feeding difficulties are apparent from birth, however, the delayed physical and mental development is accompanied by an insatiable appetite, which leads to rapid weight gain and subsequent obesity.

As the child continues to grow, there is evidence of decreased speed of growth, despite the onset of obesity, reduced lean body mass, small hands and feet, and low insulin-like growth factor-1 (Eiholzer *et al*, 2000). Adolescents and adults with Prader Willi syndrome can have a number of severe behavioural problems and a moderate to severe degree of learning disability (Gelbart, 1999).

The insatiable appetite which accompanies the condition, is thought to be caused by hypothalamic dysfunction, and the child may develop aggressive tendencies and some behavioural problems when attempts are made to reduce the intake of food consumed. There is some evidence to suggest that a deficiency in growth hormone (hypothalamic growth hormone deficiency) may be a factor in the development of Prader Willi syndrome. Partsch *et al* (2000) found that 38% of adult patients with Prader Willi syndrome had severe growth hormone deficiency and 87% had decreased levels of insulin-like growth factor. Sufferers of this condition become grossly obese, (often with body mass indices greater than thirty), morbidity occurs as a result of associated metabolic diseases, sleep apnoea, and lipo-lymphoedema (Partsh *et al*, 2000).

Administration of growth hormone therapy changes the phenotype of Prader Willi syndrome in childhood and enables height and weight to normalise with an associated reduction in body fat (Eiholzer *et al*, 2000).

Suggested further reading

Associated health problems

Haffner SM (2000) Obesity and the metabolic syndrome: the San Antonio Heart Study. *Br J Nutr* **83**(Supplement 1): S 67–70

Seidell JC (2000) Obesity, insulin resistance and diabetes: a world-wide epidemic. *Br J Nutr* **83**(Supplement 1): S5–8

Psychiatric comorbidity

Marcus MD, Wing RR, Ewing L, Kern E, Gooding W, McDermott M (1990) Psychiatric disorders among obese binge-eaters. *Int J Eat Disord* **9**: 69–77

Black DW, Goldstein RB, Mason EE (1992) Prevalence of mental disorder in 88 morbidly obese bariatric clinic patients. *Am J Psychiatry* **149**: 227–34

Differential diagnosis

Rossi R, Tauchmanova L, Luciano A, Di Martino M, Battista C, Del Viscovo L, Nuzzo V, Lombardi G (2000) Subclinical Cushing's syndrome in patients with adrenal incidentaloma: clinical and biochemical features. *J Clin Endocrinol Metab* **85**(4): 1440–8

9

Treatment and management of binge-eating disorder

Because patients with this condition present with two distinct problems (binge-eating behaviour and obesity), many of the studies conducted so far have adopted a combined approach in the hope of conferring benefits of treating both of these problems at the same time. There is still work to be done to determine optimum length of treatments and effective combinations if the patient is to achieve a successful long-term outcome. The treatment programme needs to be tailored to individual requirements, and in many sufferers will need to address associated psychiatric disorders and/or emotional symptoms for successful treatment to be accomplished (Brewerton, 1999).

Weight control programmes

In obese binge eaters normalisation of eating patterns and weight loss are among the key aims which health professionals would hope to achieve. Although the health benefits of weight loss have been extensively researched, the problems in achieving such loss are considerable, requiring a great deal of motivation and will power on the patient's part. Relatively modest weight losses have produced substantial health benefits for patients, including: lower blood pressure readings; reduced LDL cholesterol and increased HDL cholesterol; decreased blood glucose levels; and improved HBA1C levels among some diabetics (Devlin et al, 2000b). The benefits of waist reduction in those with abdominal obesity have shown that waist reduction correlates significantly with a reduction in total cholesterol and diastolic blood pressure (Han et al, 1997).

The ability to lose large amounts of weight is often achieved by substantial calorie restriction. For many obese subjects this, in itself, is a miserable project, signifying eradication from the diet of many of their favourite foods. Care is needed in the strategy adopted to encourage weight loss, given the evidence to suggest that dietary restraint or overt dieting has a disinhibiting effect on overeating or bingeing, and contributes to the marked bodyweight fluctuations that are found in the histories of these patients (Brewerton, 1999).

Evaluation of a commercially available weight ⎫
(Lowe *et al*, 1999) found that participants who
four-week programme achieved greater improvem
of areas, including weight loss and eating behaviour, w.
to subjects who undertook a self-help initiative.

Calorie counting has been found to be counterproductive in the
it promotes a higher degree of restraint (Goldfein *et al*, 2000), and
encourages the patient to focus all their attention on food and dietary
intake. In some cases it may be a useful tool in demonstrating the
parameters of normal eating (Lask and Bryant Waugh, 1997),
especially in those patients who have no concept of food values or
how many calories they consume.

The ability to sustain these changes during periods of stress and
personal difficulties requires exceptional emotional strength, particularly
given the evidence to suggest their potential ability to pre-empt a binge.

The development of a healthier attitude towards shape and weight
will hopefully encourage future weight loss through elimination of
abnormal eating patterns and a healthier lifestyle.

Educational input for these patients needs to address the episodes
of binge eating and the reasons behind them, which would explain
why dietary advice as a single form of input is often inadequate in
these patients.

Increasing physical activity

Increasing energy expenditure can be achieved successfully in the
majority of individuals without the need for rigorous exercise
programmes. For many, the mention of exercise conjures up images
of strenuous physical or sporting activity. The approach of the health
professional should aim to encourage the incorporation of more
easily accomplished inclusions to daily living (where appropriate),
which the individual can easily incorporate into their daily routine.
The effect of recreational physical activity on longer term weight
status in the obese has confirmed that physical inactivity is strongly
related to major weight gain at follow-up (Williamson *et al*, 1993).
Relatively simple measures such as using the stairs instead of the lift,
walking to the shops instead of travelling by car whenever possible,
are far less daunting than attending keep fit classes. Individual advice
should be tailored to the person's personal circumstances, taking into
account their existing pattern of daily behaviour, adopting a 'one step
at a time approach'. In studies where physical activity has been

ıuded in the weight loss strategy, keeping it up has been the ,reatest factor underlining the success and the ability to sustain long-term weight loss (Klem *et al*, 1997).

Behaviour modification

Support groups

A twelve-week programme which advocated a self-selected low calorie diet and increased activity levels was found to have substantial improvement in health and well being among obese binge eaters. At twelve-week follow-up significant improvements were seen in the intervention group when compared to the control group. Group support together with a practical approach to weight loss, yielded significant health and psychological benefits, with improved physical activity levels (Rippe *et al*, 1998).

A Norwegian survey evaluating long-term effectiveness in subjects who had maintained attendance of self-help groups for three years, reported that from the cohort of 49% who attended for follow-up, 62% had maintained their weight loss and a further 39% had continued to lose more weight (Andersen and Grimsmo, 1999).

Interpersonal psychotherapy

Interpersonal psychotherapy has been used with some success in the treatment of bulimia nervosa (Fairburn *et al*, 1995, Agras *et al*, 2000), and has aroused some interest in its potential as an option for use in binge-eating disorder, or as an alternative if first line treatments are unsuccessful.

Its application is based on the premise that the continued presence of abnormal eating behaviour is often fuelled by personal situations or conflicts which interpersonal psychotherapy might help the person to address.

Agras *et al* (1995) studied the results obtained when inter-personal psychotherapy was administered to a cohort of women who had gained little benefit from a course of cognitive behaviour therapy followed by weight loss intervention. The outcome suggested that despite this further intervention, interpersonal psychotherapy did not add anything extra to the current range of treatment options for binge-eating disorder, with little improvement seen in those who completed the additional therapy. One of the most important findings was the identification of a number of prognostic factors which were found to influence effectiveness of interpersonal psychotherapy. Poor outcome measures were found to be the severity and chronicity of the condition, severity of binge-eating behaviour and beginning binge-eating behaviour in childhood or early adolescence (Agras *et al*, 1995).

Cognitive behavioural therapy

This particular therapy has been adapted for use in binge-eating disorder, because it is hoped that it will effectively alleviate binges and encourage a more rational approach to nutritional intake. Previous studies have evaluated its efficacy when performed in a group or one-to-one setting.

A group of female subjects were assigned to receive cognitive behaviour therapy and at study completion the frequency of binge episodes had declined by 94% in treated subjects, with 79% of these subjects abstinent from binge eating by the end of treatment (Telch *et al*, 1990). The critical issue is to maintain these improvements, and at twenty weeks there was evidence of relapse, although their symptoms were less severe than they had been prior to treatment.

Loeb *et al* (2000) compared the use of cognitive behaviour therapy administered via a self-help manual. Two groups of women received treatment with a cognitive behavioural guided self-help manual, however one of these groups received additional guidance from a therapist. Women in both groups appeared to gain some benefits with an improvement seen in patterns of eating behaviour, better psychological functioning and subjects expressing less concern about their shape and weight. Additional guidance from a therapist was notably superior in reducing the occurrence of binge eating, interpersonal sensitivity and its associated symptomatology (Loeb *et al*, 2000).

A combination approach has been found to be more successful than weight control input alone.

Goldfein *et al* (2000) studied the benefits of combining drug therapy (fluoxetine, with group behavioural weight control treatment and individual cognitive behavioural therapy). By incorporating the use of self-monitoring, patients were discouraged from minimal food intake during the day, and binge eating during the evening (which is described as a typical eating pattern). Instead, emphasis was placed on three meals each day. Although initial patient concerns centred around the fear of further weight gain, believing this pattern of food intake to be higher in calories than their usual intake, these fears were reduced when this did not materialise.

Although such strategies did not achieve weight loss, weight stability was felt to be a successful accomplishment, and the combination of self-monitoring and the introduction of a regular meal pattern was sufficient to suppress binge eating at least for the short term (Goldfein *et al*, 2000). Weight loss is considered less important than normalising eating patterns and it is hoped that this will follow if abstinence from binge eating can be sustained.

Maintaining any improvement is the most difficult aspect for many subjects, and it may be that behaviour therapy for weight loss may be needed once abstinence from binge eating has been achieved with cognitive behaviour therapy (Telch *et al*, 1990).

Pharmacological therapy

The relative newness of binge-eating disorder has led to an interest in the potential of pharmacological intervention. The high rates of comorbid depression reported have evoked interest in the role of antidepressant therapy prescribed in addition to weight loss programmes or cognitive behaviour therapy. Unfortunately, it appears that such a combination does not produce any greater improvement than when cognitive behaviour therapy or weight loss treatments are used as monotherapy. The two main categories of drug therapy are:

- antidepressants
- anti-obesity agents.

Antidepressant therapy

Fluvoxamine

Fluvoxamine belongs to the same class of drugs as fluoxetine which has received encouraging reviews in the treatment of bulimia nervosa. It is used in the treatment of depressive symptoms and obsessive compulsive disorder.

Clinical trials comparing the use of this drug with placebo over a nine-week period produced potentially encouraging results. Active drug treatment was associated with a greater rate of reduction in the frequency of binges, but most encouraging was the reduction in body mass index, with weight loss after nine weeks of treatment found to correlate with the reduction in the frequency of binge episodes (Hudson *et al*, 1998).

These benefits have psychological advantages for the patient given the additional weight loss which occurred as well as a reduction in their eating disorder symptoms.

Sertraline

A trial of sertraline achieved similar benefits. When compared with placebo over a six-week period, patients who had received the active drug experienced; an improvement in binge-eating behaviour, a decrease in the severity of their illness, an increase in global improvement, and a reduction in body mass index (McElroy *et al*, 2000).

Desipramine

Trials of this drug in women who have endured their condition for twelve months or more resulted in a 63% reduction in the frequency of binge-eating episodes, while those treated with placebo were associated with a 16% reduction (McCann and Agras, 1990), although the major downfall with this treatment was that relapse occurred quite quickly following completion of treatment.

Improvement seen while taking the drug was accompanied by variable weight loss, which was not influenced by the inclusion of dietary advice or nutritional counselling. One of the main problems with this treatment is the reported association with weight gain, which probably results from a combination of induced hyperphagia via stimulation of hypothalamic noradrenergic pathways as well as a decrease in metabolic rate (Brewerton, 1999). This particular aspect may make this treatment unacceptable for those patients already distressed at their obesity. Further research is needed to establish long-term use of safe and effective treatments because, when medication was discontinued, there was a tendency by the time of the sixteen-week assessment for increased hunger, and the frequency of binge eating to return to levels comparable to those at original assessment.

Anti-obesity agents/appetite suppressants

Phentermine

Phentermine is licensed in the UK for use in the treatment of obesity, and acts as an appetite suppressant. The use of phentermine is restricted to twelve weeks, and carries a serious risk of pulmonary hypertension which may be insidious (*BNF*, 1999).

d-Fenfluramine

Both fenfluramine and d-fenfluramine were licensed as anorectic agents by the Food and Drug Administration (FDA), and fenfluramine has been used in combination with phentermine in the United States. Although this combination was not officially approved by the FDA the total number of prescriptions for this combination exceeded eighteen million in total across the States in 1996 (Connolly *et al*, 1997).

Given the clinical features of binge-eating disorder it would seem logical for research to focus on the potential for appetite suppressants to help to control the desire to binge. Eighty per cent of subjects in one trial with adequate plasma levels of d-fenfluramine stopped binge eating compared with 38% of those treated with placebo (Stunkard *et al*, 1996), although there was no reduction in body mass index which treatment with fluvoxamine and sertraline successfully accomplished.

Unfortunately fenfluramine and dexenfluramine have been removed from the market because of increasing concerns that they may be associated with valvular heart disease. Several studies have found evidence of valvular heart disease following treatment with a combination of fenfluramine and phentermine (Connolly *et al*, 1997; Boston Collaborative Drug Surveillance Program, 1998).

On the basis of evidence supplied from trials of fenfluramine and dexenfluramine used separately, both drugs have been confirmed to increase the risk of cardiac valve regurgitation (Jick *et al*, 1998; Weissman *et al*, 1998), and as a result both drugs have now been withdrawn from use.

The cessation of symptoms following treatment with placebo is somewhat puzzling, although it has been a finding in other drug trials. Hudson *et al* (1998) reported a 44% response rate in those treated with placebo, and were able to demonstrate a reduction of more than 50% in the number of binges each week.

Sibutramine

Sibutramine is a beta-phenethylamine which blocks reuptake of norephinephrine and serotonin (Bray *et al*, 1996). It has recently been licensed by the American Food and Drug administration as a weight loss agent and has been found to reduce body weight in rats by reducing energy intake and energy expenditure (Seagle *et al*, 1998).

A six-month double blind trial of this drug found it to be effective in achieving weight loss. Of those who completed the trial, the active drug was found to be particularly effective in reducing waist circumference when compared to placebo, and was well tolerated by patients (Cuellar *et al*, 2000). Weight reduction with sibutramine has been found to be dose dependent, with greatest weight loss evident in those subjects taking the highest doses (Bray *et al*, 1996). Higher drug dose also correlated with a greater likelihood of adverse effects and, in common with other studies (Marcus *et al*, 1990, Sussman and Ginsberg, 1998), weight gain recurred on discontinuation of the active treatment.

Combination therapy

Fluoxetine with behaviour modification

The addition of behaviour modification to fluoxetine achieved significantly more weight loss than those treated with a placebo substance and behaviour modification. One of the most significant findings was that there were no significant additional benefits for binge eaters, in terms of a reduction in binge-eating behaviour and the fluoxetine did not influence mood (Marcus *et al*, 1990).

Phentermine and fluoxetine

Devlin *et al* (2000a) used a combination therapy regime of phentermine and fluoxetine which were prescribed as an adjunct to cognitive behavioural therapy.

On completion of the active treatment there was a reduction in the frequency of binge episodes, reduced psychological distress and some degree of weight reduction. Significant weight gain appeared to correlate with discontinuation of the drug regime, and appeared to have occurred within approximately twelve months of completion.

Surgical Intervention

There are a number of surgical interventions which can be used in severe obesity when the patient's health is at risk, and attempts at other weight loss strategies have failed. Surgery to help severely overweight individuals has been performed for the past forty years (Fisher and Barber, 1999).

Before such drastic measures are considered certain criteria need to be taken into account, including: the well being of the patient (pre-operative assessment must confirm that surgery can be performed with relatively low risk); that the outcome will improve the patient's quality of life, and any risk will be outweighed by the expected benefits; and, of course, it is important to stress that this type of treatment will not address the binge-eating behaviour or any psychological disturbance which accompanies its presence.

Surgery is indicated for patients with a body mass index greater than forty, or for those with serious medical problems or co-morbid disease with a body mass index greater than thirty-five (Albrecht and Pories, 1999).

A survey of patients who had previously undergone gastric surgery for morbid obesity, and had successfully maintained their weight loss for a minimum of three years, described their previous obesity as extremely distressful, stating that they would rather be a normal weight with a disabling handicap than a morbidly obese millionaire (Rand and Macgregor, 1991).

Outcome

Further research is needed to evaluate long-term outlook for patients who are known to have suffered or are currently suffering from this condition, as there is very little material related to long-term prognosis.

Prognostic indicators of outcome

The wealth of material related to anorexia nervosa and bulimia nervosa has identified prognostic factors thought to be indicative of both good, and poor outcome. Peterson *et al* (1999) has recently attempted to identify similar factors in relation to binge-eating disorder which will give an insight into the identification of subjects at greater risk of relapse.

Identification of these factors might prove useful in formulating future treatment programmes so that increased risk can be eradicated.

Severity of symptoms

Assessment of subjects following a course of cognitive behaviour therapy found the severity of the patients' symptoms prior to starting their treatment to be the most likely indicator of a poor outcome (Peterson *et al*, 1999).

Psychiatric comorbidity

The level of comorbid psychiatric disturbance might be expected to influence long-term outcome and the risk of relapse. Fichter *et al* (1997) confirmed that at six-year follow-up, a proportion of subjects continued to exhibit signs of an affective disorder and anxiety disorder although the prevalence of these two conditions was lower in those with no eating disorder at follow-up, and highest in those who continued to exhibit features of binge-eating disorder or had crossed over to bulimia nervosa.

Because of the limited availability of follow-up studies there is little material with which to make comparisons. Fairburn's comparison study found that at five-year assessment, levels of psychiatric disturbance had decreased by a greater value in binge-eating disordered subjects when compared to bulimics (42% compared to 30%). Those among the bulimia group who continued to fulfil the criteria for a depressive illness were also found to continue to have eating disorder symptoms, a scenario which did not apply equally to the binge-eating disorder group.

Crossover

One of the concerns in binge-eating disorder is the potential for transmission to symptoms of bulimia nervosa. Fairburn *et al* (2000) found little evidence of movement from binge eating to bulimia (or vice versa).

At six-year follow-up, Fichter *et al* (1997) identified that; 7.4% of subjects had shifted to bulimia nervosa, while a further 11% vomited regularly, 2% were abusing laxatives, 2% were abusing diuretics and a further 5.4% were misusing appetite suppressants.

Short-term follow-up

Follow-up assessment conducted one year after treatment (cognitive behaviour therapy followed by weight loss) reported that a percentage of those included were abstinent at one-year follow-up (Agras *et al*, 1997). Although inability to change the pattern of binge-eating behaviour appeared to correlate with weight gain, with the greatest successes documented for those patients who successfully dealt with their binge eating and then subsequently lost weight via a specialist programme.

Long-term outcome

There is a limited quantity of follow-up material, and further investigation is needed to update the medical profession on long-term prognosis for those who have received treatment for this condition.

Comparison studies of binge-eating disorder and bulimia nervosa have indicated that the outlook for the former condition appeared to be more favourable than that reported for the latter, with only 18% of the original sample of binge eaters still symptomatic at five-year follow-up (Fairburn *et al*, 2000).

Sustaining weight loss

Intentional weight loss of any amount is associated with a 20% reduction in all cause mortality, and a 30–40% reduction in diabetes associated mortality (Williamson *et al*, 1995). Long-term maintenance of this is widely accepted to be a considerable accomplishment and, in several studies, is regarded as an added bonus rather than a key aim. It is important to avoid deterioration into the cycle of weight loss and weight gain and its associated detrimental effect on self-esteem.

Weight cycling is associated with decreased perceptions of health and well being, and appears to be associated with clinically significant reductions in eating, self-efficacy and weak but consistent increases in binge-eating severity (Foster *et al*, 1997). The long-term follow-up studies available have identified comparable weights at follow-up to those at the commencement of treatment.

Fairburn *et al* (2000) found that 39% of those at five-year follow-up met the criteria for obesity, Fichter *et al* (1997) found that 38% of those who were asymptomatic at follow-up remained obese.

Fairburn *et al* (2000) reported that although individuals had improved personal self-esteem and social functioning, weight gain had still occurred despite a reduction in their binge-eating behaviour.

Weight loss maintainers have been found to use more behavioural strategies to control their weight than those who regain weight or whose weight remains stable (lost no weight during active treatment) (McGuire *et al*, 1999). They reported that individuals who intentionally lost weight and had sustained this for a period of seven years reported higher levels of physical exercise, and more behavioural strategies to control dietary intake. Appropriate levels of exercise appear to be vital to sustaining weight loss. Williamson *et al* (1993) reported that low recreational physical activity at follow-up was strongly related to major weight gain.

Forty-two per cent of patients taken from the National Weight Control Registry implied that they found maintaining their weight loss less difficult than the process of losing weight itself (Klem *et al*, 1997).

Suggested further reading

Weight loss

Lowe MR, Miller Kovach K, Frye N, Phelan S (1999) An initial evaluation of a commercial weight loss program: short-term effects on weight, eating behaviour and mood. *Obesity Res* **7**: 51–9

Rippe JM, Price JM, Hess SA, Kline G, DeMers KA, Damitz S, Kreidieh I, Freedson P (1998) Improved psychological well-being, quality of life, and health practices in moderately overweight women participating in a 12-week structured weight loss programme. *Obesity Res* **6**(3): 208–18

Pharmacotherapy

Greeno CG, Wing RR (1996) A double-blind placebo-controlled trial of the effect of fluoxetine on dietary intake in overweight women with and without binge-eating disorder. *Am J Clin Nutr* **64**(3): 267–73

Hudson JI Carter WP, Pope HG (1988) Antidepressant treatment of binge-eating disorder: research findings and clinical guidelines. *J Clin Psychiatry* **57**(Supplement 8): 73–9

Abenhaim L, Moride Y, Brenot F *et al* (1996) Appetite-suppressant drugs and the risk of primary pulmonary hypertension. International Primary Hypertension Study Group. *New Engl J Med* **335**(9): 609–16

Interpersonal psychotherapy

Agras WS, Telch CF, Arnow B, Eldredge K, Henderson J, Marnell M (1995) Does interpersonal therapy help patients with binge-eating disorder who fail to respond to cognitive-behavioural therapy? *J Consult Clin Psychol* **63**(3): 356–60

Cognitive behaviour therapy

Smith DE, Marcus MD, Kaye W (1992) Cognitive behavioural treatment of obese binge eaters. *Int J Eat Disord* **12**: 257–62

Self-help groups

Loeb KL, Wilson GT, Gilbert JS, Labouvie E (2000) Guided and unguided self-help for binge eating. *Behav Res Ther* **38**: 259–72

Surgical intervention

Scheen AJ, Luyckx FH Desaive C., Lefebvre PJ (1999) Severe/extreme obesity: a medical disease requiring a surgical treatment? *Acta Clin Belg* **54**(3): 154–61

Outcome

Fichter MM, Quadflieg N, Gnutzmann A (1998) Binge-eating disorder: treatment outcome over a 6-year course. *J Psychosom Res* **44**(3–4): 385–405

Peterson CB, Crow SJ, Nugent S, Mitchell JE, Engbloom S, Pederson Mussell M, (1999) Predictors of treatment outcome for binge-eating disorder. *Int J Eat Disord* **28**: 131–8

Wadden TA, Foster GD, Letizia KA (1992) Response of obese binge eaters to treatment by behavioral therapy combined with very low calorie diet. *J Consult Clin Psychol* **60**(5): 808–11

Section IV: Other sufferers of eating disorders

10

Eating disorders in men

Because of the widely held perception that eating disorders are predominantly female conditions much of the research has centred around women. There is now widespread concern that eating disorders among men may be more common than previous statistics have suggested.

The prevalence rates of these conditions among the male population as a whole is equally difficult to assess. Statistical data remains limited, and prevalence rates are variable, but recent research appears to indicate that more males are now seeking treatment for eating disorders (Braun *et al*, 1999). American findings have indicated that each year as many as one million boys and men struggle with an eating disorder of some kind or with a borderline associated condition. A further one in four American men are estimated to be on a diet on any given day.

Others believe that men with eating disorders generally may be more reluctant than women to seek professional help and treatment (Margo, 1987; Crisp and Toms, 1972), which would suggest that the numbers of men suffering from an eating disorder may be considerably higher than current statistics imply.

Onset of symptoms

Comparison studies of males and females have identified significant differences between the two groups in the length of time between onset of symptoms and seeking treatment. In one study, binge-eating disordered males had a delay of 13.7 years before commencement of treatment, 4.3 years for the bulimic anorexic male, and 1.2 years for the anorexic male (Carlat *et al*, 1997).

The shortest delay in seeking treatment was clearly in the anorexic group, and presumably friends and relatives might have been instrumental in persuading these men to seek urgent help, particularly in cases where severe weight loss was apparent.

Several studies have looked at the clinical features exhibited by males with eating disorders with the purpose of identifying notable differences from those seen in female sufferers (Sharp *et al*, 1994;

Crisp *et al*, 1976; Lieberman, 1989) and the general consensus of opinion appears to be that both men and women display similar signs and symptoms.

Personality differences

Personality types have been found to play some part in increasing the vulnerability to develop an eating disorder. There is now evidence to support the implication that males who develop chronic bulimic symptoms appear to report more perfectionist traits, and inter- personal distrust, which differs from females with similar chronic symptoms who have been found to report a drive for thinness (Joiner *et al*, 2000).

Psychiatric comorbidity

A review of discharge summaries for 466,590 male hospitalised veterans identified ninety-eight men who were diagnosed as having an eating disorder. High rates of comorbid substance abuse and mood disorders were evident in those subjects with both anorexia nervosa, bulimia nervosa and eating disorder not otherwise specified (Striegel-Moore *et al*, 1999). Anorexic men appeared to represent a higher risk for comorbid psychotic disorder/schizophrenia as did those with eating disorder not otherwise specified, while the bulimic males appeared to be at a greater risk for comorbid personality disorder.

Body image disturbance

Eating disordered men interviewed in one study were said to exhibit a greater fear of weight gain and a distorted body image, with many expressing a feeling of being overweight despite the fact that others perceived them to be of normal weight for their height. Yager *et al* (1988) suggested that males who develop eating disorders have similar feelings of body image distortion to those exhibited by their female counterparts.

Carlat *et al* (1997) found that in some cases the onset of the eating disorder was clearly job related, with the individuals concerned working in settings which were described as 'appearance based jobs' (ie. acting, modelling), and the need to stay slim was clearly important.

Magazines targeted at a male audience are also increasing in prevalence, with many focusing on specific topics, often health or fitness related. These magazines have been found to contain more articles and advertisements related to body shape, predominantly covering such subjects as fitness, weight lifting, body building, or muscle toning (DiDomenico and Anderson, 1988). This is in contrast to those articles featured in women's magazines which tend to adopt a different approach. They also give image and body shape a high profile, but tend to focus on fashion, diet-related articles, nutrition and weight reduction advice as a tool for enhancing personal appearance, and cookery pages are used to emphasise nutritional meals.

A study of college students found that eating disordered males differed significantly from the comparison group, in that they exhibited more dissatisfaction with body image and had higher rates of comorbid psychiatric disorders than healthy males (Olivardia *et al*, 1995), however these characteristics did not differ when compared to females, which appear to support the view that aetiological factors are similar in both genders.

Anorexia nervosa

It is now estimated that approximately 5–10% of anorexia cases occur in men and young boys (Barry and Lippmann 1990), with onset of the condition possible at any time between the prepubertal years and adulthood. Assessment of clinical features at presentation, outcome studies and prognostic indicators at presentation were all found to be largely similar to those which have been reported in female anorexia nervosa, suggesting that there may be very little difference in this condition between males and females. One significant factor was the impact of psychosexual development. This single entity alone was found to influence outcome and its effect was found to be more prominent in males than females.

In men with a confirmed diagnosis of anorexia nervosa, it was revealed that lower social class featured significantly (Margo, 1987). Physiological characteristics identified that these men were small in stature, in direct contrast to the females in the comparison group who were actually tall for their age. In fact, three subjects cited teasing because of their size (in one case this was due to delayed physical development), as potentially influential in the onset of the condition.

Seven of the patients described by Margo were able to recall a significant life event, which they felt had preceded onset of their illness, and in some cases these were particularly distressing in nature.

Sharp *et al* (1994) found that many of the symptoms exhibited by anorexic males were classical of the condition, although the age of onset tended to be older than that of females. In common with other studies men were found to use excessive exercise regimes as an additional means of weight control alongside bingeing and vomiting, although were found to be less likely to use laxatives than females.

Bulimia nervosa

Carlat *et al* (1997) found that males account for 10–15% of all bulimic patients, and that a further 0.2% of all adolescent and young adult males meet the stringent criteria for bulimia nervosa.

Accurate statistical data is difficult to collate and is confounded by the same difficulties as with females: namely, because of the secrecy surrounding bulimic behaviour many patients are able to conceal their condition for many years.

Although the clinical features of bulimia nervosa appear to follow a similar pattern in males, one exception differentiating the genders is that male bulimics appear to be less concerned with strict weight control than female bulimic patients, and there is preliminary evidence that they may be less troubled by their binge-eating behaviour (Carlat and Camargo, 1991).

Methods of bingeing and purging in male bulimics also appear to be largely similar to those employed by females. Olivardia *et al* (1995) reported that 59% of subjects used laxatives, 59% used self-induced vomiting, 53% used fasting, and a further 53% cited exercise, with several subjects using more than one method as an adjunct to weight control.

Eating disorders and homosexuality

In an early study Crisp (1967) suggested that in a percentage of males conflict surrounding gender identity, or homosexual orientation might precede the initial onset of an eating disorder, implying that the emotional distress caused by this struggle may be an antecedent factor rather than an integral part of eating disorders in males.

Data relating to this issue provided by later studies has produced inconsistent evidence.

Dunkeld *et al* (1987) found no proof of homosexuality among the anorexic men in their study, although other studies have indicated otherwise. Investigation of anorexic and bulimic males comparing them to a cohort of females, all of whom were receiving treatment for their illness, reported that significantly more males than females with both conditions were found to be experiencing sexual isolation, sexual inactivity and conflicting homosexuality (Herzog *et al*, 1984). Schneider and Agras (1987) found higher rates of either homosexuality or bisexuality among bulimic males, when compared to bulimic females.

Events surrounding the onset of the illness

Dunkeld *et al* (1987) reported five cases of bulimia nervosa and the physical and psychological features characterised by them. Two cases reported that their symptoms commenced after a period of weight gain which had occurred as a result of lifestyle changes and greater inactivity. One subject started bingeing and vomiting after a prolonged period of dieting and was already below the recommended weight for his height when his illness began. Two further cases became ill following personal difficulties; one patient was receiving dialysis for a kidney problem and commenced an abnormal eating pattern with bulimia symptoms, which allowed him to continue to indulge in foods which were not allowed in the recommended dietary regime recommended as part of his treatment. The final case developed bulimic symptoms following extreme personal distress, during which his alcoholic father admitted to homosexual tendencies, which eventually led to the subsequent divorce of his parents.

Binge-eating disorder

An Austrian telephone survey of 1,000 male subjects identified that the total prevalence of eating disorders was 14.9%, with 0.8% of these meeting the full diagnostic criteria for binge-eating disorder, a further 9.4% had a subthreshold version of this condition (Kinzl *et al*, 1999). A large number of those who took part were overweight or obese, particularly the latter.

Evaluation of specific gender differences exhibited between males and females with this condition have identified that men and women do not differ on measures of eating disturbance, shape and weight concerns, interpersonal problems or self-esteem, but more men than women were found to have had a lifetime diagnosis of substance abuse (Tanofsky *et al*, 1997).

One of the most significant findings was that males were found to be less likely to binge in response to emotional problems but exhibited greater levels of psychiatric disturbance than their comparison female group.

Outcome studies

Anorexia nervosa

During the course of their illness male anorexics are known to experience similar medical complications with evidence of osteo-porosis, anaemia, and hypotension, with the need for hospitalisation in some cases for medical or psychiatric reasons during the course of their illness.

Burns and Crisps (1984) measured successful treatment outcome on a number of key areas, including nutritional status and weight regain, psychological health and psychosexual functioning, assessing patients up to twenty years after presentation.

Thirty per cent of subjects were married at follow-up, all of whom had made a good recovery, while the one patient who had been already married at entry to the study was divorced at follow-up and was considered to have an intermediate outcome with poor psychosexual adjustment (Burns and Crisp, 1984).

Bulimia nervosa

Comparison studies of bulimic men and women have tended to concentrate on shared aetiological factors and clinical features between the two groups. Similar studies comparing bulimic men with healthy controls have tended to adopt a similar approach. To date, there are few long-term outcome studies of bulimia nervosa solely applicable to males.

Complications appear to follow a similar pattern to those found in female bulimics, with recordings of dental erosion, swollen parotid glands, leg cramps due to hypokalaemia and oesophagitis (Carlat *et al*, 1997).

Reluctance to seek professional help may be a factor, with as few as four patients from a possible twenty-five subjects in one study found to have actively sought treatment for their illness. In common with female sufferers of this condition it appears that relatively few bulimic males required hospital admission during the course of their illness (1.7% of bulimics, 2.3% of those with eating disorder not otherwise specified) (Carlat *et al*, 1997).

There is clearly a need for further research into eating disorders in males to determine long-term outcome and health effects.

Suggested further reading

Men and eating disorders

Olivardia R, Pope HG (jnr), Mangweth B, Hudson JI (1995) Eating disorders in college men. *Am J Psychiatry* **152**(9): 1279–85

Carlat DJ, Camargo CA Herzog DB (1997) Eating disorders in males: A report on 35 patients. *Am J Psychiatry* **154**(8): 1127–32

Schneider JA, Agras WS (1987) Bulimia in males: a matched comparison with females. *Int J Eat Disord* **6**: 235–42

Crisp AH, Burns T (1983) The clinical presentation of anorexia nervosa in males. *Int J Eat Disord* **2**(4): 5–10

11

Eating disorders and sport

Sportsmen and women are reported to be at an increased risk of developing an eating disorder because of the need within their chosen field to achieve and maintain a certain weight. The desire to win and to succeed is high on the agenda for professional sports people, as it is for those at amateur level, who seek to reach the higher levels of achievement within their particular sport. A Scandinavian study examined the prevalence of eating disorders among a high school population of physically active athletes and non-athletes. Anorexia nervosa was found to affect 1.5% of those questioned, 2% were bulimic, and a further 0.3% were bulimic anorexic with the greatest incidence found among physically active non-athletes who were members of fitness clubs (Augestad *et al*, 1999). It is highly conceivable that amateur athletes who strive to be the best in a highly competitive environment are under considerable pressure to attain and maintain what may for some be an unrealistic weight.

Bale *et al* (1996) emphasised that there are a number of shared similarities between runners, gymnasts and dieters, in which all three groups exhibit similar attitudes and behaviours. These behaviours are primarily centred around the perceived requirement to stay slim, a persistent concern with shape and weight and an associated exercise regime.

Subclinical conditions have also been identified where a pattern of disordered eating prevails, but diagnostic criteria are not fully met.

Beals and Manore (2000) identified the following characteristics common to female athletes with these attributes:

- distorted body image
- preoccupation with food, calorie consumption
- fear of weight gain
- menstrual disturbances.

Sports such as gymnastics and athletics also place an emphasis on thinness and low body weight (Bale *et al*, 1996). Ballet dancers and gymnasts are two fields represented by notoriously slim, often quite young participants. Garner and Garfinkel (1980) compared dance students alongside music scholars, both of whom were under pressure to achieve, both in terms of personal achievement and high expectations from those close to them. The findings revealed that

those from the music cohort did not display anore
while those in the dance group did. This appeared to s
predisposition and tendency to develop anorexia was
by the need to maintain such a low body weight ra
pressure which the individual is subjected to by the very
competitive environment in which they operate.

Abraham (1996) found that 4% of ballet dancers regularly induced vomiting and appeared to be under intense pressure to diet, although their low body weight and amenorrhoea were not sufficient to confirm a diagnosis of anorexia nervosa. The pressure to retain a thin physique might increase the risk for later development of bulimic tendencies, given that a significant association has been identified between the degree of dieting and dietary restraint and the tendency towards bulimia (Kirkley *et al*, 1988).

There are also a number of sports which require an athlete to achieve a particular weight so that the sportsman or woman can enter within a particular weight specific category. Wrestling and boxing are examples of two such sports. There is a tendency for many sports orientated individuals to gain weight when the competitive season ends, and some find the constant training and adherence to a healthy diet difficult to maintain all year round. Varying degrees of weight fluctuation are often found and several studies have found this to be cause for distress and concern among those affected.

Lakin *et al* (1990) studied 716 wrestlers and found that many resorted to dieting, food restriction, and heated wrestling rooms alongside an increased exercise regime. Oppliger *et al* (1993) found that 1.7% of wrestlers in one study met the full diagnostic criteria for bulimia nervosa, but in common with other studies a number of those interviewed were found to have a partial syndrome in which they admitted to adopting more extreme behaviour as a means of weight control.

Women involved in weight lifting (particularly at competitive level) have been found likely to have a history of anorexia with current attitudes and behaviours common to eating disorder syndromes (Walberg and Johnston, 1991). Many women in this study were found to exhibit an unhealthy preoccupation with body shape and weight although they did not meet the full diagnostic criteria for anorexia or bulimia nervosa.

There is obviously a need for nutritional and weight management advice among school children who show an aptitude for sport and those who attend training and athletic clubs.

.enstrual disturbances

Menstrual irregularities which occur secondary to extensive exercise have been frequently noted in earlier studies (Myerson *et al*, 1991; Walberg and Johnston, 1991). A comparison study of ten top class female distance runners, ten female anorexics and twenty female gymnasts of a similar age suggested that the two groups of athletes and the anorexics appeared to have a later onset of menstruation, by comparison to the average age of onset of menstruation in British teenage females. In those whose monthly periods had already commenced, cessation of menstruation appeared shortly after onset of the anorexic illness or after commencement of a strenuous exercise regime.

Intense physical activity, extreme dietary practices, and low levels of body fat in combination may result in a higher prevalence of menstrual irregularity than in the normal population, with high rates found among those who frequently use aerobic activity (Walberg and Johnston, 1991).

Bale *et al* (1996) reported similar higher rates of amenorrhoea among the gymnasts and athletes which compared with those of the anorexics in their study. They suggested that in athletes and anorexics alike, the body attempts to adapt to the changed metabolic energy demands by either delaying the onset of menstruation or precipitating the onset of amenorrhoea.

Exercise dependence

An unhealthy preoccupation with exercise and primary exercise dependence have been cited as disease manifestations which may mask the underlying eating disorder (Bamber *et al*, 2000). The implication that exercise has pathogenic implications has received some consideration, particularly as a potential early prognostic factor. Davis *et al* (1994) found that 78% of eating disordered patients used current excessive exercise regimes, 60% were competitive athletes prior to the onset of their illness, a further 60% were clear in their perception that the onset of exercise predated that of dieting behaviour and a further 75% admitted that the amount of physical activity undertaken steadily increased, while at the same time food intake and body weight decreased.

Those who engage in rigorous physical activity often adhere to a particular routine, and efforts to establish motivation, daily running habits and attitudes towards their weight and eating patterns revealed that 26% of males and 25% of females were fuelled by feelings of guilt and were classed as 'obligatory runners' (Slay *et al*, 1998). Those who fell into this category had lower body weight and exhibited more eating and weight concern, and female responses in particular were felt to be indicative of the potential to develop an eating disorder. The implication that early onset of increased physical activity may have an aetiological influence has implications for future research.

The frequency of exercise may differ between anorexics and bulimics. Brewerton *et al* (1995) found a significantly greater frequency of physical activity among anorexics (38.5%) than bulimics (22.5%), while Davis *et al* (1993) found the level of exercise among anorexics was directly correlated to the existence of an obsessive compulsive personality profile.

The level of denial of symptoms of eating disorders among athletes may be no different to those displayed among the general population. Where patients present with problems which may be seen to be directly related to their training programme or performance, they may be viewed from a narrow physiological rather than a broader biopsychosocial perspective (Schwenk, 2000)

Schwenk (2000) described the case of a female athlete who presented with a history of fatigue and reduced level of motivation, sleep disturbance and associated minor health problems. The clinical features described by the patient lent themselves to a number of potential diagnoses, including depression, over training, and high stress levels induced from competing.

Schwenk proposed that athletes may be more susceptible to under-diagnosis and inadequate treatment of mental illness.

Suggested further reading

Opplinger RA, Landrey GL, Foster SW, Lambrecht AC (1993) Bulimic behaviours among interscholastic wrestlers: a state-wide survey. *Paediatrics* 91(4): 826–31

Johnson C, Powers PS, Dick R (1999) Athletes and Eating Disorders: the National Collegiate Athletic Association study. *Int J Eat Disord* 26(2): 179–88

Hobart JA, Smucker DR (2000) The female athlete triad. *Am Fam Physician* 61(11): 3357–64

Ryujin DH, Breaux C, Marks AD (1999) Symptoms of eating disorders among female distance runners: can the inconsistencies be unravelled? *Womens Health* 30(1): 71–83

Eating disorders and diabetes mellitus

Introduction

The presentation of diabetes mellitus in juveniles and adolescents is often acute. The patient may have experienced a relatively short duration of illness, with symptoms of thirst, polyuria, and rapid weight loss in the period preceding diagnosis. Excessive amounts of urine are passed in an attempt to rid the bloodstream of the excess glucose which cannot be taken up by body cell sand this, in term, depletes the tissues of the energy supplies which are needed to maintain adequate functioning.

If left untreated the patient becomes severely dehydrated and quickly deteriorates into a ketoacidotic state. Correction of the dehydration becomes a medical priority, requiring urgent attention if a life-threatening emergency situation is to be avoided.

Once a diagnosis has been confirmed and treatment commenced, the young patient and their family receive a wealth of advice with the ultimate aim of enabling the individual to lead as normal a life as possible and prevent complications in later life. For some, the suggested dietary pattern and content require making considerable lifestyle changes, with the danger that some will find the alterations needed too much to cope with. The emphasis on food management may become a major issue for youths with type 1 diabetes mellitus and result in pathological eating habits (Pitel *et al*, 1998).

The rising prevalence of eating disorders in the general population has led to an interest in their existence among young diabetics. Because diet is a key issue it is assumed that young diabetics are more prone to eating disorders (Herpetz *et al*, 1998), and there is specific interest in whether prevalence rates among this community may be greater than among the general population.

Aetiology

The weight loss which precedes onset of the condition is quickly rectified once an insulin regime is implemented. A process of weight gain commences, which has been associated with a tendency towards a higher body mass index in diabetics (Diabetes Control and Complications Trial [DCCT], 1993) once the condition becomes more stabilised.

Studies of attitudes among young, non-insulin-dependent diabetics have established that this particular aspect of their condition may have potentially significant psychological effects. Steel *et al* (1989) found that many young diabetics described the process of rapid weight gain as 'alarming', and several of these patients developed an eating disorder shortly after this had happened. The onset of the eating disorder was found to occur both in subjects who became overweight following commencement of their insulin therapy and those who were of normal weight, which would suggest that this was associated with the process of rapid weight gain and not their acquired body mass once their diabetes had been stabilised.

Vila *et al* (1995) studied eating habits and emotional distress in a group of adolescent girls, making comparisons between normal weight and obese insulin-dependent diabetics, and normal weight non-diabetics and obese non-diabetics. The highest rates of eating disorders were found among the obese subjects in both the diabetic and non-diabetic groups, although there were also eating disorders in the non-obese diabetic group. Vila *et al* (1995) concluded that obesity in both groups was a significant predisposing factor and was linked to significantly lower self-esteem and mild anxiety states.

Many teenagers experience a period of rebellion during the transition from adolescence to adulthood, which may cause significant problems as they attempt to cope with the diagnosis. Despite advice and emphasis on dietary control, many teenagers do not want to be seen as different from their peers and may choose to defy such information.

Some studies have indicated that the aetiological factors associated with eating disorders in diabetes are similar to those in the general population, and that many of those who develop them will share a number of the predisposing factors described in other studies of non-diabetic eating disordered individuals. Vila *et al* (1997) identified that 63% of eating disordered diabetics had experienced a number of family problems (conflicts, separations, economical difficulties), and several of these children met the criteria for DSM 111-R mental disorders, the most common of which was emotional disorder. The onset and atiology surrounding eating disorders in young diabetics appears to be multifactorial and requires further investigation.

Prevalence rates

The question of higher prevalence rates among young diabetics than those reported among the general population remains an issue that is presently unresolved. The data remains controversial. Statistics obtained are influenced by the methodology and the sample selection used to collect relevant data. Many studies use samples collected from centres where treatment is either implemented or is already underway. Szmuckler (1984) suggested that where the diabetic sample has been taken from a tertiary treatment centre, it is likely that eating disorders will be more prevalent among this group, based on the likelihood that the undiagnosed eating disorder will result in greater problems with diabetic control which, in turn, will have resulted in referral for investigation.

A Canadian study compared female diabetics with non-diabetic females and reported that those with diabetes were approximately two to four times more likely to have an eating disorder than their non-diabetic controls (Jones, 2000). In common with other studies, (Friedman *et al*, 1998), eating disorder not otherwise specified was the most frequent finding, and no individuals were found to exhibit symptoms of anorexia. This particular research used females only, but where males have been included in the participant group, it appears that diabetic men are far less likely to develop an eating disorder. Fairburn *et al* (1991) found no association between male diabetics and eating disorders, similarly, Friedman *et al* (1998) found no evidence of anorexia nervosa or bulimia nervosa, current or lifetime in male patients with insulin-dependent diabetes mellitus.

A large scale study of diabetic patients estimated the prevalence of eating disorders to be 5.9% which was irrespective of the gender or the type of diabetes (Herpetz *et al*, 1998). Bulimia nervosa was more frequent in insulin-dependent diabetics, while binge-eating disorder was more frequent among non-insulin-dependent subjects (Herpetz *et al*, 1998).

Anorexia nervosa

The combination of anorexia nervosa and insulin-dependent diabetes, although rare is potentially fatal, and presents a considerable challenge (Fairburn and Steel, 1980).

Pitel *et al* (1998) described the case of a seventeen-year-old girl who presented with poorly controlled type 1 diabetes, with significant weight loss which was found to be secondary to anorexia nervosa. The patient was admitted for treatment and received intensive input from the multidisciplinary team.

She was found to have used some unconventional methods of weight control, with her mother reporting that she suspected her daughter of tampering with her insulin regime (which she felt might involve diluting the dose). Poor metabolic control was reflected in high glycosolated haemoglobin (Hba1c) levels, with the associated concern that this might lead to an earlier onset of diabetic complications (Steel *et al*, 1987).

As a result of the girl's suspected role in influencing these high readings all insulin injections following admission were supervised by staff. A highly structured behaviour modification programme to promote diabetes management skills and weight gain was introduced, with family therapy to focus on the family's denial of the seriousness of her condition and the long-term consequences of poor management (Pitel *et al*, 1998).

Despite these interventions weight gain was not evident and weight loss, in fact, continued. This appeared to be related to weekend visits home, during which time the staff suspected laxative abuse took place. (Laxative abuse can be detected by biochemical screening, and has its own medical complications [Turner *et al*, 2000].) It is often associated with longer duration of disease.

More intensive treatment was implemented (including naso-gastric feeding, and a 24-hour fully supervised monitoring regime). Weight gain ensued, reflected in improved HBA1C results and additional improvements in cognitive function. The girl made a substantial recovery and was eventually discharged home. Follow-up assessments indicated weight maintenance with no symptoms of depression and family communication continued to be addressed in outpatient therapy (Pitel *et al*, 1998).

Bulimia nervosa

The detection of bulimia nervosa is no easier among the diabetic population and it is suspected that the number of undetected cases, which are believed to exist in society as a whole, may feasibly extend to a similar number of undiagnosed subjects among the diabetic population. Seven per cent of patients attending a diabetes clinic in Edinburgh were found to have clinical evidence of an eating disorder (Steel *et al*, 1987). Anorexia was the easiest to identify because of the unexplained weight loss, however bulimia was only detected when sufferers were questioned intensively about the reasons for their poor glycaemic control.

Peveler and Fairburn (1990) identified cases of bulimia nervosa where eating disorders had developed prior to the onset of diabetes, which confirms that in these cases the diabetes itself had no part in the aetiology. The patients were found to exhibit many clinical features in common with other eating disordered individuals (Peveler and Fairburn, 1990), with disordered eating patterns evident in all cases.

Binge-eating disorder

Binge-eating disorder has been found to be more prevalent among type 2 diabetics, with the suggestion that binge-eating behaviour may be one of the causes of obesity which precedes the onset of this classification of diabetes (Herpetz *et al*, 1998). However, its existence in type 1 diabetes has also been reported.

Mannucci (1995) described the case of a patient who developed insulin-dependent diabetes at the age of seventeen, and appeared to be in relatively good health on clinical examination. The only clue to her eating disorder came from extremely high HBA1C results which could not be explained and warranted further investigation. It then became apparent that the girl suffered from disturbed thoughts relating to her shape and weight and admitted to having had regular and frequent episodes of nocturnal binge eating for the past three years. On further examination she was found to meet the diagnostic criteria for binge-eating disorder, but was not overweight. In patients with insulin-dependent diabetes mellitus, overeating in any form, unless it is accompanied by an increase in insulin doses does not usually lead to weight gain, but to glycosuria and impaired metabolic control (Mannucci *et al*, 1995), which was evident in this case study.

Disordered eating patterns among diabetics are always a concern for health professionals and the effect of binge eating among diabetics has been compared to the effect of bulimia. Takii *et al* (1999) found that bulimia nervosa was associated with more emotional and psychological disturbance (including depression and anxiety), while the binge-eating disorder group had poorer glycaemic control, a factor further complicated by the omission and misuse of their insulin regime as a means of attempted weight control.

Subthreshold disorders

In common with the general population there is reason to believe that a number of diabetics may have a subthreshold eating disorder. Bryden *et al* (1999) found that milder forms of disordered eating patterns were common among adolescent diabetics, and had implications for diabetes management, but full-blown eating disorders were no more prevalent than those found in non-diabetic subjects.

Insulin misuse

Misuse of insulin (by deliberately reducing the prescribed dose or omitting it altogether), is a strategy that diabetic women have been found to adopt in an attempt to lose weight although, once again, prevalence statistics are variable and remain a topic for future research. Rydall *et al* (1997) found that 14% of the women in their study admitted to adopting these practices at baseline, a statistic which had increased to 34% at follow-up. Jones *et al* (2000) reported a much higher figure, with 42% of diabetics in their study admitting to misuse of insulin at the time of screening which was reflected in high HBA1C values. Females in particular adopted dietary restraint and patterns of disordered eating, and 30% of females admitted to under-using insulin to assist in weight control. The lack of evidence for eating disorders among male diabetics supports other previous studies (Fairburn *et al*, 1991; Friedman *et al*, 1998), and indicates the need to seek an alternative reason for poor diabetic control and high HBA1C levels in diabetic men, when an eating disorder cannot be confirmed.

Diabetic complications

HBA1C levels are used to assess diabetic control, a poor result suggests to the health professional that dietary intake has not followed the recommended balance of foodstuffs.

Several studies have provided evidence that hyperglycaemia is a risk factor for early development of diabetic complications (Wing *et al*, 1986; Steel *et al*, 1989; Rydall *et al*, 1997; Diabetes Control and Complications Trial, 1993). Diabetics who develop an eating disorder will require a greater level of professional input if potentially preventable complications are to be avoided.

The recent United Kingdom Prospective Diabetes Study (UKPDS) was able to confirm that poor control of blood glucose levels is reflected in an increased risk of macrovascular and micro-vascular complications, while the lower the level of glycaemia, the lower the risk of complication (Stratton *et al*, 2000). Microvascular complications have been found to be a particularly high risk. Eighty-six per cent of diabetics in one study with highly disordered eating patterns developed retinopathy after four years of the onset of the eating disorder. Forty-three per cent of those with a lesser degree of disordered eating behaviour compared to 24% of those with a regular eating pattern developed this complication (Rydall *et al*, 1997).

Diabetes and hyperlipidaemia are associated with an increased risk of macrovascular complications, cerebrovascular, cardiovascular and peripheral vascular disease (Gatling *et al*, 1997). Bulimics and binge eaters have been found to consume large quantities of foods during binge episodes which are high in fat and carbohydrate which has led to interest in whether disordered eating patterns among diabetics further enhances the prevalence of hyperlipidaemia.

Anorexia nervosa, although rarer among diabetics is already associated with disturbed lipid metabolism among the non-diabetic population (Holman *et al*, 1995).

Estimation of glycosalated haemoglobin levels and triglycerides and cholesterol confirmed that those with subthreshold eating disorders had raised triglycerides levels when compared to controls, while women who intentionally reduced or omitted their insulin dose had both cholesterol and triglyceride values above the recommended level (Affenito *et al*, 1997).

Rydall *et al* (1997) demonstrated that the greater the degree of disordered eating, the greater the likelihood of developing an associated problem.

Associated psychopathology

Subjects with both type 1 and type 2 diabetes have been found to

exhibit a more severe level of psychopathology than diabetics with no eating disorder symptoms (Herpetz *et al*, 2000).

Interestingly, those individuals with type 2 diabetes exhibited greater levels of psychiatric comorbidity than those with type 1.

The interaction of both an eating disorder and diabetes requires expert intervention for successful treatment and management of the combined effects which these two conditions bring.

Suggested further reading

Diabetes

Mannucci E, Ricca V, Mezzani B, Di Bernardo M, Piani F, Vannini R *et al* (1995) Eating attitudes and behaviour in IDDM patients: a case control controlled study. *Diabetes Care* **18**: 1503–5

Fairburn CG, Peveler RC, Davies B, Mann JI, Mayou RA (1991) Eating disorders in young adults with insulin-dependent diabetes mellitus: a controlled study. *Br Med J* **303**: 17–20

Anorexia nervosa

Gomez M, Dally P, Isaacs AM (1980) Anorexia nervosa in diabetes mellitus. *Br Med J* **281**: 61–2

Powers PS, Malone ML, Duncan MA (1983) Anorexia nervosa and diabetes mellitus. *J Clin Psychiatry* **44**: 133–5

Bulimia nervosa

Hillard JR, Hillard PJA (1984) Bulimia, anorexia nervosa and diabetes — deadly combinations. *Psychiatr Clin North Am* **7**: 367–79

Wing RR, Nowalk MP, Marcus MD, Koeske R, Finegold D (1986) Subclinical eating disorders and glycaemic control in adolescents with type 1 diabetes. *Diabetes Care* **9**: 162–7

Binge-eating disorder

Mannucci E, Ricca V, Rotella CM (1997) Clinical features of binge-eating disorder in type 1 diabetes. *Int J Eating Disorder* **21**(1): 99–102

Complications

Rydall AC, Rodin GM, Olmsted MP, Devenyi RG, Daneman D (1997) Disordered eating behaviour and microvascular complications in young women with insulin dependent diabetes mellitus. *New Engl J Med* **336**: 1849–54

Steel JM, Young RJ, Lloyd GG, Clarke BF (1987) Clinically apparent eating disorders in young diabetic women: associations with painful neuropathy and other complications. *Br Med J* **294**: 859–62

Conclusion: Future directions

Recent years have seen a growing volume of research material related to aetiology, epidemiology, treatment and outcome studies relating to the field of eating disorders, yet still there remain a number of unanswered questions.

In other areas of healthcare provision, preventative strategies have taken a lead in formulating plans to reduce morbidity and mortality from specific diseases. Such strategies are not specific to the United Kingdom and have been implemented in other countries around the world to tackle such problems as heart disease, cancer and obesity: conditions which are seen to cause considerable human suffering, often for a prolonged period of time. Despite this, less than two dozen prevention intervention studies to reduce the prevalence of eating disorders have been conducted to date, with little emphasis on leverage points for intervention in the larger social environment (Austin, 2000).

The recent acknowledgement that eating disorders across the spectrum of currently recognised conditions, are becoming evident in nations where they were previously rare or non-existent raises concern over their impact in future years.

These concerns encompass both the effects on the health of young sufferers, and the potential rise in long-term associated morbidity and mortality.

The ability to put a significant strain on healthcare resources is recognised, as is the concern that rising incidence will pose a considerable public health challenge in years to come (Lee, 2000). Future research will need to address multicultural issues, given the confounding evidence to support the notion that eating disorders are no longer confined to white middle class females (Yanovski, 2000), as portrayed by early research.

In relation to anorexia nervosa and bulimia nervosa, the role of the media and fashion industries, especially those targeting women and young girls by promoting unrealistic standards of female beauty (Austin, 2000), has been called to question. The BMA in the United Kingdom has recently called for the media to adopt 'a more responsible attitude towards body image' suggesting that the constant portrayal of thin women can lead to low self-esteem, which with associated aetiological factors may lead to the onset of an eating

(Morant, 2000). Similar concerns have arisen with Asian , with the implication that media advertising is the only social determinant of eating disorders and that among these communities, societal modernisation intensifies vulnerability to eating disorders in young women (Lee, 2000).

The research material to date suggests that the early adolescent years may hold the key to identification and early intervention of those who are at risk of developing an eating disorder. There is considerable scope for individuals who have contact with this age group to exercise vigilance and maintain a high level of suspicion, a feat which can only be accomplished with increased awareness.

In relation to anorexia nervosa, early dieting behaviour has been cited as highly relevant, with statistics indicating that young girls who have dieted severely, have a one in five chance of developing an eating disorder over the course of a twelve-month period (Patton *et al*, 1999). The other factor surrounds the issue of excessive physical activity. Davis *et al* (1994) suggested that in anorexia nervosa, overactivity should not be regarded as a secondary symptom and may be an integral part of the pathogenesis and progression of self-starvation. These two additions to the range of aetiological factors already identified have connotations for early suspicion of impending problems among young adolescents. The need for parental awareness is as great as the need for a high level of suspicion among health professionals from all disciplines, and to this end the American Psychiatric Association cite linkages between the physiological and psychological processes of puberty as important areas for further evaluation, with a need for preventative intervention through the development of earlier screening and risk factor identification (American Psychiatric Association, 2000). Young children in the transition from adolescence to adulthood undergo a wealth of physical and emotional changes which they endure alongside additional pressures and responsibility. The teenage years are for many associated with the first introduction to alcohol, smoking and first sexual relationships. Any programme that seeks to change the eating and exercise patterns of young people may have to address the problems many children have with unhealthy dieting, bingeing, weight-related stigma and disturbed relationships within their bodies (Austin, 2000).

School-based intervention programmes have already been implemented in some parts of the world, aiming to change eating attitudes and behaviours in young adolescent males and females. An American project enlisted 470 volunteers, aged between eleven and fourteen, who were subdivided into a control and intervention group. Early mediation through a programme which addressed body image issues was deemed successful in improving self-esteem, feelings towards social acceptance and physical appearance (O'Dea and Abraham, 2000). These improvements appeared to be sustained when subjects were assessed twelve months later. Particularly encouraging was the outcome for the cohort of females who were considered to be at a high risk of developing an eating disorder, but who were found to respond in a similar way to the other improved adolescents and were successful in sustaining their improvement at follow-up assessment. A Swiss intervention study aimed at adolescents aged fourteen years of age achieved similar benefits. The sessions took place on a monthly basis over a period of three months and covered a range of issues relating to psychological and social health and well being. Concepts of health and ill health were addressed, and adolescents were encouraged to reflect upon their own desire, motives and actions while at the same time improving their own self-esteem (Buddeberg-Fischer *et al*, 1998).

Psychoeducational interventions delivered via the internet have also been found to achieve some success in reducing the risk factors which may potentiate the onset of an eating disorder. When compared to a classroom delivered programme, the internet delivered intervention achieved significant reductions in weight and shape concerns and disordered eating attitudes (Celio *et al*, 2000), suggesting that its use may have a useful role to play in educating young people who may be at risk.

The number of cases which remain undiagnosed are a cause for concern given the data to support the suspected prevalence of the many individuals who have some, but not all of the criteria and are labelled as having a subthreshold eating disorder. Detection of these cases is particularly difficult, and has led to a call for a greater degree of flexibility in the application of the diagnostic criteria, which may be required to allow for the identification and treatment of such atypical cases (American Psychiatric Association, 2000).

Complex screening tools may be difficult for non-specialist staff to utilise and require specialist interpretation (Morgan *et al*, 1999), making their use impractical in the primary care setting. The need for a simple tool that allows early suspicions to be confirmed would be beneficial in detecting currently undiagnosed cases in primary care. Such cases would then be referred for early specialist assessment and treatment.

The relative 'newness' of binge-eating disorder leaves the

condition poorly understood. The obesity with which it is associated has received considerably more attention with far more being known about the long-term health risks, and the accompanying morbidity and mortality. While in many cases the onset of the binge-eating behaviour itself does not commence until late adolescence or the early twenties (American Psychiatric Association, 1995), childhood obesity has been cited as a risk factor (Fairburn *et al*, 1998). Arguably, school-based intervention programmes need to focus on prevention of obesity and healthy eating as a further tool in the prevention of eating disorders. Steiner-Adair (1994) suggests a need for school policies to deal with teasing which is weight orientated and might constitute harassment of the individual.

There is considerable scope for further work on all aspects of this condition's aetiology, evaluation and treatment. Progress has been made in an effort to improve treatment options, although there is still debate as to the length of treatment required and suitable combinations of treatments which will improve recovery rates and long-term outlook. This is increasingly important in those individuals who have a high risk of relapse, appear resistant to treatment, have had several attempts at recovery or who possess comorbid conditions (American Psychiatric Association, 2000), which may require separate, additional treatment to the eating disorder itself.

Advances in genetic science have been heralded as a major advancement in a range of medical conditions. The rapid developments in molecular genetics are forcing the field of psychiatry to define more specifically the phenotypes of the mental disorders, with anorexia, bulimia and their variants being relative latecomers to the arena of investigation (Halmi, 1999).

Genetic studies of psychiatric disorders in the relatives of anorexics and bulimics have made major advances in the heritability of eating disorders with evidence now available to support the notion that there is a risk of major depressive illness, subthreshold eating disorders, generalised anxiety disorder and obsessive compulsive disorder in relatives of these sufferers (Lilenfield *et al*, 1998). Recent research has identified that obsessive compulsive personality disorder may share some genetic risk factors with anorexia nervosa and be a risk factor for its development (Woodside, 1999).

Further work is needed to confirm the exact nature of genetic predisposition, more importantly whether anorexia nervosa and bulimia share genetic vulnerabilities or are inherited as separate conditions (Woodside, 1999).

This work needs to extend to binge-eating disorder since there is already identification of several gene products including leptin (the leptin receptor) that are associated with obesity (Devlin *et al*, 2000b). It would seem useful to examine a possible genetic predisposition in this particular illness, given the tendency of binge eaters to have a history of obesity.

Treatment programmes are under constant review and the nature of these interventions has changed as knowledge levels have increased. Yet, there are still unsatisfactory end points which have to be addressed. The risk of relapse has been discussed and appears to be a danger in all eating disordered patients. The different stages at which patients present for treatment, and their willingness to participate have implications for both the type of treatment, treatment venue and the duration required. More refined clinical indicators and a better understanding of the stages of these disorders, including follow-up issues for short-term and long-term studies (American Psychiatric Association, 2000), might be invaluable in helping to tailor treatment programmes more effectively to individual needs, so that the risk of recurrence or transmission to other conditions can be avoided.

To date, eating disorders appear to have received a relatively low profile in the healthcare arena in Britain; the recent emphasis on public health initiatives offers scope to rectify this situation. The cost of intensive alterations to current ways of working is always an issue which causes concern, and the resources required to implement intervention programmes, improve knowledge among nursing and medical staff, and offer the best available treatment programmes would need to be justified in terms of long-term health improvement. It is clear that there remains a considerable amount of work to be done if these issues are to be addressed.

Evidence-based medicine and research-based practice are an integral part of nursing and medical practice and Austin (2000) suggests that extending research collaborations across disciplinary lines, especially with public health, may be the most promising course to take at this moment in eating disorders prevention.

Suggested further reading

Austin SB (2000) Prevention research in eating disorders: theory and new directions. *Psychol Med* **30**(6): 1249–62

Neumark-Sztainer D (1996) School-based program for preventing eating disturbances. *J School Health* **66**: 64–71

Seidell JC (1999) Obesity: a growing problem. *Acta Paediatr* **88**(Suppl 428): 46–60

O'Dea JA, Abraham S (2000) Improving the body image, eating attitudes, and behaviours of young male and female adolescents: A new educational approach that focuses on self esteem. *Int J Eat Disorder* **28**(1): 43–57

References

Abraham S, Jones L (1984) *Eating disorders: The facts.* Oxford University Press, Oxford

Abraham S (1996) Characteristics of eating disorders among young ballet dancers. *Psychopathology* **29**(4): 223–9

Abraham S (1998) Sexuality and reproduction in bulimia nervosa patients over ten years. *J Psychosom Res* **44**(3–4): 491–502

Adami GF, Gandolfo P, Campastano A, Cocchi F, Bauer B, Scopinaro N (1995) Obese binge eaters: metabolic characteristics, energy expenditure and dieting. *Psychol Med* **25**(1): 195–8

Adams K, Sargent RG, Thompson SH, Richter D, Corwin S, Rogan TJ (2000) A study of body weight control and weight control practices in 4th and 7th grade adolescents. *Ethn Health* **5**(1): 79–94

Affenito SG, Lammi-Keefe CJ, Vogel S, Backstrand JR, Welch GW, Adams CH (1997) Women with insulin-dependent diabetes mellitus (IDDM) complicated by eating disorders are at risk for exacerbated alterations in lipid metabolism. *Eur J Clin Nutr* **51**(7): 462–6

Agras WS, McCann U (1987) The efficacy and role of antidepressants in the treatment of bulimia nervosa. *Ann Behav Med* **9**(18): 18–22

Agras WS, Rossiter EM, Arnow B, Schneider JA, Telch CF, Raeburn SD, Bruce B, Perl M, Koran LM (1992) Pharmacological and cognitive behavioural treatment for bulimia nervosa: A controlled comparison. *Am J Psychiatry* **149**: 82–7

Agras WS, Telch CF, Arnow B, Eldredge K, Detzer MJ, Henderson J, Marnell M (1995) Does interpersonal therapy help patients with binge-eating disorder who fail to respond to cognitive behavioural therapy? *Am Psychological Association* **63**(3): 356–60

Agras WS, Telch CF, Arnow B, Eldridge K Marnell M (1997) One-year follow-up of cognitive-behaviour therapy for obese individuals with binge-eating disorder. *J Consult Clin Psychol* **65**(2): 343–7

Agras WA, Walsh T, Fairburn CG, Wilson TG, Kraemer HC (2000) A multi-centre comparison of cognitive-behavioral therapy and interpersonal psychotherapy for bulimia nervosa. *Arch Gen Psychiatry* **57**(5): 459–66

Agras WS, Crow SJ, Halmi KA Mitchell JE, Wilson G, Kraemer H (2000) Outcome predictors for the cognitive behaviour treatment of bulimia nervosa: data from a multisite study. *Am J Psychiatry* **157**(8): 1302–8

Albrecht RJ, Pories WJ (1999) Surgical intervention of the severely obese: Best practice and research. *Clin Endocrinol Metabolism* **13**(1): 149–72

Allison DB, Kaprio J, Korkeila M, Koskenvuo M, Neale MC, Hayakawa K (1996) The heritability of body mass index among an international sample of monozygotic twins reared apart. *Int J Obes Relat Metab Disord* **20**(6): 501–6

Altemus M, Hetherington M, Kennedy B, Licinio J, Gold PW (1996) Thyroid function in bulimia nervosa. *Psychoneuroendocrinology* **21**(3): 249–61

American Dietetic Association (1988) Position of the American Dietetic Association: Nutrition intervention in the treatment of anorexia nervosa and bulimia nervosa. *J Am Diet Assoc* **88**(1): 68–71

American Psychiatric Association (1993) Practice guideline for eating disorders. *Am J Psychiatry* **150**: 212–28

American Psychiatric Association (1994) *Diagnostic and Statistical Manual of Mental Disorders.* 4th edn. Washington DC

American Psychiatric Association (1995) *Diagnostic and Statistical Manual of Mental Disorders.* 4th edn. International Version, Washington DC

American Psychiatric Association (2000) *Practice guideline for the treatment of patients with eating disorders.* (Revision) 157, 1(Supplement): 1–39

Andersen E, Grimsmo A (1999) Long-term results of treatment of overweight in self help groups. *Tiddskrift for den Norske Laegseforening* **119**(1): 14–17

Andersen AE, Watson T, Schlecte J (2000) Osteoporosis and osteoporosis in men with eating disorders. *The Lancet* **355**: 1967–8

Andersen AE, Bowers WE, Evans K (1997) Inpatient treatment of anorexia nervosa. In: Garner DM, Garfinkel PE, eds. *Handbook of Treatment for Eating Disorders.* 2nd edn. The Guildford Press, London: 327–53

Anderson P (1998) Spiritual hunger. *Nurs Times* **94**(38): 34–5

Aperia A, Broberger O, Fohlin L (1978) Renal function in anorexia nervosa. *Acta Paediatr Scand* **67**(2): 219–24

Argente J, Caballo N, Barrios V, Munoz MT, Pozo J, Chowen JA, Hernandez M (1997) Disturbances in the growth hormone insulin like growth factor axis in children and adolescents with different eating disorders. *Horm Res* **48**(Suppl 4): 16–18

Attia E, Haiman C, Walsh T Flater SR (1998) Does fluoxetine augment the inpatient treatment of anorexia nervosa? *Am J Psychiatry* **155**(4): 548–51

Augestad LB, Saether B, Gotestam KG (1999) The relationship between eating disorders and personality in physically active women. *Scand J Med Sci Sports* **9**(5): 304–12

Austin SB (2000) Prevention research in eating disorders: theory and new directions. *Psychol Med* **30**(6): 1249–62

Bachrach LK, Guido D, Katzman D, Litt IF, Marcus R (1990) Decreased bone density in adolescent girls with anorexia nervosa. *Paediatrics* **86**(3): 440–5

Bailly D (1993) Epidemiological research, eating disorders, and addictive behaviours. *Encephale* **19**(4): 285–92

Bale P, Doust J, Dawson D (1996) Gymnasts, distance runners, anorexics body composition and menstrual status. *J Sports Med Phys Fitness* **36**(1): 49–53

Bamber D, Cockerill IM, Carroll D (2000) The pathological status of exercise dependence. *Br J Sports Med* **34**: 125–32

Bannai C, Kuzuya N, Koide Y, Fujita T, Itakura M, Kawai K, Yamashita K (1988) Assessment of the relationship between serum thyroid hormone levels and peripheral metabolism in patients with anorexia nervosa. *Endocrinol Japan* **35**(3): 455–62

Baran SA, Weltzin TE, Kaye WH (1995) Low discharge weight and outcome in anorexia nervosa. *Am J Psychiatry* **152**(7): 1070–72

Barry A, Lippmann SB (1990) Anorexia nervosa in males. *Postgrad Med* **87**(8): 161–5

Bastiani AM, Rao R, Weltzin T, Kaye WH (1995) Perfectionism in anorexia nervosa. *Int J Eat Disord* **17**(2): 147–52

Baumgarten HG, Grozdanovic Z (1998) Role of serotonin in obsessive-compulsive disorder. *Br J Psychiatry* **173**(Suppl 35): 13–20

Beals KA, Manore MM (2000) Behavioural, psychological, and physical characteristics of female athletes with subclinical eating disorders. *Int J Sport, Nutr Exercise Metabolism* **10**(2): 128–43

Beary MD, Lacey JH, Merry J (1986) Alcoholism and eating disorders in women of fertile age. *Br J Addiction* **81**: 685–9

Beglin SJ, Fairburn CG (1992) What is meant by the binge? *Am J Psychiatry* **149**: 123–4

Benjamin S (1988) Crohn's disease presenting as anorexia nervosa. *Br Med J* **296**: 2006

Bergh C, Sodersten P (1998) Anorexia nervosa: rediscovery of a disorder. *The Lancet* **351**: 1427–9

Beumont PJ, George GC Smart DE (1976) Dieters, vomiters and purgers in anorexia nervosa. *Psychol Med* **6**: 617–22

Beument PG, Large M (1991) Hypophosphataemia, delirium and cardiac arrhythmia in anorexia nervosa. *Med J Australia* **155**(8): 519–22

Beumont PJV, Beumont CC, Touyz SW, Williams H (1997) Nutritional counselling and supervised exercise In: Garner DM, Garfinkel PE, eds. *Handbook of Treatment for Eating Disorders.* 2nd edn. The Guildford Press, London

Biebl W, Kinzl JF (1996) Hypokalaemia in eating disorders. *Am J Psychiatry* **153**(2): 296

Birketvedt GS, Florholmen J, Sundsfjord J, Osterud B, Dinges D, Bilker W, Stunkard A (1999) Behavioural and neuroendocrine characteristics of the night-eating syndrome. *Jama* **282**(7): 657–63

Birmingham CL, Alothman AF, Goldner EM (1996) Anorexia nervosa: refeeding and hypophosphataemia. *Int J Eat Disord* **20**(2): 211–3

Birmingham CL, Goldner EM, Bakan R (1994) Controlled trial of zinc supplementation in anorexia nervosa. *Int J Eat Disord* **15**(3): 251–255

Blades M (1997) Eating disorders: A growing trend among young people. *Community Nurse* **3**(9): 27–28

Blouin A, Blouin J, Aubin P, Carter J, Goldstein C, Boyer H, Perez E, (1992) Seasonal patterns of bulimia nervosa. *Am J Psychiatry* **149**(1): 73–81

Blundell JE (1990) How culture undermines the biopsychological system of appetite control. *Appetite* **14**(2): 113–15

Boag F, Weerakoon J, Ginsburg J, Havard CWH, Dandona P (1985) Diminished creatinine clearance in anorexia nervosa: reversal with weight gain. *J Clin Pathol* **38**(1): 60–3

Bolton D, Luckie M, Steinberg D (1995) Long term course of obsessive compulsive disorder treated in adolescence. *J Am Acad Child Adolesc Psychiatry* **34**: 1441–1450

Boston Collaborative Drug Surveillance Program (1998) Further cases of valvular heart disease associated with fenfluramine-phentermine. *New Engl J Med* **337**(9): 719–24

Bradley J, Rubenstein D, Wayne D (1994) *The Clinical Manual*. Blackwell Scientific Publications, London

Braun DL, Sunday SR, Huang A, Halmi KA (1999) More males seek treatment for eating disorders. *Int J Eat Disord* **25**(4): 415–24

Bray GA, Ryan DS, Gordon D, Heidingsfelder S, Cerise F, Wilson K (1996) A double-blind randomised placebo-controlled trial of sibutramine. *Obesity Res* **4**: 263–70

Brewerton TD (1995) Towards a unified theory of serotonin dysregulation in eating and related disorders. *Psychoendocrinology* **20**: 561–590

Brewerton TD (1999) Binge eating disorder: Diagnosis and treatment options. *CNS Drugs* **11**(5): 351–61

Brewerton TD, Stellefson EJ, Hibbs N, Hodges EL, Cochrane CE (1995) Comparison of eating disordered patients with and without compulsive exercising. *Int J Eat Disord* **17**(4): 413–16

Brion LP, Boeck MA, Gauthier B, Nussbaum MP, Schwartz GJ (1989) Estimation of glomerular filtration rate in anorectic adolescents. *Paediatr nephrology* **3**(1): 16–21

British Medical Association and the Royal Pharmaceutical Society of Great Britain (1999) *British National Formulary*. BMJ Books, London

Brotman AW, Stern TA (1985) Osteoporosis and pathological fractures in anorexia nervosa. *Am J Psychiatry* **142**(4): 495–6

Brotman AW, Rigotti N, Herzog W (1985) Medical complications of eating disorders: outpatient evaluation and management. *Compr Psychiatry* **26**(3): 258–72

Brotman AW, Stern TA, Brotman DL (1986) Renal disease and dysfunction in two patients with anorexia nervosa. *J Clin Psychiatry* **47**: 495–496

Browne A, Finkelhor D (1986) Impact of child sexual abuse: a review of the research. *Psychol Bull* **99**: 66–7

Brzozowska A, Wolanczyk T, Komender J (1998) Schizophrenia, schizophrenia-like disorders and delusional disorders in patients with anorexia nervosa: literature review and report of three cases. *Psychiatr Pol* **32**(3): 265–27

Bryden KS, Neil A, Mayou RA, Pevelar RC, Fairburn CG, Dunger DB (1999) Eating habits, body weight and insulin misuse: A longitudinal study of teenagers and young adults with type 1 diabetes. *Diabetes Care* **22**(12): 1956

Buddeberg-Fischer B, Bernet R, Sieber M, Schmidt J, Budderberg C (1996) Epidemiology of eating behaviour and weight distribution in 14–19 year old Swiss students. *Acta Psychiatr Scand* **93**(4): 296–304

Budderberg-Fischer B, Klaghofer R, Gnam G, Budderberg C (1998) Prevention of disturbed eating behaviour: a prospective intervention study in 14–19-year-old Swiss students. *Acta Psychiatr Scand* **98**(2): 146–55

Bulik CM (1987) Drug and alcohol abuse by bulimic women and their families. *Am J Psychiatry* **144**: 1604–6

Bulik CM, Sullivan PF, Nckee M, Weltzen TE, Kaye WH (1994) Characteristics of bulimic women with and without alcohol abuse. *Am J Drug Alcohol Abuse* **20**(2): 273–83

Bulik CM, Sullivan PF, Fear JL, Joyce PR (1997a) Eating disorders and antecedent anxiety disorders: a controlled study. *Acta Psychiatr Scand* **96**(2): 101–7

Bulik C, Sullivan PF, Fear J, Pickering A (1997b) Predictors of the development of bulimia of bulimia nervosa in women with anorexia nervosa. *J Nerv Ment Disorder* **185**: 704–7

Bulik CM, Sullivan PF, Carter FA, Joyce PR (1996) Lifetime disorders in women with bulimia nervosa. *Compr Psychiatry* **37**(5): 368–374

Bulimia nervosa collaborative study group (1992) Fluoxetine in the treatment of bulimia nervosa: A multi centre placebo-controlled double blind trial. *Arch Gen Psychiatry* **49**: 139–47

Burden M (1995) Obesity and diabetes: Aetiology and pathophysiology. Part 1. *Diabetic Nurs* **20**: 994–7

Burns T, Crisp AH (1984) Outcome of anorexia nervosa in males. *Br J Psychiatry* **145**: 319–25

Button EJ, Sonuga-Barke EJS, Davies J, Thompson M (1996) A prospective study of self-esteem in the prediction of eating problems in adolescent schoolgirls: questionnaire findings. *Br J Clin Psychol* **35**(Pt 2): 193–203

Button EJ, Whitehouse A (1981) Subclinical anorexia nervosa. *Psychol Med* **11**: 509–16

Calam RM, Slade PD (1989) Sexual experience and eating problems in undergraduates. *Int J Eat Disorder* **8**: 391–7

Cameron FJ,Warne GL (1997) Familial Cushing's disease with severe weight loss occurring in late childhood. *J Paediatr Child Health* **33**(1): 74–7

Caprio S, Tamborlane WV (1999) Metabolic impact of obesity in childhood. *Endocrinol Metab Clin North Am* **28**(4): 731–47

Cargill BR, Clark MM, Pera V, Niaura RS, Abrams DB (1999) Binge eating, body image, depression, and self-efficacy in an obese clinical population. *Obesity Res* **7**: 379–86

Carlat DJ, Camargo CA (1991) Review of bulimia nervosa in males. *Am J Psychiatry* **148**(7): 831–43

Carlat DJ, Camargo CA, Herzog DB (1997) Eating disorders in males: A report on 135 patients. *Am J Psychiatry* **154**(8): 1127–32

Casper RC, Offer D (1990) Weight and dieting in adolescents: fashion or symptom? *Paediatrics* **86**: 384–90

Casper RC (1990) Personality features of women with good outcome from restricting anorexia nervosa. *Psychosom Med* **52**: 156–70

Casper RC (1998) Depression and eating disorders. *Depression, Anxiety* **8**(Suppl 1): 96–104

Castonguay LG, Eldridge KL, Agras WS (1995) Binge-eating disorder: current state and future directions. *Clin Psychol Rev* **15**: 865–90

Castro J, Toro J, Cruz M (2000) Quality of rearing practices as a predictor of short term outcome in adolescent anorexia nervosa. *Psychol Med* **30**(1): 61–7

Celio AA, Winzleberg AJ, Wilfley DE, Eppstein-Herald D, Springer EA, Dev P, Taylor CB (2000) Reducing risk factors for eating disorders: comparison of an Internet and a classroom delivered psychoeducational program. *J Clin Psychol* **68**(4): 650–7

Chan JM, Rimm EB, Colditz GA, Stampfer MJ, Willett WC (1994) Obesity, fat distribution and weight gain as risk factors for clinical diabetes in men. *Diabetes Care* **17**(9): 961–9

Chipkevitch E (1994) Brain tumours and anorexia nervosa syndrome. *Brain Development* **16**(3): 175–9

Cnattingius S, Hultman CM, Dahl M, Sparen P (1999) Very preterm birth, birth trauma, and the risk of anorexia nervosa among girls. *Arch Gen Psychiatry* **56**(7): 634–8

Collings S, King M (1994) Ten-year follow-up of 50 patients with bulimia nervosa. *Br J Psychiatry* **164**(1): 80–7

Connolly HM, Crary JL, McGoon MD, Hensrud DD, Edwards BS, Edwards WD, Schaff HV (1997) Valvular heart disease associated with fenfluramine-phentermine. *New Engl J Med* **337**(9): 581–8

Cooke AK, Striegel-Moore R (1997) The aetiology and treatment of body image disturbance. In: Garner DM, Garfinkel PE, eds. *Handbook of Treatment for Eating Disorders*. 2nd edn. The Guildford Press, London

Cooper PJ, Fairburn CG (1983) Binge eating and self-induced vomiting in the community: a preliminary study. *Br J Psychiatry* **142**: 139–44

Copeland PM (1994) Renal failure associated with laxative abuse. *Psychother Psychosom* **62**(3–4): 200–2

Copeland PM, Sacks NR, Herzog DR (1995) Longitudinal follow-up of amenorrhoea in eating disorders. *Psychosom Med* **57**(2): 121–6

Corcos M, Flament MF, Giraud MJ, Paterniti S, Ledoux S, Atger F, Jeammet P (2000) Early psychopathological signs in bulimia nervosa. A retrospective comparison of the period of puberty in bulimic and control girls. *Eur Child Adolesc Psychiatry* **9**(2): 115–21

Couzinet B, Young J, Brailly S, Le Bouc Y, Chanson P, Schaison G (1999) Functional hypothalamic amenorrhoea: a partial and reversible gonadotrophin deficiency of nutritional origin. *Clin Endocrinol* **50**(2): 229–35

Crisp AH (1967) Anorexia nervosa. *Hospital Med* **1**: 713–8

Crisp AH (1997) Anorexia nervosa as flight from growth. In: Garner DM, Garfinkel PE, eds. *Handbook of Treatment for Eating Disorders*. 2nd edn. The Guildford Press, London

Crisp AH, Toms DA (1972) Primary anorexia nervosa or weight phobia in the male: report on 13 cases. *Br Med J* **1**: 334–8

Crisp AH, Palmer RL,Kalucy RS (1976) How common is anorexia nervosa: A prevalence study. *Br J Psychiatry* **128**: 549–54

Crisp AH (1977) Some psychobiological aspects of adolescent growth and their relevance for the fat/thin syndrome (anorexia nervosa). *Int J Obes* **1**(3): 231–8

Croner S, Larsson J, Schildt, Symreng T (1985) Severe anorexia nervosa treated with parenteral nutrition: Clinical course and influence on chemical analyses. *Acta Paediatr Scand* **74**(2): 230–6

Cuellar RE, Kaye WH, Hsu LK, Van Thiel DH (1988) Upper gastrointestinal tract dysfunction in bulimia nervosa. *Dig Disease Sci* **33**(12): 1459–53

Cuellar GEM, Ruiz AM, Monsalve MCR, Berber A (2000) Sixth-month treatment of obesity with sibutramine 15mg: a double-blind placebo-controlled monocenter clinical trial in a Hispanic population. *Obesity Res* **8**: 71–82

Daluiski A, Rahbar B, Meals RA (1997) Russell's sign: Subtle hand changes in patients with bulimia nervosa. *Clinical Orthop* **343**: 107–9

Daniels SR, Morrison JA, Sprecher DL, Khoury P, Kimball TR (1999) Association of body fat distribution and cardiovascular risk factors in children and adolescents. *Circulation* **99**(4): 541–545

Danziger Y, Mukamel M, Zeharia A, Dinari G, Mimouni M (1994) Stunting of growth in anorexia during the prepubertal and pubertal period. *Isr J Med Sci* **30**(8): 581–4

Davies E, Furnham A (1986a) The dieting and body shape concerns of adolescent teenagers. *J Child Psychol Psychiatry* **27**: 417–28

Davies E, Furnham A (1986b) Body satisfaction in adolescent girls. *Br J Med Psychol* **59**: 279–87

Davis C, Katzman DK, Kirsch C (1999) Compulsive physical activity in adolescents with anorexia: a psychobehavioural spiral of pathology. *J Nerv Ment Disorder* **187**(6): 336–42

Davis C, Brewer H, Ratusny D (1993) Behavioural frequency and psychological commitment: necessary concepts in the study of excessive exercising. *J Behav Med* **16**(6): 611–28

Davis C, Kennedy SH, Ravelski E, Dionne M (1994) The role of physical activity in the development and maintenance of eating disorders. *Psychol Med* **24**(4): 957–67

Deckelman MC, Dixon LB, Conley RR (1997) Comorbid bulimia and schizophrenia. *Int J Eat Disord* **1**: 101–105

Deep AL, Nagy LM, Weltzin TE, Rao R, Kaye WH (1995) Premorbid onset of psychopathology in long-term recovered anorexia nervosa. *Int J Eat Disorder* **17**(3): 291–7

Dennis AB, Sansone RA (1997) Treatment of patients with personality disorders. In: Garner DM, Garfinkel PE, eds. *Handbook of Treatment of Eating Disorders*. 2nd edn. The Guildford Press, London

DeVile CJ, Sufraz R, Lask BD, Stanhope R (1995) Lesson of the week: Occult intracranial tumours masquerading as early onset anorexia nervosa. *Br Med J* **311**: 1359–60

Devlin MJ, Goldfein JA, Carino JS, Wolk SL (2000a) Open treatment of overweight binge-eaters with phentermine and fluoxetine as an adjunct to cognitive behavioural therapy. *Int J Eat Disord* **28**(3): 325–32

Devlin MJ, Yanovski SZ, Wilson GT (2000b) Obesity: What mental health professionals need to know. *Am J Psychiatry* **157**: 854–66

Devuyst O, Lambert M, Rodhain J, Lefebvre C, Coche E (1993) Haematological changes and infectious complications in anorexia nervosa: A case control study. *Q J Med* **86**(12): 791–9

De Zwaan M, Nutzinger DO, Schonbeck G (1992) Binge-eating in overweight females. *Compre Psychiatry* **33**: 256–61

De Zwaan M, Mitchell JE, Raymond NC, Spitzer RL (1994) Binge eating disorder: Clinical features and treatment of a new diagnosis. *Harvard Review of Psychiatry* **1**(6): 310–325

Diabetes Control and Complications Trial Research Group (1993) Weight gain associated with intensive therapy in the diabetes control and complication's trial. *Diabetes Care* **11**: 567–73

DiDomenico L, Anderson AE (1988) Sociocultural considerations and sex differences in anorexia nervosa. In: Anderson A, ed. *Males with Eating Disorders*. Brunner/Mazel, New York

Dolan RJ, Mitchell J, Wakeling A (1988) Structural brain changes in patients with anorexia nervosa. *Psychol Med* **18**(2): 349–53

Dunkeld Turnbull J, Freeman CPL, Barry F, Annandale A (1987) Physical and psychological characteristics of five male bulimics. *Br J Psychiatry* **150**: 25–9

Edelman B (1982) Developmental differences in the conceptualization of obesity. *J Am Diet Assoc* **80**(2): 122–7

Eiholzer U, Bachmann S, L'Allemand (2000) Is there growth hormone deficiency in Prader Willi syndrome? Six arguments to support the presence of hypothalamic growth hormone deficiency in Prader Willi syndrome. *Horm Res* **53**(Suppl 3): 44–52

Eisler I, Dare C, Russell GFM, Szmuckler G, Le Grange D, Dodge E (1997) Family and individual therapy in anorexia nervosa. *Arch Gen Psychiatry* **54**(11): 1025–30

Fahy TA, Eisler I, Russell GFM (1993) Personality disorder and treatment response in bulimia nervosa. *Br J Psychiatry* **162**: 765–70

Fairburn CG (1997) Interpersonal psychotherapy for bulimia nervosa. In: Garner DM, Garfinkel PE, eds. *Handbook of Treatment for Eating Disorders*. 2nd edn. The Guildford Press, London

Fairburn CG, Cooper Z (1993) The eating disorders examination, 12th edition. In: Fairburn CG, Wilson GT, eds. *Binge Eating: Nature Assessment and Treatment*. Guildford Press, New York

Fairburn CG, Steel JM (1980) Anorexia nervosa in diabetes mellitus. *Br Med J* **280**: 1167–8

Fairburn CG, Cooper PJ (1982) Self-induced vomiting and bulimia nervosa: an undetected problem. *Br Med J* **284**: 1153–5

Fairburn CG, Cooper PJ (1984) The clinical features of bulimia nervosa. *Br J Psychiatry* **144**: 238–46

Fairburn CG, Garner DM (1986) The diagnosis of bulimia nervosa. *Int J Eat Disord* **5**: 403–19

Fairburn CG (1990) Bulimia Nervosa: Antidepressant or cognitive therapy is effective. *Br Med J* **300**: 485–6

Fairburn CG, Jones R, Peveler RC, Carr SJ, Soloman RA, O'Connor ME, Burton J, Hope RA (1991) Three psychological treatments for bulimia nervosa: A comparative trial. *Arch Gen Psychiatry* **48**: 463–9

Fairburn CG, Peveler RC, Davies B, Mann JI, Mayou RA (1991) Eating disorders in young adults with insulin-dependent diabetes mellitus: a controlled study. *Br Med J* **303**: 17–20

Fairburn CG, Jones R, Peveler RC, Hope RA, O'Connor M (1993) Psychotherapy and bulimia nervosa. Longer-term effects of interpersonal psychotherapy, behavior therapy, and cognitive therapy. *Arch Gen Psychiatry* **50**(6): 419–28

Fairburn CG, Welch SL, Hay PJ (1993) The classification of recurrent overeating: the 'binge-eating disorder' proposal. *Int J Eat Disord* **13**(2): 155–9

Fairburn CG, Norman PA, Welch SL, O'Connor ME Doll HA, Peveler RC (1995) A prospective study of outcome in bulimia nervosa and the long-term effects of three psychological treatments. *Arch Gen Psychiatry* **52**: 304–12

Fairburn CG, Welch SL, Norman PA, O'Connor ME, Doll HA (1996) Bias and bulimia nervosa: How typical are clinic cases? *Am J Psychiatry* **153**(3): 386–91

Fairburn CG, Welch SL, Doll HA, Davies BA, O'Connor BE (1997) Risk factors for bulimia nervosa: A community-based case-control study. *Arch Gen Psychiatry* **54**(6): 509–17

Fairburn CG, Doll HA, Welch SL, Hay PJ, Davies BA, O'Connor ME (1998) Risk factors for binge-eating disorder: A community-based case-control study. *Arch Gen Psychiatry* **55**(5): 425–32

Fairburn CG, Cooper Z, Doll HA, Welch SL (1999) Risk factors for anorexia nervosa: Three integrated case-control comparisons. *Arch Gen Psychiatry* **56**(5): 468–476

Fairburn CG, Cooper Z, Doll HA, Norman P, O'Connor M (2000) The natural course of bulimia nervosa and binge-eating disorder in young women. *Arch Gen Psychiatry* **57**(7): 659–65

Feillet F, Feillet-Coudrey C, Bard JM, Parra HJ, Favre E, Kabuth B, Fruchart JC, Vidailhet M (2000) Plasma cholesterol and endogenous cholesterol synthesis during refeeding in anorexia nervosa. *Clin Chim Acta* **294**(1–2): 45–56

Ferron SF (1999) Occult gastrointestinal bleeding with anorexia nervosa. *Am J Psychiatry* **156**(5): 801

Fichter MM, Quadflieg N, Gnutzman A (1997) Binge-eating disorder: Treatment outcome over a six-year course. *J Psychosom Res* **44**(3/4): 385–405

Fichter MM, Quadflieg N, Brandl B (1993) Recurrent overeating: An empirical comparison of binge eating disorder, bulimia nervosa and obesity. *Int J Eat Disord* **14**(1): 1–16

Field AE, Camargo CA, Barr Taylor C, Berkey CS, Colditz GA (1999) Relation of peer and media influences to the development of purging behaviours among pre-adolescent and adolescent girls. *Arch Paediatr Adolesc Med* **153**(11): 1184–9

Field AE, Colditz GA, Herzog DB, Heatherton TF (1996) Disordered eating: can women accurately recall their bingeing and purging behaviours ten years later? *Obesity Res* **4**: 153–9

Field AE, Wolf AM, Herzog DB, Cheung L, Colditz GA (1993) The relationship of calorific intake to frequency of dieting among pre-adolescent and adolescent girls. *J Am Acad Child Adolesc Psychiatry* **32**: 1246–52

Field AE, Colditz GA, Peterson KE (1997) Racial/ethnic and gender differences in concern with weight and in bulimic behaviours among adolescents. *Obesity Res* **5**: 447–54

Fisher M, Simpser E, Schneider M (2000) Hypophosphataemia secondary to oral refeeding in anorexia nervosa. *Int J Eat Disord* **28**(2): 181–7

Fisher BL, Barber AE (1999) Gastric bypass procedures. *Eur J Gastroenterol Hepatol* **11**(2): 93–7

Fitzgibbon ML, Spring B, Avellone ME, Blackman LR, Pingitore R, Stolley MR (1998) Correlates of binge eating in Hispanic, black and white women. *Int J Eat Disord* **24**(1): 43–52

Folsom AR, Kushi LH, Anderson KE, Mink PJ, Olsen JE, Hong CP, Sellars TA, Lazovich D, Prineas RJ (2000) Associations of general and abdominal obesity with multiple health outcomes in older women: the Iowa women's health study. *Arch Intern Med* **160**(14): 2117–28

Fombonne E (1995) Anorexia nervosa: No evidence of an increase. *Br J Psychiatry* **166**(4): 462–71

Ford ES, Williamson DF, Liu S (1997) Weight change and diabetes incidence: findings from a national cohort of US adults. *Am J Epidemiol* **146**(3): 214–22

Fornari V, Kaplan M, Sandberg E, Matthews M, Skolnick N, Katz JL (1992) Depressive and anxiety disorders in anorexia nervosa and bulimia nervosa. *Int J Eat Disord* **12**(1): 21–9

Foster GD, Sarwar DB, Wadden TA (1997) Psychological effects of weight cycling in obese persons: a review and research agenda. *Obesity Res* **5**: 474–88

Freeman C, Newton R (1995) Eating disorders. In: Macpherson A, ed. *Women's Problems in General Practice*. 3rd edn. Oxford General Practice Series. Oxford University Press, Oxford

Friedman JM, Halaas JL (1998) Leptin and the regulation of body weight in mammals. *Nature* **395**: 673

Friedman S, Vila G, Timsit J, Boitard C, Mouren-Simeoni MC (1998) Eating disorders and insulin-dependent diabetes mellitus (IDDM): relationships with glycaemic control and somatic complications. *Acta Psychiatr Scand* **97**(3): 206–12

Garfinkel PE, Garner DM (1982). *Anorexia nervosa: A multi-dimensional perspective*. Bruner Mazel, New York

Garfinkel PE, Moldofsky H, Garner DM (1980) The heterogenicity of anorexia nervosa: bulimia as a distinct subgroup. *Arch Gen Psychiatry* **37**: 1036–40

Garfinkel PE, Lin E, Goering P, Spegg C, Goldbloom DS, Kennedy S, Kaplan AS, Woodside DB (1995) Bulimia nervosa in a Canadian community sample: prevalence and comparison of subgroups. *Am J Psychiatry* **152**: 1052–8

Garner DM, Olmsted MP, Polivy J (1983) Development and validation of a multidimensional eating disorder for anorexia and bulimia. *Int J Eat Disord* **2**: 15–34

Garner DM, Vitousek KM, Pike KM (1997) Cognitive behavioural therapy for anorexia nervosa. In: Garner DM, Garfinkel PE, eds. *Handbook of Treatment for Eating Disorders*. 2nd edn. The Guildford Press, London

Garner DM, Olmsted MP, Bohr Y, Garfinkel PE (1982) The Eating Attitudes Test: psychometric features and clinical correlates. *Psychol Med* **12**(4): 871–8

Garner DM, Garfinkel PE (1980) Socio-cultural factors in the development of anorexia nervosa. *Psychol Med* **10**(4): 647–57

Garner DM (1991) *The Eating Disorders Inventory-2 Professional Manual*. Psychological Assessment Resources, Odessa, FL

Garner DM, Needleman LD (1997) Sequencing and Integration of Treatments. In: Garner DM, Garfinkel PE, eds. *Handbook of Treatment for Eating Disorders*. 2nd edn. The Guildford Press, London

Garner DM, Garfinkel PE (1979) The Eating Attitudes Test: An index of the symptoms of anorexia nervosa. *Psychol Med* **9**(2): 273–9

Garner DM, Rockert W, Olmsted MP, Johnson CL, Coscina DV (1985) Psychoeducational principles in the treatment of bulimia and anorexia nervosa. In: DM Garner, PE Garfinkel, eds. *Handbook of Psychotherapy for Anorexia and Bulimia*. Guildford Press, New York: 513–72

Garner DM (1997) Psychoeducational principles in treatment. In: Garner DM, Garfinkel PE, eds. *Treatment and Management of Eating Disorders*. 2nd edn. The Guildford Press, London

Garrow JS (1980) Dietary management of obesity and anorexia nervosa. *J Hum Nutr* **34**(2): 131–8

Gartner AF, Marcus RN, Halmi K, Loranger AW (1989) DSM-111-R personality disorders in patients with eating disorders. *Am J Psychiatry* **146**(12): 1585–1591

Gatling W, Hill R, Kirby M (1997) *Shared Care for Diabetes*. Isis Medical Media, Oxford

Geist R, Heinmaa M, Stephens D, Davis R, Katzman DK (2000) Comparison of family therapy and family group psychoeducation in adolescents with anorexia nervosa. *Can J Psychiatry* **45**(2): 173–8

Gelbart M (1999) Prader Willi syndrome. *Nurs Times* **9**(2): 36

Gelder M, Gath D, Mayou R (1991) *Oxford Textbook of Psychiatry*. Oxford University Press, Oxford

Gillberg IC, Rastam M, Gillberg C (1995) Anorexia nervosa 6 years after onset: Part 1. Personality disorders. *Compre Psychiatry* **36**(1): 61–9

Girardin E, Garoscio-Cholet M, Dechaud Lejeune H, Carrier E, Tourniaire J, Pugeat M (1991) Glucocorticoid receptors and lymphocytes in anorexia nervosa. *Clin Endocrinol* **35**(1): 79–84

Goldbloom DS, Olmsted MP (1993) Pharmacotherapy of bulimia nervosa with fluoxetine: Assessment of clinically significant attitudinal change. *Am J Psychiatry* **150**(5): 770–4

Golden NH, Jacobsen MS, Schebendach J, Solanto MV, Hertz SM, Shenker IR (1997) Resumption of menses in anorexia nervosa. *Arch Paediatr Adolesc Med* **151**(1): 16–21

Golden NH, Kreitzer P, Jacobsen MS, Chasalow FI, Schebendach J, Freedman SM, Shenker IR (1994) Disturbances in growth hormone secretion and action in adolescents with anorexia nervosa. *J Paediatr* **125**(4): 655–60

Golden NH, Ashtari M, Kohn MR, Patel M, Jacobson MS, Fletcher A, Shenker IR (1996) Reversibility of cerebral ventricular enlargement in anorexia nervosa, demonstrated by quantitative magnetic resonance imaging. *J Paediatr* **128**(2): 296–301

Goldfein JA, Devlin MJ, Spitzer RL (2000) Cognitive behavioural therapy for the treatment of binge-eating disorder: What constitutes success? *Am J Psychiatry* **157**(7): 1051–6

Gordon RA (1990) *Anorexia and bulimia: Anatomy of a social epidemic.* Blackwell, Oxford

Greenfield D, Mickley D, Quinlan DM, Roloff P (1995) Hypokalaemia in outpatients with eating disorders. *Am J Psychiatry* **152**(1): 60–3

Greenfield D, Quinlan D, Harding P (1987) Eating behaviour in an adolescent population. *Int J Eat Disord* **6**: 99–111

Grinspoon S, Miller K, Coyle C, Krempin J Armstrong C, Pitts S *et al* (1999) Severity of osteopenia in oestrogen deficient women with anorexia nervosa and hypothalmic amenorrhoea. *J Clin Endocrinol Metab* **84**(6): 2049–55

Gwirtsman HE, Kaye WH, George DT, Jimerson DC, Ebert MH, Gold PW (1989) Central and peripheral ACTH and cortisol levels in anorexia nervosa and bulimia. *Arch Gen Psychiatry* **46**: 61–9

Haffner SM (2000) Obesity and the metabolic syndrome: the San Antonio heart study. *Br J Nutr* **83**(Suppl 1): S67–70

Hall A, Crisp HA (1987) Brief psychotherapy in the treatment of anorexia nervosa: outcome at one year. *Br J Psychiatry* **151**: 185–91

Hall RCW, Hoffman RS, Beresford TP, Wooley B, Klassen-Hall A, Kubasak L (1989) Physical illness encountered in patients with eating disorders. *Psychosomatics* **30**(2): 174–91

Halmi KA, Eckert E, Lodu TJ, Cohen J (1986) Anorexia nervosa: Treatment efficacy of cyproheptadine and amitryptalline. *Arch Gen Psychiatry* **43**: 117–81

Halmi KA (1995) Current concepts and definitions. In: Szmukler G, Dare C, Treasure J, eds. *Handbook of Eating Disorders: Theory , treatment and research.* Wiley, Chichester

Halmi KA, Eckert E, Marchi P, Sampugnaro V, Apple R, Cohen J (1991) Comorbidity of psychiatric diagnoses in anorexia nervosa. *Arch Gen Psychiatry* **48**: 712–8

Halmi KA, Long M, Stunkard AJ, Mason E (1980) Psychiatric diagnosis of morbidly obese gastric bypass patients. *Am J Psychiatry* **137**: 470–472

Halmi KA (1997) Models to conceptualize risk factors for bulimia nervosa. *Arch Gen Psychiatry* **54**(6): 507–8

Halmi KA (1999) Eating disorders: Defining the phenotype and reinventing the treatment. *Am J Psychiatry* **156**(11): 1673–5

Hamburger WH (1951) Emotional aspects of obesity. *Med Clin North Am* **35**: 483–9

Han TS, Richmond P, Avenall A, Lean ME (1997) Waist circumference reduction and cardiovascular benefits during weight loss in women. *Int J Obesity Related Metabolic Disorders* **21**(2): 127–34

Harries AD, Fitzsimons E, Fifield R, Dew MJ, Rhodes J (1983) Platelet count: a simple measure of activity in Crohn's disease. *Br Med J* **286**: 1476

Hartman D, Crisp A, Rooney B, Rackow C, Atkinson R, Patel S (2000) Bone density of women who have recovered from anorexia nervosa. *Int J Eat Disord* **28**(1): 107–12

Hawley RM (1985) The outcome of anorexia nervosa in younger subjects. *Br J Psychiatry* **146**: 657–60

Hay PJ, Fairburn CG, Doll HA (1996) The classification of bulimic eating disorders: a community-based cluster analysis study. *Psychol Med* **26**(4): 801–12

Hebebrand J, Wehmeier PM, Remschmidt H (2000) Weight criteria for diagnosis of anorexia nervosa. *Am J Psychiatry* **157**(6): 1024

Hediger C, Rost B, Itin P (2000) Cutaneous manifestations in anorexia nervosa. *Schweiz Med Wochenschr* **130**(16): 565–75

Henderson M, Freeman CPL (1987) A self-rating scale for bulimia. The 'Bite'. *Br J Psychiatry* **150**: 18–24

Hendren RL, De Backer I, Pandina GJ (2000) Review of neuroimaging studies of child and adolescent psychiatric disorders from the past 10 years. *J Am Acad Child Adolesc Psychiatry* **39**(7): 815–28

Herman P, Polivy J (1991) Fat is a psychological issue. *New Scientist,* 16 November: 41–5

Herpetz S, Wagener R, Albus C, Kocnar M, Wagner R *et al* (1998) Diabetes mellitus and eating disorders: A multicentre study on the comorbidity of the two diseases. *J Psychosom Res* **44**(3–4): 503–15

Herpetz S, Albus C, Wagener R, Kocnar M, Wagner R Henning A *et al* (1998) Comorbidity of diabetes and eating disorders. *Diabetes Care* **21**(7): 1110

Herpetz S, Albus C, Lohff S, Michalski K, Masrour M, Lichtblau K *et al* (2000) Characteristics of diabetic patients with and without an eating disorder. *Psychother Psychosom Med Psychol* **50**(3–4): 161–168

Herpetz-Dahlmann B (1998/1999) Course and outcome in adolescent anorexia nervosa: Psychiatric morbidity and psychosocial functioning in adults with former anorexia nervosa. *Fortschr Fortbildung Med* **22**: 193–198+336

Herzog DB, Norman DK, Gordon C, Pepose M (1984) Sexual conflict and eating disorders in 27 males. *Am J Psychiatry* **141**: 989–990

Herzog DB, Keler MB, Lavori PW, Sacks NR (1991) The course and outcome of bulimia nervosa. *J Clin Psychiatry* **52**(Suppl 10): 4–8

Herzog DB, Sacks NR, Keller MB, Lavori PW, von Ranson KB, Gray HM (1993) Patterns and predictors of recovery in anorexia nervosa and bulimia nervosa. *J Am Acad Child Adolesc Psychiatry* **32**: 835–42

Herzog W, Deter HC, Fiehn W, Petzold E (1997) Medical findings and predictors of long-term outcome in anorexia nervosa: a prospective 12-year follow-up study. *Psychol Med* **27**(2): 269–79

Ho PC, Dweik R, Cohen MC (1998) Rapidly reversible cardiomyopathy associated with chronic ipecac ingestion. *Clin Cardiol* **21**(10): 780–3

Hoek HW (1991) The incidence and prevalence of anorexia nervosa and bulimia nervosa in primary care. *Psychol Med* **21**(2): 455–60

Hoek HW, Bartelds AI, Bosveld JJ, Van Der Graaf Y, Limpens VE, Maiwald M, Spaaij CJ (1995) Impact of urbanisation on detection rates of eating disorders. *Am J Psychiatry* **152**(9): 1272–8

Holderness CC, Brooks-Gunn J, Warren MP (1994) Co-morbidity of eating disorders and substance abuse, review of the literature. *Int J Eat Disord* **16**(1): 1–34

Holman RT, Adams CE, Nelson RA, Grater SJ, Jaskiewicz JA, Johnson SB, Erdman JW Jr (1995) Patients with anorexia nervosa demonstrate deficiencies of selected essential fatty acids, compensatory changes in non-essential fatty acids and decreased fluidity of plasma lipids. *J Nutr* **125**(4): 901–7

Hope RA, Longmore JM, Hodgetts TJ, Ramrakha PS (1994) *Oxford Handbook of Clinical Medicine.* 3rd edn. Oxford University Press, Oxford

Horesh N, Apter A, Lepkifker E, Ratzoni G, Weizmann R, Tyano S (1995) Life events and severe anorexia nervosa in adolescence. *Acta Psychiatr Scand* **91**(1): 5–9

Howard WT, Evans KK, Quintero-Howard CV, Bowers WA, Anderson AE (1999) Predictors of success or failure of transition to day hospital treatment for inpatients with anorexia nervosa. *Am J Psychiatry* **156**: 1697–1702

Hsu LKG, Chesler BE, Santhouse R (1990) Bulimia nervosa in eleven sets of twins: a clinical report. *Int J Eat Disord* **9**: 275–82

Hsu LKG (1982) Outcome in anorexia nervosa: a review of the literature (1954–1978). *Arch Gen Psychiatry* **37**(9): 1041–6

Hsu LK, Clement L, Santhouse R, Ju ES (1991) Treatment of bulimia nervosa with lithium carbonate: A controlled study. *J Nerv Ment Disord* **179**(6): 351–5

Hubert HB, Feinleib M, Mcnamara PM, Castelli WP (1983) Obesity as an independent risk factor for cardiovascular disease: a 26-year follow-up of patients in the Framingham study. *Circulation* **67**: 968–77

Hudson JI, Pope HG, Jonas JM, Yurgelun-Todd D, Frankenburg FR (1987) A controlled family history study of bulimia. *Psychol Med* **17**(4): 883–90

Hudson JI, Pope HG, Jonas JM *et al* (1989) Family history study of anorexia nervosa and bulimia. *Br J Psychiatry* **142**: 133–138

Hudson JI, Mcelroy SL, Raymond NC, Crow S, Keck PE, Carter WP *et al* (1998) Fluvoxamine in the treatment of binge-eating disorder: A multicentre placebo-controlled double-blind trial. *Am J Psychiatry* **155**(12): 1756–62

Isner JM, Roberts WC, Heymsfield SB, Jager J (1985) Anorexia nervosa and sudden death. *Ann Int Med* **102**: 49–52

Jackson TD, Grilo CM, Masheb M (2000) Teasing history, onset of obesity, current eating disorder psychopathology, body dissatisfaction, and psychological functioning in binge eating disorder. *Obesity Res* **8**: 451–8

Jenkins AP, Treasure J, Thompson RPH (1988) Crohn's disease presenting as anorexia nervosa. *Br Med J* **296**: 699–70

Jick H, Vasilakis C, Weinrauch LA, Meier CR, Jick SS, Derby LE (1998) A population based study of appetite suppressant drugs and the risk of cardiac valve regurgitation. *New Engl J Med* **339**(11): 719–24

Jimerson DC, Wolfe BE, Metzger ED, Finkelstein DM, Cooper TD, Levine JM (1997) Decreased serotonin function in bulimia nervosa. *Arch Gen Psychiatry* **54**(6): 529–34

Johnson-Sabine E, Reiss D, Dayson D (1992) Bulimia nervosa: a 5-year follow-up study. *Psychol Med* **22**(4): 951–9

Joiner TE, Jnr Katz J, Heatherton TF (2000) Personality features of late adolescent females and males with chronic bulimic symptoms. *Int J Eat Disord* **27**(2): 191–7

Jones JM, Lawson ML, Daneman D, Olmsted MP, Rodin G (2000) Eating disorders in adolescent females with and without type 1 diabetes: cross-sectional study. *Br Med J* **320**: 1563–6

Jones SL, O'Bryan M, Doheny RN, Jones PK, Bradley N (1986) Binge eaters: a comparison of eating patterns of those who admit to bingeing and those who do not. *J Adv Nurs* **11**(5): 545–52

Joos A, Steinert T (1997) Comorbidity of schizophrenia and anorexia nervosa, bulimic type: A forensic study. *Nervenarzt* **68**(5): 417–20

Joughan NA, Crisp AH, Gowers S., Bhat AV (1991) The clinical features of late onset anorexia nervosa. *Postgrad Med J* **67**(793): 973–7

Kaltiala-Heino R, Rissanen A, Rimpela M, Rantanen P (1999) Bulimia and bulimic behaviour in middle adolescence: more common than thought? *Acta Psychiatr Scand* **100**(1): 33–9

Kamal N, Chami T, Anderson A, Rossell FA, Schuster MM, Whitehead WE (1991) Delayed gastro-intestinal transit times in anorexia nervosa and bulimia nervosa. *Gastroenterology* **101**(5): 1320–4

Kannel WB, Larson M (1993) Long-term epidemiologic prediction of coronary disease: The Framingham experience. *Cardiology* **82**(2–3): 137–52

Kassett JA, Gwirtsman HE, Kaye WH, Brandt HA, Jimerson DC (1988) Pattern of onset of bulimic symptoms in anorexia nervosa. *Am J Psychiatry* **145**(10): 1287–8

Katzman DK, Lambe EK, Mikulis DJ, Ridgely JN, Goldbloom DS, Zipursky RB (1996) Cerebral grey and white matter volume deficits in adolescent females with anorexia nervosa. *J Paediatr* **129**: 794–803

Kaye WH (1993) Relationship between anorexia and obsessive and compulsive behaviours. *Psychiatric Annals* **23**: 365–73

Keel PK, Mitchell JE (1997) Outcome in bulimia nervosa. *Am J Psychiatry* **154**(3): 313–21

Keel PK, Mitchell JE, Miller KB, Davis TL, Crow SJ (1999) Long term outcome of bulimia nervosa. *Arch Gen Psychiatry* **56**(1): 63–9

Keel PK, Mitchell JE, Miller KB, Davis TL, Crow SJ (2000) Predictive validity of bulimia nervosa as a diagnostic category. *Am J Psychiatry* **157**(1): 136–8

Keller MB, Herzog DB, Lavori PW, Bradburn IS, Mahoney EM (1992) The naturalist history of bulimia nervosa: extraordinarily high rates of chronicity, relapse, recurrence and psychosocial morbidity. *Int J Eat Disord* **12**: 1–10

Kendler KS, Maclean C, Neale M, Kessler R, Heath A, Eaves L (1991) The genetic epidemiology of bulimia nervosa. *Am J Psychiatry* **148**(12): 1627–37

Kennedy SH, Goldbloom DS (1991) Current perspectives on drug therapies for anorexia nervosa and bulimia nervosa. *Drugs* **41**(3): 367–77

Kennedy SH, Garfinkel PE (1992) Advances in diagnosis and treatment of anorexia nervosa and bulimia nervosa. *Can J Psychiatry — Revue Canadienne de Psychiatrie* **37**(5): 309–15

Kennedy SH, Kaplan AS, Garfinkel PE, Rockert W, Toner B, Abbey SE, (1994) Depression in anorexia nervosa and bulimia nervosa:discriminating depressive symptoms and episodes. *J Psychosom Res* **38**(7): 773–82

Kenny T (1991) Anorexia nervosa: a nursing challenge that can bring results. *Prof Nurse* **7**(7): 666–9

Kholy ME, Job JC, Chaussain JL (1986) Growth of anorexic adolescents. *Arch French Paediatrics* **43**(1): 35–40

King MB (1989) Eating disorders in a general practice population: prevalence, characteristics and follow up at twelve to eighteen months. *Psychol Med* (Suppl) **14**: 1–34

Kingston K, Szmukler G, Andrewes D, Tress B, Desmond P (1996) Neuropsychological and structural brain changes in anorexia nervosa before and after refeeding. *Psychol Med* **26**(1): 15–28

Kinzl JF, Traweger C, Trefalt E, Mangweth B, Biebl W (1999) Binge-eating disorder in males: a population based investigation. *Eating Weight Disorders* **4**(4): 169–74

Kirkley BG, Burge JC, Ammerman A (1988) Dietary restraint, binge eating and dietary behaviour patterns. *Int J Eat Disord* **7**: 771–8

Kiss A, Wiesnagrotzki S, Abatzi T, Meryn S, Haubenstock A, Base W (1989) Upper gastrointestinal endoscopy findings in patients with long standing bulimia nervosa. *Gastrointest Endosc* **35**(6): 516–18

Klem ML, Wing RR, Mcguire MT, Seagle HM, Hill JO (1997) A descriptive study of individuals successful at long-term maintenance of substantial weight loss. *Am J Clin Nutr* **67**(5): 946

Kobrin S (1999) Preventing progression of diabetic nephropathy. *Hospital Med* February: 44–53

Kollai M, Bonyhay I, Jokkel G Szonyi L (1994) Eating and Weight Disorders. *Eur Heart J* **15**(8): 1113–8

Kolotkin RL, Revis ES, Kirkley BG, Janick L (1987) Binge eating in obesity. *J Consult Clin Psychol* **55**(6): 872–6

Lacey JH (1992) The treatment demands for bulimia: a catchment area report of referral rates and demography. *Psychiatr Bull* **16**: 203–5

Lacey H, Smith G (1987) Bulimia nervosa: The impact of pregnancy on mother and baby. *Br J Psychiatry* **150**: 777–81

Lacey J, Crisp A, Hart G, Kirkwood B (1979) Weight and skeletal maturation — a study of radiological and chronological age in an anorexia population. *Postgrad Med J* **55**: 381–5

Laessle RG, Kittle S, Fichter MM, Wittchen HU, Pirke KM (1987) Major affective disorder in anorexia nervosa and bulimia: a descriptive diagnostic study. *Br J Psychiatry* **151**: 785–9

Laessle RG, Beumont PJV, Butow P, Lennerts W, O'Connor M, Pirke KM *et al* (1991) A comparison of nutritional management with stress management in the treatment of bulimia nervosa. *Br J Psychiatry* **159**: 250–61

Lakin JA, Steen SN, Oppliger RA (1990) Eating behaviours, weight loss methods, and nutrition practices among high school wrestlers. *J Community Health Nurs* **7**(4): 223–34

Lam RW, Goldner EM, Solyom L, Remick RA (1994) A controlled study of light therapy for bulimia nervosa. *Am J Psychiatry* **151**(5): 744–50

Lambe EK, Katzman DK, Mikulis DJ, Kennedy SH, Zipursky RB (1997) Cerebral grey matter volume deficits after weight recovery from anorexia nervosa. *Arch Gen Psychiatry* **54**(6): 537–42

Lambert MJ, DeJulio SS, Stein DM (1978) Therapist interpersonal skills: process, outcome, methodological considerations and recommendations for future research. *Psychol Bull* **85**(3): 467–89

Lask B, Bryant Waugh R (1997) Preburtal eating disorders. In: Garner DM, Garfinkel PE, eds. *Handbook of Treatment for Eating Disorders*. 2nd edn. The Guildford Press, New York, London

Lee S (2000) Eating disorders are becoming more common in the East too. *Br Med J* **321**: 1023

Lee S, Lee AM (2000) Disordered eating in three communities of China: a comparative study of female high school students in Hong Kong, Shenzhen, and rural Hunan. *Int J Eat Disord* **27**(3): 317–27

Legge A (2000) Approaches to preventing an epidemic of obesity. *Community Nurse* **6**(8): 13–14

Le Heuzey MF, Mouren Simeoni MC (1999) Abdelfattah Perdrizet Velrat Koupernik. *An Med Psycholog* **157**(10): 717–21

Levin PA, Falko J, Dixon K, Gallup EM, Saunders W (1980) Benign parotid enlargement in bulimia. *Ann Intern Med* **93**(6): 827–9

Lieberman S (1989) A family with four bulimic children. *Int J Eat Disord* **8**: 101–4

Lilenfield LR, Kaye WH, Greeno CG, Merikangas KR, Plotnicov KH, Pollice C *et al* (1998) A controlled family study of anorexia nervosa and bulimia nervosa: psychiatric disorders in first degree relatives and affects of proband comorbidity. *Arch Gen Psychiatry* **55**(7): 603–10

Lilenfield L, Kaye W, Greeno C Merikangas KR, Plotnicov KH, Pollice C *et al* (1997) Psychiatric disorders in women with bulimia nervosa and their first degree relatives: effects of comorbid substance dependence. *Int J Eat Disord* **22**: 253–64

Loeb KL, Wilson GT, Gilbert JS, Labouvie E (2000) Guided and unguided self-help for binge eating. *Behav Res Ther* **38**: 259–72

Lowe MR, Miller Kovach K, Frye N, Phelan S (1999) An initial evaluation of a commercial weight loss program: short-term effects on weight, eating behaviour and mood. *Obesity Res* **7**: 51–59

Lucas AR (1993) Has the incidence of anorexia nervosa increased since the 1930s? *Neuropsychiatric de l'Enfance et de l'Adolescence* **41**(5–6): 260–3

Lyketsos GC, Paterakis P, Beis A (1985) Eating disorders in schizophrenia. *Br J Psychiatry* **146**: 255–61

Lyritis GP, Schoenau E, Skarantavos G (2000) Osteopaenic syndromes in the adolescent female. *Ann N Y Acad Sci* **900**: 403–8

Maloney MJ, McGuire J, Daniels SR, Specker B (1989) Dieting behaviour and eating attitudes in children. *Paediatrics* **8**(3): 482–7

Mannucci E, Ricca Rotella CM (1995) Clinical features of binge eating disorder in type 1 diabetes: A case report. *Int J Eat Disord* **21**(1): 99–102

Mannucci E, Ricca V, Barcuilli E, Di Bernardo M, Travaglini R, Cabras PL, Rotella CM (1999) Quality of life and overweight: the obesity related well-being (Orwell 97) questionnaire. *Addictive Behaviours* **24**(3): 345–57

Manson JE, Colditz GA, Stamper MJ, Willett WC, Rosner B, Monson RR *et al* (1990) A prospective study of obesity and risk of coronary heart disease in women. *New Engl J Med* **322**(13): 882–9Marcus MD, Wing RR, Hopkins J (1988) Obese binge eaters: affect, cognition's, and response to behavioural weight control. *J Consult Clin Psychol* **3**: 433–9

Marcus MD, Wing RR, Hopkins J (1988) Obese binge eaters: affect, cognitions and response to behavoural weight control. *J Consult Clin Psychol* **56**(3): 433–9

Marcus MD, Wing RR, Ewing L, Kern E, Mcdermott M, Gooding W (1990) A double blind placebo-controlled trial of fluoxetine plus behaviour modification in the treatment of obese binge eaters and non-binge eaters. *Am J Psychiatry* **147**(7): 876–81

Marcus MD, Smith D, Santelli R, Kaye W (1992) Characterisation of eating disordered behaviour in obese binge eaters. *Int J Eat Disord* **12**: 249–55

Marcus MD (1993) Binge-eating in obesity. In: Fairbur CG, Wilson GT, eds. *Binge Eating: Nature, Assessment and Treatment*. Guildford Press, New York

Marcus MD (1997) Adapting treatment for patients with binge-eating disorder. In: Garner DM, Garfinkel PE, eds. *Handbook of Treatment for Eating Disorders*. 2nd edn. The Guildford Press, London

Margo JL (1987) Anorexia nervosa in males: a comparison with female patients. *Br J Psychiatry* **151**: 80–3

Marrazzi MA, Bacon JP, Kinzie J, Luby ED (1995) Naltrexone use in the treatment of anorexia nervosa and bulimia nervosa. *Int Clin Psychopharmacol* **10**(3): 163–172

Matsunaga H, Kiriike N (1997) Personality disorders in patients with treatment resistant disorders. *Jpn J Psychosom Med* **37**(1): 61–8

Matsunaga H, Kiriike N, Iwasake Y, Miyati A, Yamagami S (1999) Clinical characteristics in patients with anorexia nervosa and obsessive-compulsive disorder. *Psychol Med* **29**(2): 407–14

McCallum RW, Grill BB, Lange R, Planky M, Glass EE *et al* (1985) Definition of a gastric emptying abnormality in patients with anorexia nervosa. *Dig Dis Sci* **30**(8): 713–722

McCann UD, Agras WS (1990) Successful treatment of non-purging bulimia nervosa with desipramine: a double blind placebo-controlled study. *Am J Psychiatry* **147**(11): 1509–13

McClain CJ, Humphries LL, Hill KK, Nicki NJ (1993) Gastro-intestinal and nutritional aspects of eating disorders. *J Am College Nutrition* **12**(4): 466–74

McClain MR, Srinivasan SR, Chen W, Steinmann WC, Berenson GS (2000) Risk of type 2 diabetes mellitus in young adults from a biracial community: the bogalusa heart study. *Prev Med* **31**(1): 1–7

McElroy SM, Casuto LS, Nelson EB, Lake KA, Soutullo CA *et al* (2000) Placebo-controlled trial of sertraline in the treatment of binge-eating disorder. *Am J Psychiatry* **157**(6): 1004–6

McGuire MT, Wing RR, Klem ML, Hill JO (1999) Behavioural strategies of individuals who have maintained long-term weight losses. *Obesity Res* **7**: 334–41

McLoughlin DM, Wassif WS, Morton J, Spargo E, Peters TJ *et al* (2000) Metabolic abnormalities associated with skeletal myopathy in severe anorexia nervosa. *Nutrition* **16**(3): 192–6

McSherry JA (1984) The diagnostic challenge of anorexia nervosa. *Am Fam Physician* **29**(2): 141–5

Meadows GN, Palmer RL, Newball EUM, Kenrick JMT (1986) Eating attitudes and disorder in young women: a general practice based survey. *Psychol Med* **16**(2): 351–7

Mitchel JE, Pyle RL, Miner RA (1982) Gastric dilatation as a complication of bulimia. *Psychosom* **23**: 96–9

Mitchell JE, Pyle RL, Eckert ED, Hatsuka D, Lentz R (1983) Electrolyte and other physiological abnormalities in patients with bulimia. *Psychol Med* **13**(2): 273–8

Mitchell JE, Hatsukami D, Eckert ED Pyle RE (1985) Characteristics of 275 patients with bulimia. *Am J Psychiatry* **142**: 482–5

Mitchell JE, Fletcher L, Pyle RL, Eckert ED, Hatsukami DK *et al* (1989) The impact of treatment on meal patterns in patients with bulimia nervosa. *Int J Eat Disord* **8**: 167–72

Mitchell JE, Hatsukami D, Pyle RL, Eckert ED, Soll (1987) Late onset bulimia. *Compre Psychiatry* **28**: 323–8

Mitchell JE, Pomeroy C, Adson DE (1997) Managing medical complications. In: Garner DM, Garfinkel PE, eds. *Handbook of Treatment for Eating Disorders*. 2nd edn. The Guildford Press, London

Moodie DS (1987) Anorexia and the heart. Results of studies to assess the effects. *Postgrad Med* **81**(8): 46–48, 51–55

Moodie DS, Salcedo E (1983) Cardiac function in adolescents and young adults with anorexia nervosa. *J Adolesc Health Care* **4**(1): 9–14

Moore R, Mills JH (1981) Naloxone in the treatment of anorexia nervosa: effect on weight gain and lipolysis. *J Proc R Soc Med* **74**: 129–131

Morant H (2000) British Medical Association demands a more responsible media attitude on body image. *Br Med J* **320**: 1495

Morgan JF, Lacey H, Sedgewick PM (1999) Impact of pregnancy on bulimia. *Br J Psychiatry* **174**: 135–40

Morgan JF (1999) Eating disorders and gynaecology: knowledge and attitudes among clinicians. *Acta Obstet Gynecol Scand* **78**(3): 233–9

Morgan JF, Reid F, Lacey JH (1999) The SCOFF questionnaire: assessment of a new screening tool for eating disorders. *Br Med J* **319**: 1467–8

Morgan HG, Russell GFM (1975) Value of family background and clinical features as predictors of long term outcome in anorexia nervosa: four-year follow-up study of forty-one patients. *Psychol Med* **5**: 355–71

Mumford DB, Whitehouse AM (1988) Increased prevalence of bulimia nervosa among Asian schoolgirls. *Br Med J* **297**: 718

Murakami A, Suwaki H (1999) A study of anorexia nervosa, especially on the shifts of its subtypes and psychiatric comorbidity in the clinical course. *Jpn J Psychosom Med* **39**(7): 515–523

Murciano D, Rigaud D, Pingleton S, Armengaud MH, Melchior JC, Aubier M (1994) Diaphramatic function in severely malnourished patients with anorexia nervosa: Effects of renutrition. *Am J Respir Crit Care Med* **150**(6 Pt 1): 1569–74

Mussell MP, Mitchell JE, Weller CL, Raymond NC, Crow SJ, Crosby RD (1995) Onset of binge-eating, dieting, obesity, and mood disorders among subjects seeking treatment for binge eating disorder. *Int J Eat Disord* **17**: 395–401

Mussell MP, Peterson CB, Weller CL, Crosby RD, de Zwaan M, Mitchell JE (1996a) Differences in body image and depression among obese women with and without binge eating disorder. *Obesity Res* **4**(5): 431–9

Mussell MP, Mitchell JE, de Zwaan M, Crosby RD, Seim HC Crow SJ (1996b) Clinical characteristics associated with binge eating in obese females: a descriptive study. *Int J Obesity* **20**: 324–31

Mussell MP, Mitchell JE, Crosby RD, Fulkerson JA, Hoberman HM, Romano JL (2000) Commitment to treatment goals in prediction of group behavioural therapy treatment outcome for women with bulimia nervosa. *J Consult Clin Psychol* **68**(3): 432–7

Must A, Spadano J, Coakley E, Field AE, Colditz G, Dietz WH (1999) The disease burden associated with overweight and obesity. *JAMA* **282**(16): 1523–9

Myerson M, Gutin B, Warren MP, May MT, Contento I, Lee M *et al* (1991) Resting metabolic rate and energy balance in amenorrhoeic and eumenorrhoeic runners. *Med Sci Sports Exerc* **23**(1): 15–22

Nadaoka T, Oiji A, Takahashi S, Moriaka Y, Kashiwakura M, Totsuka S (1996) An epidemiological study of eating disorders in a Northern area of Japan. *Acta Psychiatr Scand* **93**(4): 305–10

Natori Y, Yamaguchi N, Koike S, Aoyama A, Tsuchibuchi S *et al* (1994) Thyroid function in patients with anorexia nervosa and depression. *Rinsho Byori* **42**(12): 1268–72

Nestel PJ (1973) Cholesterol metabolism in anorexia nervosa and hypercholesteraemia. *J Clin Endocrinol Metab* **38**(2): 325–8

Neumark-Sztainer D, Hannan PJ (2000) Weight related behaviours among adolescent girls and boys. Results from a national survey. *Arch Paediatr Adolesc Med* **154**(6): 569–577

Newman MM, Gold MS (1992) Preliminary findings of patterns of substance abuse in eating disorder patients. *Am J Drug Alcohol Abuse* **18**: 207–11

Newton JR, Freeman CP, Hannan WJ, Cowen S (1993) Osteoporosis and normal weight bulimia nervosa — which patients are at risk? *J Psychosom Res* **37**(3): 239–47

Norring CEA, Sohlberg SS (1993) Outcome, recovery, relapse and mortality across six years in patients with clinical eating disorders. *Acta Psychiatr Scand* **87**(6): 437–44

North C, Gowers S, Byram V (1997) Family functioning and life events in the outcome of adolescent anorexia nervosa. *Br J Psychiatry* **171**: 545–9

Nylander I (1971) The feeling of being fat and dieting in a school population: epidemiologic interview investigation. *Acta Sociomedica Scandinavica* **3**: 17–26

O'Brien ET, Beevers DG, Marshall HJ (1995) *ABC of Hypertension*. 3rd edn. British Medical Journal Publishing Group, London

O'Dea JA, Abraham S (1999) Onset of disordered eating attitudes and behaviours in early adolescence: interplay of pubertal status, gender, weight and age. *Adolescence* **34**(136): 671–79

O'Dea JA, Abraham S (2000) Improving the body image, eating attitudes, and behaviours of young male and female adolescents: A new educational approach that focuses on self esteem. *Int J Eat Disord* **28**: 43–57

Oka Y, Ito T, Sekine I, Sada T, Okabe F, Naito *et al* (1984) Mitral valve prolapse in patients with anorexia nervosa. *J Cardiography* **14**(3): 483–91

Olivardio R, Pope HG, Mangweth B, Hudson JI (1995) Eating disorders in college men. *Am J Psychiatry* **152**(9): 1279–85

Olmsted MP, Kaplan AS, Rockert W (1994) Rate and prediction of relapse in bulimia nervosa. *Am J Psychiatry* **151**(5): 738–43

Oppliger RA, Landry GA, Foster SW Lambrecht AC (1993) Bulimic behaviours among interscholastic wrestlers: a state-wide survey. *Paediatrics* **91**(4): 826–31

Osona Rodriguez B, Gonzalez Vicent M, Mencia Bartolome S, Casada Flores J (2000) Suicide in paediatric patients: thirty cases. *An Espana Pediatria* **52**(1): 31–5

Palla B, Litt IF (1988) Medical complications of eating disorders in adolescents. *Paediatr* **81**(5): 613–23

Palmer EP, Guay AT (1985) Reversible myopathy secondary to abuse of ipecac in patients with major eating disorders. *N Engl J Med* **313**(23): 1457–9

Palmer RL, Oppenheimer R, Dignon D, Chaloner DA, Howells K (1990) Childhood sexual experiences with adults reported by women with eating disorders: an extended series. *Br J Psychiatry* **156**: 699–703

Palmer TA (1990) Anorexia nervosa, bulimia nervosa, causal theories and treatment. *Nurse Pract* **15**(4): 12–21

Panagiotopoulos C, McCrindle BW, Hick K, Katzman DK (2000) Electrocardiographic findings in adolescents with eating disorders. *Paediatrics* **105**(5): 1100–5

Partsch CJ, Lammer C, Gillessen-Kaesbach G, Pankau R (2000) Adult patients with Prader Willi syndrome: clinical characteristics, life circumstances and growth hormone secretion. *Growth Hormone IGF Research*, 10 April: Suppl B, S81–5

Patton GC (1988) Mortality in eating disorders. *Psychol Med* **18**: 947–51

Patton GC, Johnson Sabine E, Wood K, Mann AH, Wakeling A (1990) Abnormal eating attitudes in London schoolgirls — a prospective epidemiological study: outcome at twelve-month follow-up. *Psychol Med* **20**: 383–94

Patton GC, Selzer R, Coffey C, Carlin JB, Wolfe R (1999) Onset of adolescent eating disorders: population based cohort study over three years. *Br Med J* **318**: 765–8

Pazzagli A, Monti M (2000) Dysphoria and aloneness in borderline personality disorder. *Psychopathology* **33**(4): 220–6

Perry IJ, Wannamethee SG, Walker MK, Thompson AG, Whincup PH, Shaper AG (1995) Prospective study of risk factors for the development of non-insulin-dependent diabetes in middle-aged British men. *Br Med J* **310**: 560–4

Peterson CB, Crow SJ, Nugent S, Mitchell JE, Engbloom S, Pederson Mussell M, (1999) Predictors of treatment outcome for binge-eating disorder. *Int J Eat Disord* **28**(2): 131–8

Peveler R, Fairburn C (1990) Eating disorders in women who abuse alcohol. *Br J Addiction to Alcohol & Other Drugs* **85**(12): 1633–8

Piggott TA (1996) Obsessive compulsive disorder: Where the serotonin selectivity story begins. *J Clin Psychiatry* **57**: 11–20

Pitel AU, Monaco L, Geffken GR, Silverstein JH (1998) Diagnosis and treatment of an adolescent with comorbid type 1diabetes mellitus and anorexia nervosa. *Clin Paediatr*, August: 491–5

Polito A, Fabbri A, Ferro-Luzzi A, Cuzzolaro M, Censi L, Ciarapica D *et al* (2000) Basal metabolic rate in anorexia nervosa: relation to body composition and leptin concentrations. *Am J Clin Nutr* **71**(6): 1495–502

Pollice C, Kaye WH, Greeno CG, Weltzin TE (1997) Relationship of depression, anxiety and obsessionality to the state of illness in anorexia nervosa. *Int J Eat Disord* **21**(4): 367–76

Pope HG, Hudson JI (1992) Is childhood sexual abuse a risk factor for bulimia nervosa? *Am J Psychiatry* **149**(4): 455–64

Powers PS (1982) Heart failure during the treatment of anorexia nervosa. *Am J Psychiatry* **139**(9): 1167–70

Pryor T, Wiederman MW, Mcgilley B (1996) Laxative abuse among women with eating disorders: An indication of psychology? *Int J Eat Disord* **20**(1): 13–19

Pyle RL, Mitchell JE, Eckert ED, Hatsukami D, Pomeroy C, Zimmerman R (1990) Maintenance treatment and six-month outcome for bulimic patients who respond to initial treatment. *Am J Psychiatry* **147**(7): 871–5

Ramsey R, Treasure J (1996) Treating anorexia nervosa. *Br Med J* **312**: 182

Ramsey R, Ward A, Treasure J, Russell GFM (1999) Compulsory treatment in anorexia nervosa: Short-term benefits and long-term mortality. *Br J Psychiatry* **175**: 147–53

Ramsey LE, Williams B, Johnston GD, Macgregor GA, Poston L, Potter JF, Poulton NR, Russell G (1999) British Hypertension Society guidelines for hypertension management (1999): summary. *Br Med J* **319**: 630–5

Rand CS, Macgregor AM (1991) Successful weight loss following obesity surgery and the perceived liability of morbid obesity. *Int J Obesity* **9**: 577–9

Rastam M (1992) Anorexia nervosa in 51 Swedish adolescents: premorbid problems and comorbidity. *J Am Acad Child Adolesc Psychiatry* **31**(5): 819–29

Ratcliffe PJ, Bevan JS (1985) Severe hypoglycaemia and sudden death in anorexia nervosa. *Psychol Med* **15**(3): 679–81

Ratnasuriya RH, Eisler I Scmuckler GT, Russell GFM (1991) Anorexia nervosa, outcome and prognostic factors after 20 years. *Br J Psychiatry* **158**: 495–512

Rickards H, Prendergast M, Booth IW (1994) Psychiatric presentation of Crohn's disease: Diagnostic delay and increased morbidity. *Br J Psychiatry* **164**(2): 256–61

Rigotti NA, Nussbaum SR Herzog DB, Neer RM (1984) Osteoporosis in women with anorexia nervosa. *N Engl J Med* **311**: 1601–6

Rigotti N, Neer R, Skates S *et al* (1991) The clinical course of osteoporosis in anorexia nervosa. *J Am Med Assoc* **265**(9): 1138

Rippe JM, Price JM, Hess SA, Kline G, DeMers KA, Damitz S, Kriedieh I, Freedson P (1998) Improved psychological well-being, quality of life, and health practices in moderately overweight women participating in a 12-week structured weight loss programme. *Obes Res* **6**(3): 208–18

Roberts MW, Tylenda CA (1989) Dental aspects of anorexia and bulimia. *Paediatrician* **16**(3–4): 178–84

Rogol AD, Clark PA, Roemmich JN (2000) Growth and pubertal development in children and adolescents: effects of diet and physical activity. *Am J Clin Nutr* **72**(2) (2 Suppl): 521S–8S

Rorty M, Yager J, Rossotto E, Buckwalter G (2000) Parental intrusiveness in adolescence recalled by women with a history of bulimia nervosa and comparison. *Int J Eat Disord* **28**(2): 202–8

Rorty M, Yager J, Rossoto E (1994) Childhood sexual, physical and psychological abuse in bulimia nervosa. *Am J Psychiatry* **151**(8): 1122–6

Rosch DS, Crowther JH,Graham JR (1992) MMPI derived personality description and personality subtypes in bulimia. *Psychol Addic Behav* **5**: 15–22

Rosenthal NE, Sack DA, Gillin JC, Lewy AJ, Goodwin FK, Davenport Y *et al* (1984) Seasonal affective disorder. A description of the syndrome and preliminary findings with light therapy. *Arch Gen Psychiatry* **41**(1): 72–80

Rossi R, Tauchmanova L, Luciano A, DiMartino M, Battista C, Del Viscovo L *et al* (2000) Subclinical Cushing's syndrome in patients with adrenal incidentalomas: biochemical features. *J Clin Endocrinol Metab* **85**(4): 1440–8

Russell G (1979) Bulimia nervosa: an ominous variant of anorexia nervosa. *Psychol Med* **9**(3): 429–48

Russell GF, Szmukler GI, Dare C, Eisler I (1987) An evaluation of family therapy in anorexia nervosa and bulimia nervosa. *Arch Gen Psychiatry* **44**(12): 1047–56

Russell GF, Treasure J, Eisler I (1998) Mothers with anorexia nervosa who underfeed their children: their recognition and management. *Psychol Med* **28**(1): 93–108

Russell GF (1988) The diagnostic formulation in bulimia nervosa. In: Garner DM, Garfinkel PE, eds. *Diagnostic Issues in Anorexia Nervosa and Bulimia Nervosa*. Bruner/Mazel, New York: 3–25

Russell J, Baur L, Beumont P, Byrnes S, Zipfel S (1998) Refeeding of anorexics: wasteful not wilful. *The Lancet* **352**: 1445–6

Russell J (1995) Treating anorexia nervosa. *Br Med J* **311**: 584

Rydall AC, Rodin GM, Olmsted MP, Devenyi RG, Daneman D (1997) Disordered eating behaviour and microvascular complications in young women with insulin-dependent diabetes mellitus. *N Engl J Med* **336**(26): 1849–54

Rytomaa I, Jarvinen V, Kanerva R, Heinonen OP (1998) Bulimia and tooth erosion. *Acta Odontologica Scand* **56**(1): 36–40

Saccomani L, Savoini M, Cirrincione M, Vercellino F, Ravera G (1998) Long term outcome of children and adolescents with anorexia nervosa: study of comorbidity. *J Psychosom Res* **44**(5): 565–71

Scheuble KJ, Dixon KN (1987) Premature termination: A risk in eating disorder groups. *Group* **11**(2): 85–93

Schmidt U, Hodes M, Treasure J (1992) Early onset bulimia nervosa: who is at risk? A retrospective case control study. *Psychol Med* **22**(3): 623–8

Schmidt U, Tiller J, Treasure J (1993) Setting the scene for eating disorders:childhood care, classification and course of illness. *Psychol Med* **23**(3): 663–72

Schmidt U, Tiller J, Blanchard M, Andrews B, Treasure J (1997) Is there a specific trauma precipitating anorexia nervosa? *Psychol Med* **27**(3): 523–30

Schneider JA, Agras WS (1987) Bulimia in males: a matched comparison with females. *Int J Eat Disord* **6**: 235–42

Schultz UME Pettke-Rank CV, Kreienkamp M, Hamm H, Brocker EB, Wewetzer C, Trott GE, Warnke A (1999) Dermatologic findings in anorexia and bulimia nervosa of childhood and adolescence. *Paediatr Dermatol* **16**(2): 90–4

Schwenk TL (2000) The stigmatisation and denial of mental illness in athletes. *Br J Sport Med* **34**(1): 4–5

Seagle HM, Bessesen DH, Hill J, (1998) Effects of Sibutramine on resting metabolic rate and weight loss in overweight women. *Obesity Res* **6**: 115–21

Seidell JC (2000) Obesity, insulin resistance and diabetes — a world-wide epidemic. *Br J Nutr* **83**(Suppl 1): S5–8

Sharp CW, Freeman PL (1993) The medical complications of anorexia nervosa. *Br J Psychiatry* **162**: 452–62

Sharp CW, Clark SA, Dunan JR, Blackwood DHR, Shapiro CM (1994) Clinical presentation of anorexia nervosa in males: 24 new cases. *Int J Eat Disord* **15**(2): 125–34

Shisslak CM, Mckeon RT, Crago M (1990) Family dysfunction in normal weight bulimic and bulimic anorexic families. *J Clin Psychol* **46**(2): 185–9

Shoebridge PJ, Gowers SG (2000) Parental high concern and adolescent anorexia nervosa. *Br J Psychiatry* **176**: 132–7

Shur E, Alloway R, Obrecht R, Russell GFM (1988) Physical complications in anorexia nervosa: Haematological and neuromuscular changes in 12 patients. *Br J Psychiatry* **153**: 72–5

Siegal JH, Hardoff D, Golden NH, Shenker IR (1995) Medical complications in male adolescents with anorexia nervosa. *J Adolesc Health* **16**(6): 448–53

Silber TJ, Kass EJ (1984) Anorexia nervosa and nephrolithiasis. *J Adolesc Health Care* **5**(1): 50–52

Skodol AE, Oldham JM, Hyler SE, Kellman HD, Doidge N, Davies M (1993) Comorbidity of DSM-111-R eating disorders and personality disorders. *Int J Eat Disord* **14**(4): 403–16

Slay HA, Hayaki J, Napolitano MA, Brownell KD (1998) Motivations for running and eating attitudes in obligatory versus non-obligatory runners. *Int J Eat Disord* **23**(3): 267–75

Slupik RJ (1999) Managing adolescents with eating disorders. *Int J Fertil Women's Med* **44**(3): 125–30

Smith J (1988) Hypoglycaemic coma associated with anorexia nervosa. *Aust N Z Psychiatry* **22**(4): 448–53

Spalter AR, Gwirtsman HE, Demitrack MA, Gold PW (1993) Thyroid function in bulimia nervosa. *Biol Psychiatry* **33**(6): 408–414

Spitzer RL, Devlin MJ, Walsh BT Hasin D (1992) Binge-eating disorder: a multisite field site of the diagnostic criteria. *Int J Eat Disord* **11**: 191–203

Spitzer RL, Yanovski S, Wadden T, Wing R, Marcus MD, Stunkard A *et al* (1993) Binge-eating disorder: its further validation in a multisite study. *Int J Eat Disord* **13**(2): 137–53

Srinivasagam NM, Kaye WH, Plotnicov KH, Greeno C, Weltzin TE, Radhiko R (1995) Persistent perfectionism, symmetry and exactness after long-term recovery from anorexia nervosa. *Am J Psychiatry* **152**(11): 1630–5

Stangler RS, Printz AM (1980) Psychiatric diagnosis in a university population. *Am J Psychiatry* **137**(8): 937–40

Steel JM, Young RJ, Lloyd GG, Macintyre CA (1989) Abnormal eating attitudes in young insulin-dependent diabetics. *Br J Psychiatry* **155**: 515–21

Steel JM, Young RJ, Lloyd GG, Clarke BF (1987) Clinically apparent eating disorders in young diabetic women: associations with painful neuropathy and other complications. *Br Med J* **294**: 859–62

Stein D, Meged S, Bar Hanin T (1997) Partial eating disorders in a community sample of female adolescents. *J Am Acad Child Adolesc Psychiatry* **36**(8): 1116–23

Steiner-Adair C (1994) The politics of prevention. In: Fallon P, Katzman MA, Woolley SC, eds. *Feminist Perspective on Eating Disorders*. Guildford Press, New York: 381–94

Steinhausen H, Rauss-Mason C, Seidel R (1991) Follow-up studies of anorexia nervosa: a review of four decades of outcome research. *Psychol Med* **21**: 447–54

Steinhausen HC (1997) Annotation: outcome of anorexia nervosa in the younger patient. *J Child Psychol Psychiatry* **38**(3): 271–6

Stewart DE, Robinson GE, Goldbloom DS, Wright C (1990) Infertility and eating disorders. *Am J Obstet Gynecol* **163**(41): 1196–9

Stratton IM, Adler AI, Neil HAW, Matthews DR, Manley SE, Cull CA *et al* (2000) Association of glycaemia with macrovascular and microvascular complications of type 2 diabetes (UKPDS 35): prospective observational study. *Br Med J* **321**: 405–12

Striegel-Moore RH, Wilson GT, Wilfley DE, Elder KA, Brownell K (1998) Binge-eating in an obese community sample. *Int J Eat Disord* **23**(1): 27–37

Striegel-Moore RH, Garvin V, Dohn FA, Rosenheck RA (1999) Psychiatric comorbidity of eating disorders in men: A national study of hospitalised veterans. *Int J Eat Disord* **25**(4): 399–404

Striegel-Moore R, Wilfley D, Pike K, Dohm FA, Fairburn CG (2000) Recurrent binge eating in black American women. *Arch Fam Med* **9**(1): 83–7

Strober M, Lampert C, Morrell W, Burroughs J, Jacobs C (1990) A controlled family study of anorexia nervosa: evidence of familial aggregation and lack of shared transmission with affected disorders. *Int J Eat Disord* **9**: 239–53

Strober M, Freeman R, Lampert C, Diamond J, Kaye W (2000) Controlled family study of anorexia nervosa and bulimia nervosa: evidence of shared liability and transmission of partial syndromes. *Am J Psychiatry* **157**(3): 393–401

Strober M (1997) Consultation and therapeutic engagement in severe anorexia. In: Garner DM, Garfinkel PE, eds. *Handbook of Treatment for Eating Disorders*. 2nd edn. The Guildford Press, London

Stunkard A, Berkowitz R, Wadden T, Tarikut C, Reiss E, Young L (1996) Binge-eating disorder and the night-eating syndrome. *Int J Obesity Related Metabolic Disorders* **20**: 1–6

Stunkard A, Berkowitz R, Tanrikut C, Reiss E, Young L (1996) d-fenfluramine treatment of binge-eating disorder. *Am J Psychiatry* **153**(11): 1455–9

Sullivan PF (1995) Mortality in anorexia nervosa. *Am J Psychiatry* **152**(7): 1073–4

Sullivan PJ, Bulik CM, Fear JL, Pickering A (1998a) Outcome of anorexia nervosa: a case-control study. *Am J Psychiatry* **155**(7): 939–46

Sullivan PF, Bulik CM, Kendler KS (1998b) Genetic epidemiology of bingeing and vomiting. *Br J Psychiatry* **173**: 75–9

Sussman N, Ginsberg D (1998) Rethinking side-effects of the selective serotonin reuptake inhibitors: Sexual dysfunction and weight gain. *Psychiatr Ann* **28**: 89–97

Swayze VW, Anderson A, Arndt S, Rajarethinam R, Fleming F, Sato Y (1996) Reversibility of brain tissue loss in anorexia nervosa assessed with a computerised Talairach 3-D proportional grid. *Psychol Med* **26**(2): 381–90

Swenne I, Larsson PT (1999) Heart risk associated with weight loss in anorexia nervosa and eating disorders: risk factors for QTc interval prolongation and dispersion. *Acta Paediatr* **88**(3): 304–9

Szmukler GI (1984) Anorexia and bulimia in diabetes. *J Psychosom* **28**: 365–9

Tai ES, Lau TN, Ho SC, Fok AC, Tan CE (2000) Body fat distribution and cardiovascular risk in normal weight women. Associations with insulin resistance, lipids and plasma leptin. *Int J Obesity Related Metabolic Disord* **24**(6): 751–7

Takii M, Komaki G, Uchigata Y, Maeda M, Omori Y, Kubo C (1999) Differences between bulimia nervosa and binge-eating disorder in females with type 1 diabetes: the important role of insulin omission. *J Psychosom Res* **47**(3): 221–331

Takei M, Nozoe S, Tanaka H, Soejima Y, Manuabe Y, Takayama I, Yamanaka T (1989) Clinical features in anorexia nervosa lasting ten years or more. *Psychother Psychosom* **52**(1–3): 140–5

Tanofsky MB, Wilfley DE, Spurrel EB, Welch R, Brownell KD (1997) Comparison of men and women with binge eating disorder. *Int J Eat Disord* **21**(1): 49–54

Telch TF, Agras WS, Rossiter EM (1988) Binge-eating increases with increasing adiposity. *Int J Eating Disord* **7**: 115–9

Telch CF, Agras WS, Rossiter EM, Wilfley D, Kenardy J (1990) Group cognitive behavioural treatment for the non-purging bulimic: an initial evaluation. *J Consult Clin Psychiatry* **58**(5): 629–35

Telch CF, Agras WS (1994) Obesity, binge eating and psychopathology: are they related? *Int J Eat Disord* **15**(1): 53–61

Theander S (1985) Outcome and prognosis in anorexia nervosa and bulimia: some results of previous investigations, compared with those of a Swedish long-term study. *J Psychiatry Res* **19**: 493–508

Thiels C, Schmidt U, Treasure J, Garthe R, Troop N (1998) Guided self-change for bulimia nervosa incorporating use of a self-care manual. *Am J Psychiatry* **155**(7): 947–53

Thompson D, Edelsburg J, Colditz GA, Bird AP, Oster G (1999) Lifetime health and economic consequences of obesity. *Arch Intern Med* **159**(18): 2177–83

Thompson SBN (1993) *Eating Disorders*. Chapman & Hall, London

Thompson JK, Coovert MD, Richards KJ, Johnson S, Cattarin J (1995) Development of body image, eating disturbance, and general psychological functioning in female adolescents: covariance structure modelling and longitudinal investigation. *Int J Eat Disord* **14**: 221–36

Tiller J, Schmidt U, Treasure J (1993) Compulsory treatment for anorexia nervosa: Compassion or coercion? *Br J Psychiatry* **162**: 679–80

Touyz SW, Beumont PJV, Glaun D, Phillips T, Cowie I (1984) A comparison of lenient and strict operant conditioning programmes in refeeding patients with anorexia nervosa. *Br J Psychiatry* **144**: 517–20

Treasure JL, Russell GF, Fogelman I, Murby B (1987) Reversible bone loss in anorexia nervosa. *Br Med J* **295**: 473–5

Treasure JL, Russell GFM (1988) Intrauterine growth and neonatal weight gain in babies of women with anorexia nervosa. *Br Med J* **296**: 1038

Treasure J, Schmidt U, Troop N, Tiller J, Todd G, Keilen M, Dodge E (1994) First step in managing bulimia nervosa: controlled trial of therapeutic manual. *Br Med J* **308**: 686–9

Troop NA, Treasure JL (1997) Psychological factors in the onset of eating disorders: responses to life-events and difficulties. *Br J Med Psychol* **70**(4): 373–85

Tsuchiya K, Nakauchi M, Hondo I, Nihei H (1995) Nephropathy associated with electrolyte disorders. *Nippon Rinsho* **53**(8): 1995–2000

Turnbull S, Ward A, Treasure J, Jick H, Derby L (1996) The demand for eating disorder care. An epidemiological study using the General Practice Research Database. *Br J Psychiatry* **169**(Dec): 705–12

Turner J, Batik M, Palmer LJ, Forbes D, Mcdermott BM (2000) Detection and importance of laxative use in adolescents with anorexia nervosa. *J Am Acad Child Adolesc Psychiatry* **39**(3): 378–85

Valleni-Basile LA, Garrison CZ, Jackson KL, Waller JL, Mckeown RE, Addy CL *et al* (1994) Frequency of obsessive-compulsive disorder in a community sample of young adolescents. *J Am Acad Child Adolesc Psychiatry* **33**: 782–91

van der Ham T, van Strien DC, van Engeland H (1994) A four-year prospective follow-up study of 49 eating-disordered adolescents: differences in course of illness. *Acta Psychiatr Scand* **90**(3): 229–35

Vander AJ, Sherman JH, Luciano DS (1994). *Human Physiology*. 6th edn. McGraw-Hill, Inc London

Vaz FJ, Penas EM (1998) Borderline personality and bulimia nervosa: A clinical study. *Revista de psiquiatria de la Facultad de Medicina de Barcelona* **25**(1): 10–18

Vila G, Robert JJ, Jos J, Mouren-Simeoni MC (1997) Insulin dependent diabetes mellitus in children and adolescents: value of pedopsychiatric follow-up (French). *Arch Pediatr* **4**(7): 615–22

Vila G, Robert J-J, Nollet-Clemencon C, Vera L, Crosnier H, Rault G *et al* (1995) Eating and emotional disorders in adolescent obese girls with insulin dependent diabetes mellitus. *Eur Child Adolesc Psychiatry* **4**(4): 270–9

Vitousek K, Manke F (1994) Personality variables and disorders in anorexia nervosa and bulimia nervosa. *J Abnormal Psychol* **103**: 137–47

Vize CM, Cooper PJ (1995) Sexual abuse in patients with eating disorders, patients with depression, and normal controls. A comparative study. *Br J Psychiatry* **167**(1): 80–5

Wade TD, Bulik CM, Sullivan PF, Neale MC, Kendler KS (2000) The relation between risk factors for binge-eating and bulimia nervosa: a population-based female twin study. *Health Psychol* **19**(2): 115–23

Walberg JL, Johnston CS (1991) Menstrual function and eating behavior in female recreational weight lifters and competitive body builders. *Med Sci Sports Exerc* **23**(1): 30–6

Waldholtz BD, Andersen AE (1990) Gastrointestinal symptoms in anorexia nervosa: A prospective study. *Gastroenterol* **98**(6): 1415–9

Waller D (1997) Eating Disorders: In: Mcpherson A, Waller D, eds. *Women's Health*. 4th edn. Oxford University Press, Oxford

Walsh AES, Oldman AD, Franklin M, Fairburn CG, Cowen PJ (1995) Dieting decreases plasma tryptophan and increases the prolactin response to d-fenfluramine in women, but not in men. *J Affect Disord* **33**(2): 89–97

Walsh BT, Hadigan CM, Devlin MJ, Gladis M, Roose SP (1991) Long-term outcome of antidepressant treatment for bulimia nervosa. *Am J Psychiatry* **148**(9): 1206–11

Walsh BT, Garner DM (1997) Diagnostic issues. In: Garner DM, Garfinkel PE, eds. *Handbook of Treatment for Eating Disorders*. 2nd edn. The Guildford Press, London

Walters EE, Kendler KS (1995) Anorexia nervosa and anorexic-like syndromes in a population-based female twin sample. *Am J Psychiatry* **152**(1): 64–71

Wareham NJ, Wong MY, Day NE (2000) Glucose intolerance and physical inactivity: the relative importance of low habitual energy expenditure and cardiorespiratory fitness. *Am J Epidemiol* **152**(2): 132–9

Warren MP, Vande Wiele RL (1973) Clinical and metabolic features of anorexia nervosa. *Am J Obstet Gynecol* **117**: 435–49

Webster JJ, Palmer RL (2000) The childhood and family background of women with clinical eating disorders: a comparison with women with major depression and women without psychiatric disorder. *Psychol Med* **30**: 53–60

Weeks AD (2000) Menorrhagia and hypothyroidism. *Br Med J* **320**: 649

Weissman NJ, Tighe JF, Gottdeiner JS, Gwynne JT (1998) An assessment of heart valve abnormalities in obese patients taking dexfenfluramine, sustained release dexfenfluramine or placebo. *N Engl J Med* **339**(11): 725–32

Welch SL, Fairburn CG (1994) Sexual abuse and bulimia nervosa: Three integrated case control comparisons. *Am J Psychiatry* **151**(3): 402–407

Welch SL, Doll A, Fairburn CG (1997) Life events and the onset of bulimia nervosa: a controlled family study. *Psychol Med* **27**: 515–22

Whitehouse AM, Cooper PJ, Vize CV, Hill C, Vogel L (1992) Prevalence of eating disorders in three Cambridge practices: hidden and conspicuous mortality. *Br J Gen Pract* **42**: 57–60

Whittal ML, Agras WS, Gould RA (1999. Bulimia nervosa: a meta analysis of psychosocial and psychopharmacologic treatments. *Behav Ther* **30**: 117–35

Willard SG, Anding RH, Winstead DK (1983) Nutritional counselling as an adjunct to psychotherapy in bulimia treatment. *Psychosom* **24**: 545–51

Williams CJ, Piero L, Sims A (1998) Does palliative care have a role in the treatment of anorexia nervosa? *Br Med J* **317**: 195–7

Williams GJ, Power KG, Millar HR *et al* (1993) Comparison of eating disorders and other dietary/weight groups on measures of perceived control, assertiveness, self-esteem, and self-directed hostility. *Int J Eat Disord* **14**(1): 27–32

Williamson DF, Pamuk E, Thun M, Flanders D, Byers T, Heath C (1995) Prospective study of intentional weight loss and mortality in never smoking, overweight US white women aged 40–64. *Am J Epidemiol* **141**(1): 1128–41

Williamson DF, Madans J, Anda RF, Kleinman JC, Kahn HS, Byers T (1993) Recreational physical activity and ten-year weight change in a US national cohort. *Int J Obesity Related Metabolic Disord* **17**(5): 279–86

Wilson GT, Fairburn CG, Agras WS (1997) Cognitive behavioural therapy for bulimia nervosa. In: Garner DM, Garfinkel PE, eds. *Handbook of Treatment for Eating Disorders*. 2nd edn. The Guildford Press, London

Wing RR, Nowalk MP, Marcus MD, Koeske R, Finegold D (1986) Subclinical eating disorders and glycaemic control in adolescents with type 1 diabetes. *Diabetes Care* **9**: 162–7

Wolff GE, Crosby RD, Roberts JA, Wittrock DA (2000) Differences in daily stress, mood, coping, and eating behaviour in binge eating and non-binge eating college women. *Addict Behav* **25**(2): 205–16

Wonderlich S, Ukestad L, Perzacki R (1994) Perceptions of non-shared childhood environment in bulimia nervosa. *J Am Acad Child Adolesc Psychiatry* **33**(5): 740–7

Woodside B (1999) Commentary. *Evidence-Based Mental Health* **2**(1): 29

Wurtman RJ, Wurtman JJ (1995) Brain serotonin, carbohydrate craving, obesity and depression. *Obesity Res* **3**: 477S–480S

Yager J (1999) Nocturnal eating syndromes. *JAMA* **282**(7): 689

Yager J, Landsverk J, Edelstein C (1989) Help seeking and satisfaction with care in 641 women with eating disorders. *J Nerv Ment Disord* **177**: 632–7

Yager J, Kurtzman F, Landsverk J, Weismeier E (1988) Behaviours and attitudes related to eating disorders in homosexual male college students. *Am J Psychiatry* **145**: 495–7

Yanovski SZ, Leet M, Yanovski JA, Flood M, Gold PW, Kissilheff HR, Walsh BT (1992) Food selection and intake of obese women with binge-eating disorder. *Am J Clin Nutr* **56**(6): 975–80

Yanovski SZ (2000) Eating disorders, race and mythology. *Arch Fam Med* **9**(1): 88–90

Yanovski SZ, Nelson JE, Dubbert BK, Spitzer RL (1993) Association of binge-eating disorder and psychiatric comorbidity in obese subjects. *Am J Psychiatry* **150**: 1472–9

Zucchi T, Mannucci E, Ricca V, Giardinelli L, Di Bernardo M, Pieroni V *et al* (2000) Eating attitudes and behaviour throughout the menstrual cycle in obese women: a case control study. *Eat Weight Disord* **5**(1): 31–7

Appendix: Useful addresses

Self help groups

Anorexia and bulimia care (ABC)
PO box 30
Ormskirk
Lancashire L38 5JR
Tel: 01695 422479 Best time to
contact: Monday–Wednesday,
ansaphone at all other times
www: anorexiabulimiacare.co.uk

*Offers a Christian perspective and
aims to offer help and support to
the whole family*

Caraline
25 Upper George Street
Luton
Bedfordshire LU1 2RD
Helpline: 01582 457474 Best time
to contact: 10.00am–3.00pm,
Monday–Friday

*Offers counselling and advice
across the United Kingdom but
predominantly to those who reside
in Bedfordshire*

Eating Disorders Association
1st Floor, Wensum House
103 Prince of Wales Road
Norwich NR1 1DW
Tel Helpline: 01603 765050 Best
time to contact: 4.00pm–6.00pm,
Monday to Wednesday
Office 01603 621414 Best time to
contact: normal office hours
www.edauk.com

*Offers advice and help across the
United Kingdom, runs local self
help groups*

Eating Disorders Club
Stricklandgate House
92,Stricklandgate
Kendal
Cumbria
Tel 01383 728672 Best time to
contact: 6.00pm–8.00pm, seven
days a week.

*Based in the Lake District but has
members across the country*

First Steps to Freedom
7 Avon Court
School Lane
Kenilworth
Warwickshire CV8 2GX
Tel: 01926 851608 (helpline)
Office: 01926 864473 Best time to
contact 10.00am–10.00pm, seven
days per week
www.firststeps.demon.co.uk

*Offers advice across a range of
conditions including obsessive
compulsive disorder, panic attacks,
anxiety anorexia and bulimia*

National Centre for Eating
Disorders
54, New Road
Esher
Surrey KT10 9NU
Tel: 01372 469493 Best time to
contact: 10.00am–1.00pm,
Monday–Friday
www.eating-disorders.org.uk

*Has counsellors in a number of
regions of the United Kingdom and
can offer one-to-one support across
a range of eating disorders*

Websites for health professionals

American Journal of Psychiatry
www.appi.org

Archives of General Psychiatry
www.archpsyc.com

Behaviour research and therapy;
Behavioural Psychology journals
www.clas.ufl.edu/users/gthursby/
psi/journals.htm

This site gives access to a huge
number of journals including:

*Addiction Research
Addictive behaviour
Behaviour Therapy
Canadian Journal of Psychiatry
Child and Adolescent Psychiatric
Clinics*

British Journal of Psychiatry
www.bjp.rcpsych.org

British Medical Journal
www.bmj.com

International Journal of Obesity
www.stockton-press.co.uk

Journal of Clinical Psychiatry
www.psychiatrist.com/

Obesity Research
www.obesityresearch.org/

Psychology Press
www.psypress.co.uk/journals.html

This site gives access to:
*International Journal of
Psychology
International Journal of
Behavioural Medicine
Cognition and Emotion
European Journal of Cognitive
Psychology*

Pubmed (medline)
www.ncbi.nlm.nih.gov./PubMed/

Sciencekomm
www.sciencekomm.at/journals/med
icine/psych.html

Gives access to four journal
subtypes:
Addiction and substance abuse
journals
Behavioural Science Journals
Cognitive Science Journals
Psychology Journals

The list from this site is huge and
includes:
*Australian and New Zealand
Journal of Psychiatry
Australian and New Zealand
Journal of Psychology
Behaviour Modification
Behaviour Therapy
British Journal of Guidance and
Counselling
Canadian Journal of Psychiatry
Child and Family Behaviour
Therapy*

Index